A Tapestry of Knowledge

VOLUME III

VOLUME III

Written by Virginia Beach City Public School Educators

Virginia Beach City Public Schools

Timothy R. Jenney, Ph.D., Superintendent

Compiled and Edited by Lorna S. Roberson

Published by the Virginia Beach City Public Schools
2512 George Mason Drive
Virginia Beach, VA 23456-0038

Printed in the United States of America

Printed by Letton Gooch Printers, Inc.
700 West 21ST Street
Norfolk, VA 23517

First Edition
Volume III

ISBN 0-9666992-3-8

Front Cover Art by Edward A. Obermeyer, 1998
Computer Bug Series #2, Vertical Takeoff

Book Design by Ravinder Singh
Produced by Letton Gooch Printers

Body copy typeset in Goudy
Additional copy typeset in Delphin, Mona Lisa, and Universe

This book is dedicated
to teachers
who continuously strive to bring the "magic"
of learning to all students.

Jennifer Call
Artificial Intelligence

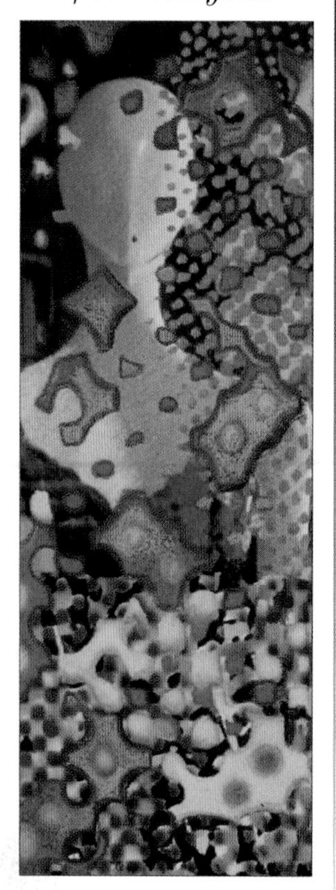

Description: A computer may be able to play chess, but will it ever have the life force necessary to breathe vitality and individuality into a work of art? The digital collage, *Artificial Intelligence*, fuses traditional photography and drawing with digital byproducts and was printed by a Colorspan Giclee printer.

Medium Used: Digital Collage/ Colored Pencil

Educational Background: Ms. Call received a Bachelor of Fine Arts degree from Virginia Commonwealth University. Recently, she has taken graduate courses at the Institute for Electronic Arts in Alfred, New York.

Teaching Experience: Ms. Call has taught students for twelve years at the middle and elementary school level.

Awards: Ms. Call was awarded Teacher of the Year at North Landing Elementary School and received the Glenn Hamm Academic Achievement Award from Virginia Commonwealth University.

A Tapestry of Knowledge, Volume III

Weaving Technology Into Instruction to Improve Learning

CONTENTS

C O N T E N T S

C O N T E N T S

ACKNOWLEDGEMENTS

This third volume of articles written by teachers and administrators from the Virginia Beach City Public Schools illustrates the varied and informed perspectives about the best uses of technology that can be found in the Beach's 86 schools. The book includes articles about the use of software programs, the Internet, computers, Musical Instrument Digital Interface (MIDI) files, digital cameras, and calculators. All these electronic devices and more are used to optimize educational experiences for all students from the gifted to the learning impaired. The educators featured in this book are devoted to making sure that these extraordinary assets do not go to waste, but are used to empower teachers as they lead students to understand how their education is connected to the world outside of school and how their education prepares them for their role in that future world.

While it is impossible to thank all the individuals who have contributed in some way to the creation of this book, I would like to extend a special thanks to Dr. Leila Christenbury for her support on this project. By working with me in the writing workshops that I coordinated for this project, she helped many contributors to focus on their topics and revise their initial drafts. Without her help and support in the beginning stages, some wonderful stories may have been lost. Also, thanks to Ms. Fran Sharer, Ms. Nancy Moskway, Mrs. Linda Koutoufas, and Ms. Lannah Hughes, for their tireless reading and commentary on this manuscript; Dr. Anne Wolcott, for her expert advice on the artwork; to Mrs. Barbara Thompson, Administrative Office Associate, for her typing and expert eye for detail; and, to Dr. Sheila S. Magula, Associate Superintendent for Curriculum and Instruction, for her support and encouragement; and, finally, a special thanks to Dr. Timothy R. Jenney, for providing this opportunity to showcase the expertise, talent, and dedication of teachers and administrators in the Virginia Beach City Public Schools.

Lorna Roberson

ARTWORK

Cover Art *Computer Bug Series #2, Vertical Takeoff*, Edward Obermeyer, Larkspur Middle School

Front Piece *Artificial Intelligence*, Jennifer Call, Rosemont Forest Elementary School

Section One: **Moving Into the Gossamer World of Technology With Fine Arts Teachers**
If We Removed, Carole Gutterman, Kempsville High School

Section Two: **From Elephants to Odysseys: English Teachers Entwine Technology With Reading and Writing**
Rose in Water: Inner Secrets, Gwen Stevens, Linkhorn Park Elementary School

Section Three: **Spinning Lessons From the Web to Enhance Student Involvement**
Flower Fusion, Anne Wolcott, Fine Arts Coordinator

Section Four: **Stitching Technology Into the Structure of Mathematics**
Blue Mood, Edward Obermeyer, Larkspur Middle School

Section Five: **Creating Designs to Understand Science**
Growth, Caroline Thietje, Salem Elementary School

Section Six: **Envisioning Real-World Experiences Through the Web**
Old World Journey of the Elusion, Sue Frost, Cox High School

Section Seven: **Interlacing Technology With Instruction in Support Services**
The Connection, Nan Leach, Princess Anne Middle School

Section Eight: **Building a Technology Framework for the Future**
Puzzle Pieces, Sharon Clohessy, Art Teacher Specialist

FOREWORD

These are exciting times for all of us involved in public education. Given the impact of technological advancement and its attendant effect on today's information age, access to knowledge has never been greater. Certainly this is true in our public schools. In fact, over the past several years, we in Virginia Beach City Public Schools have, with an eye to continuous improvement, wholeheartedly embraced technology as a means to an end, that of improving teaching and learning for the express purpose of raising levels of student achievement.

Not only has this strategy brought about the desired effect, it has also created what I believe to be a Renaissance in learning for many in our school division. One need only flip through the pages of this volume of *A Tapestry of Knowledge* to understand the truth of this statement. That educators have creatively and expertly used technology in the classroom to enhance learning and as the basis for instructional renewal is a fact. Teachers are excited about teaching, and students are excited about learning. We are well beyond the stage where many educators still find themselves—making conflicting decisions about whether to embrace technology. Fortunately, Virginia Beach School professionals crossed that point of reasoning quite some time ago. This book gives evidence to the reality that best practices are both inspiring and motivating.

A Tapestry of Knowledge: Weaving Technology into Instruction to Improve Learning is the third in a series of books by educators in Virginia Beach schools. I am extremely proud not only of the depth of knowledge and experience exhibited in these articles, but also of the incredibly original images inherent in the art. When exceptional colleagues such as these come together to create a work of this sort, I can have no doubt that the future of public education is in good hands.

Timothy R. Jenney,
Superintendent

PREFACE

Weaving Technology Into Instruction to Improve Learning

> *Leadership and learning are indispensable to each other.*
> *John F. Kennedy*

"Technology represents perhaps the greatest opportunity to advance learning since the invention of the printing press," commented Dr. Timothy Jenney when he was honored as the top administrator in the nation in the area of technology education. His belief and leadership has been made a reality in a number of initiatives, many of which are showcased in this third edition of *A Tapestry of Knowledge*.

Throughout the pages of this book, teachers and administrators of the Virginia Beach City Public Schools share their own Renaissance journeys as they utilize the technology resources that are increasingly available. Distance Learning, computer resource labs, Computer Resource Specialists in every school, the Advanced Technology Center, and the establishment of a Technology Academy at Landstown High School are but a few of these resources described in this volume. From art classrooms to mathematics classrooms and across the entire spectrum of student abilities, technology is rapidly making a crucial difference not only in the way teachers teach, but in the way students learn. Teachers are now taking up the leadership role initiated by Dr. Jenney and playing the pivotal role of ensuring that all students reap the benefits that technology can bring to their education.

Work Cited

"Timothy Jenney." *Technology and Learning*. December 2002. 24.

Section One

Moving Into the Gossamer World of Technology With Fine Arts Teachers

Carole Gutterman

If We Removed

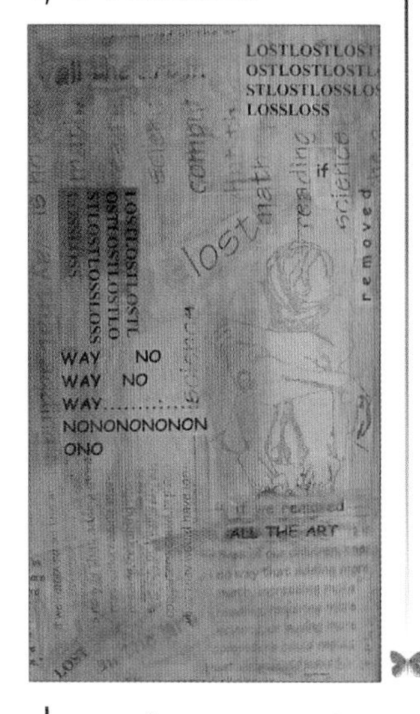

Description: This piece was created out of my frustration with what I see as a trend toward a more narrow, less whole focus on a child's total learning experience. If my nineteen years in art education have done nothing else, these years have proven to me time and time again that art can reach the most closed off, uncommunicative student; can open hearts and minds and eyes and ears to more experiences; will provide a path to college careers through the means of an art portfolio as an entrance to college, instead of an SAT score; will allow for opportunities for adolescents to express their beliefs and their feelings in socially acceptable ways; will give us all something to discuss; and will sometimes makes us uncomfortable; and will sometimes fill us with joy.

> *If we removed all the art in the lives of our children, there is no way that adding more math, increasing more reading, requiring more science, or buying more computers could replace what they would have lost.*
>
> *National Art Education Association*

When I came across the above quotation from the National Art Education Association, it seemed to speak to all of my concerns and inspired this work. By using a combination of color, printed material, fonts, and an image I had created some years previously, the piece really designed itself.

Medium Used: Mixed

Educational Background: Ms. Gutterman graduated from Virginia Wesleyan College in 1983 with a Bachelor of Arts in Education degree. In 1994, she received a Master of Arts in Humanities from Old Dominion University.

Teaching Experience: Ms. Gutterman taught at Shelton Park Elementary School from 1984-1987 and Kempsville High School from 1987-2003.

Awards: Ms. Gutterman received a Presidential Citation from the Governor's School for the Visual and Performing Arts of Richmond in 1997, 2000, and 2002. She is listed among *Who's Who Among America's Teachers* in 1992, 2000, and 2002. She received the Barbarini Faun Award from the Virginia Beach City Public Schools Fine Arts program in 2001.

LOSTLOSTLOS
OSTLOSTLOST
STLOSTLOSSL
LOSSLOSS

all the art in

lost math reading if science

LOSTLOSTL
OSTLOSTLO
STLOSTLOSS
LOSSLOSS

WAY NO
WAY NO
WAY..............
NONONONONON
ONO

if we removed
ALL THE ART

...ed all the art in
...r children, there
...at adding more
...reasing more
...quiring more
...r buying more
... could replace
...ould have lost."

LOST

Moving Into the Gossamer World of Technology With Fine Arts Teachers

Gossamer, a fine film of cobwebs, often seen floating through the air, creates illusions of enchantment and softness that belies its woven strength. Just as spiders work many hours to create the intricate patterns of their web to create the illusion of an enchanted world, students of music and art spend years learning the skills needed to sing in choirs, play instruments, create musical compositions, and produce works of art. Through their music and art these students will create moments of enchantment for others, but unlike gossamer some of these works will last forever.

The teachers who weave together the objectives, lessons, and activities that need to be in place for these students to achieve the excellence they desire are featured in this section. Here the teachers describe how they use technology to make the hard work and practice needed for students to succeed in these two disciplines more beneficial, exciting, and rewarding.

An experience with Paint Shop Pro™ led Fine Arts Coordinator, Anne Wolcott, to realize how technology could be used to enhance the art classroom. In her article, Wolcott describes how she worked with the art teachers in Virginia Beach to restructure the dynamics of learning by incorporating technology tools such as the computer, scanners, and digital cameras into the conventional learning processes in art. She concludes that the art classroom provides the optimal place to provide new ways of learning through technology because the computer allows students to explore composition, design, and technical processes more fully. She also points out that works created on computers are now recognized as an art form in galleries, museums, and school art exhibits.

Art students in Carolyn Jo Corso's class find that by manipulating self-portraits using computer graphics they can change their images in much the same way that Lewis Carroll changed Alice in his book *Alice's Adventures in Wonderland*. She presents an engaging series of lessons in which she combines technology with higher order thinking and writing. These

Front to Back: Gwen Stevens, Anne Wolcott, Jo Corso, Kenneth Smead

lessons incorporate self-identity questions that lead the students to think more deeply before they begin to create their self-portraits. She then uses the answers to these questions to help students analyze and reflect on their work. Finally, in a follow-up lesson she assigns a writing task in which they explain their self-portraits by describing the emotions they were attempting to portray and the effects they used to create the piece.

Cindy Copperthite compares her journey to integrate technology into her instruction to the fictional adventures of Alice in Wonderland. As she sorts through all the possible educational technology programs, she describes her frustration and confusion. In the midst of this confusion, Copperthite decided to heed the advice of a colleague... "Keep it Simple Sweetheart" (KISS) and implement technology into just one course, Advanced Placement Art History. Her article describes the steps she took to accomplish this and details her conclusions that technology provides her with yet another tool to reach all her students and to accommodate numerous learning styles.

"Art and computer technology are natural partners," claims Gwen Stevens in her article, *Visual Communication Rules!* She uses examples from her elementary classroom, furnished with only two computers, to illustrate how she planned quick and easy lessons using Kid Pix® to meet curriculum goals and to provide rewarding and positive experiences for her students.

Kenneth Smead, a music teacher at Larkspur Middle School, explains in his article how he uses word processing to organize and complete administrative tasks, such as keeping lesson plans, recording grades, creating activity worksheets, and designing tests. He goes on to describe how he creates professional looking singing handouts to reinforce the comprehension of reading music with notation software. Another innovative piece of software he uses is the Musical Instrument Digital Interface (MIDI) which allows him to perform several complicated tasks at the same time. Using the MIDI, Smead can prerecord his accompaniment for the choir before he meets with his students. Then, when he rehearses with the students in chorus class, he does not have to divide his attention between the keyboard and the students. He can give the students his complete attention. His article describes other adjustments he has made to his instruction by using technology to improve the learning experiences for students in his classes.

As Whitman observes in his poem "A Noiseless Patient Spider," the spider must release filament after filament from itself before it can create its web. Just like the spider, the fine arts teachers have been tenacious in their attempts to use technology in meaningful ways in their classrooms.

Mona Lisa in the Digital Age: Is She High Tech, High Wired for the Twenty-first Century?

by Anne G. Wolcott

An Epiphany! I sat transfixed in front of the computer, suddenly realizing the possibilities of a computer graphics program. I had spent the afternoon learning how to manipulate one of my personal photographs on the computer in Jo Corso's graduate computer graphics class.

"You need to come to the rest of the sessions," remarked Jo looking at me with the wisdom of a teacher who knew what I had just experienced. Realizing how much I would enjoy it, she had invited me to participate in the computer graphics class she was teaching.

"You've wanted me to do that for years," I replied, "and I always avoided it, but now that I have experimented with the Paint Shop Pro™ Program, I realize how much can be done with computer graphics, and I realize how important this training can be."

> *I realized that the time had come to immerse myself in the high- tech art classroom of the twenty-first century.*

Using the program had been so much fun! I had scanned one of my photographs into the computer and manipulated it in various ways. The afternoon flew by as I scanned, colored, erased, and duplicated the images in various forms and printed each version to my own delight. During that time, Jo had been kind enough to teach me how to use the computer graphics program. She even told me that I was a "quick learner" which encouraged me to take her up on her offer to attend the remaining sessions of her computer graphics class at Princess Anne High School. Yes, now I had the confidence and motivation to learn about computer graphics. My thinking about computers as a tool for creating art had changed. After this experience, I realized that the time had come to immerse myself in the high-tech art classroom of the twenty-first century.

Before my experience in Jo's class, I asked myself if the art teachers in Virginia Beach were ready for the high tech, "wired" art classroom. As the Fine Arts Coordinator, I also wondered if technology was just another trend or was it here to stay in art education? And what kind of technology were we talking about: computers, scanners, digital cameras, and what else? My experience with these tools was limited, and I believed the same was true for most teachers. Many art teachers do not use the tools of technology, unlike paint and clay; it is alien to them (Matthews 1). For this reason I began to investigate and ask teachers if they used technology in their classrooms. I learned that many teachers had varied levels of expertise. They told me that some of the barriers they faced were the lack of system-wide staff development, release time to learn how to use computers and software programs, and experienced faculty to teach computer technology. At that time I realized that I had a goal for the art teachers and for me. We would become wired for the future through revising the curriculum and providing staff development activities in technology.

Big Ideas and Essential Questions

For the past five years many art teachers have been working together on revising each art curriculum from a skills-based to a concept-based curriculum. Using the national and state art standards as a guide, as well as the ideas from Grant Wiggin's *Understanding by Design*, we examined and rewrote the scope and sequence, the objectives in grades 1-12, as well as the teaching and assessment strategies. During this process, many teachers' philosophies of teaching art had to be gently readjusted to accept this new approach. The major philosophy behind this approach to teaching focuses on a curriculum which addresses life-centered themes and integrates into the curriculum universal concepts, essential questions, skills, knowledge, and creative activities that draw from the four disciplines of art (art history, art production, art criticism, and aesthetics). This approach makes it possible to relate art to other school subjects as well as to the wide range of personal interests and abilities of students. The curriculum identifies important concepts that transfer to other examples across time and cultures, which results in a natural learning process for the students. Acquiring simple concepts before more complex ones enables students to build their knowledge, skills, and understanding in a clear and logical fashion. Appropriate activities are constructed to maximize students' inquiry-based learning and to enhance their ways of knowing about art. In other words, this curriculum model is structured around big ideas/concepts using the disciplines of art as well as art skills and activities to support interdisciplinary learning about art and life. For example, an instructional unit might be designed around the concept of Identity with a lesson theme of *Who Is a Hero?* The concept is used to focus on significant aspects of life, a universal idea that translates across time and cultures. Using a concept invites "inquiry rather than suggesting ready answers" and encourages students to ask questions about the world. The more specific theme of *Who Is a Hero?* might be used to capture the interests and needs of the students, relating to events or people with whom they are familiar. The concept and theme are supported by the disciplines of aesthetics, art criticism, art history and studio which serve as the vehicles of learning about art and artists. Activities are constructed in a way that require students to study certain artists and works of art that exemplify and illustrate the concept and theme. Studio projects are devised that allow students to express what they have learned about Identity and more specifically about heroes. Studio projects might address such questions as "Who is a hero to me?" Teachers are given flexibility to design studio projects to address the theme through various media such as painting, printmaking, or ceramics.

Integrating Technology Into the Curriculum Truthfully, finding a place for technology in the curriculum was a component on which I did not focus until curriculum revision was well underway. I knew a few teachers were already competent in technology, so I knew my vision for inclusion of technology was an attainable goal. With their help we began to develop technology objectives for the curriculum and to plan staff development activities that would support these objectives. In the revised curriculum, technology is included as part of the goals and objectives of learning about art in most grade levels.

As the teachers use this revised curriculum in the elementary grades, students are guided to develop basic technology skills through suggested instructional activities. The instructional activities provide strategies for using the computer to promote problem solving and critical thinking. Just think! Fifth-graders are using the computer as a tool in an art class. I observed a fifth-grade class in which students created "embellished" self-portraits using the computer. After learning traditional approaches to creating self-portraits, the teacher allowed the students to create their portraits on the computer. Students took turns using the computer in the classroom to scan their sketched image into the computer and then to color, draw, and distort the image to their liking. After all the students completed their portraits, the teacher put the portraits together in a slide presentation.

In high school, students involved in the Painting, Drawing, and Printmaking class will master two objectives connected to technology: Drawing, Painting, Printmaking (DPP) 30: Students will recognize and understand how technology advances have affected the making of art over time and across cultures, and DPP 48: Students will investigate and understand the role of technology in drawing, painting, and printmaking. In another high school art class, students investigate the ways the printing press, video camera, and computer have changed the way artists express themselves. Also in this printmaking class students combine linoleum block printed images with digital and newspaper images to create their interpretation of a hero. Technology enables them to combine multiple images from various sources to construct their own knowledge and explore new tools to create their own art.

In another high school art class, students investigate the ways the printing press, video camera, and computer have changed the way artists express themselves.

Throughout history artists have always embraced new ideas and media to express themselves. Similar to these historical models, Virginia Beach art teachers have not been deterred in the use of technology. For instance, another form of self-portrait involves high school students creating "famous" self-portraits using the digital camera and the computer. Using a digital camera, students were photographed and then the images were downloaded into the computer. Using graphic design software, they inserted the photographs of their faces into famous works of art. Once the portrait was inserted into the work of art, the students altered and embellished the image to the point that it looked as if their faces really did belong in the portrait. Thus, a traditional means of expression was transformed by integrating traditional media and tools with new technology. Students were able to engage in a unique, creative form of artistic expression by using a contemporary medium that is relevant to their lives.

Bits, Bytes, and Binary Logic

In studio production, the computer has added a new dimension as a wonderful catalyst for learning about art. It can be used to teach students general and theoretical skills such as color, composition, and design. It can also be used to facilitate exploration, experimentation, and research about art and artists. Students can explore ideas, create and manipulate, and start over again without committing to paper. For example, sketches on paper or photographs can be scanned into the computer and then manipulated until the desired effect is reached (Walling 15). The computer enables students to work at any stage of the creative process by re-using images or creating multiple images much more quickly than traditional methods. In the past, using traditional media such as pencil and paper, students would never have been able to create so many diverse images in such a short time.

The computer enables students to work at any stage of the creative process by re-using images or creating multiple images much more quickly than traditional methods.

Browsing Through New Technologies Through new technologies, interactive media allows teachers and students to share in the inquiry and discovery process. Oftentimes the roles can be reversed; the teacher becomes the student. In this sense teachers can join students in learning new technology that expands learning in art. Through the Internet teachers and students are exposed to a greater variety of works of art, artists, and different ideas and issues in the art world. What better way to examine and discuss issues in aesthetics or art history than having the "world" of art at one's fingertips? The Internet provides a vast array of resources for teachers and students to research historical information, museum collections, and works of art which can be downloaded into personal files. One example of this is an elementary teacher who uses the Internet as her resource to collect works of art. She has collected numerous images off the Internet to use in her classroom to teach about famous artists. One example she shared with me is her lesson about Vincent Van Gogh. She realized that she did not have a print of Van Gogh's most famous work, *Starry Night*. She searched the Internet and downloaded the image to use in her lesson. By using the Internet as a resource, she has put together an entire file of Van Gogh images to show her students when they study about portraits, color and Expressionism. As she stated, "The world is at my fingertips, and I am no longer limited to the resources only available in my classroom." Also, she acknowledged how the Internet provides opportunities for networking and sharing information. Often she shares her ideas, resources, and lesson plans by emailing them to other teachers. In this sense teachers can collaborate on a unit without ever leaving their classrooms. This is especially helpful to elementary teachers who are usually isolated from one another but really enjoy sharing ideas. Teachers and students can share strategies and techniques for any creative process and/or create a "collaborative" work of art online. In the past this was done via sending letters and images in the mail. Now computer technology enables students to explore numerous possibilities with one digital image.

Computer as Catalyst Interactive computer technology provides endless possibilities for art teachers. The development of multi-media and interactive, interdisciplinary units is spreading throughout the educational field. Through the use of hypertext, teachers can create broad and flexible instructional units that can be linked to other lessons within and across disciplines. Hypertext is a term used to describe "any computer program or application that involves linking and connecting" (Taylor and Carpenter 7). Software programs such as Hypermedia® allow teachers to create a series of linked cards that can be accessed to view other links or connections. Links can take the teacher from the lesson plan to other resources, images, references or activities on the Web. For instance, linking an art lesson about a contemporary painting to current events or images from the news can help make the lesson more relevant to the students. The links in hypertext give the teacher a much broader expanse of information and resources. In the past, instructional units written in notebooks were difficult to change; now hypertext allows the teacher to move from lesson to lesson linking to and connecting within the subject area or with multiple disciplines and to see the relationships among the various parts. A unit of instruction can be linked to artists, events, photography, literature, or poetry that deals with the unit concept. Links may also be set up with other teachers using the same concept within the school or beyond. Throughout the year a teacher may continue to add and/or change links and information to the "ever-evolving and growing unit of instruction" (Taylor and Carpenter 9). With the click of a button instructional units can be continuously expanded, rearranged and/or modified (Taylor and Carpenter 8). Through technology, teachers are no longer limited to the resources in their classroom or school. For teachers, developing units of instruction and resources in the twenty-first century has entered cyberspace.

For teachers, developing units of instruction and resources in the twenty-first century has entered cyberspace.

Virtual Interaction Another way to create, synthesize, and store images and information is to use Microsoft PowerPoint®. In the past, traditional classroom art history presentations included showing slides or hanging reproduction prints in the classroom. Today, a teacher can use PowerPoint® as a tool for teaching about art and artists. Two elementary teachers have shared with me how they use PowerPoint® in their classrooms. One teacher uses PowerPoint® to present lessons on Picasso and portraiture. She told me that the resources in her classroom were limited, so she searched the Internet for images and information to use in her presentation. She collected a "folder" full of images by Picasso and put them together in a Microsoft PowerPoint® presentation. She said she uses the presentation to introduce students to Picasso, Cubism, and self-portraits. To her amazement the students were much more interested and involved than they had been in prior years with this lesson. The presentation was supposed to take twenty minutes, but instead it took the entire forty-minute class period. Her students did not want to stop; they were intrigued not only by the information, but also by the presentation itself. The teacher explained to me that since so many students were already technologically proficient, they were more familiar with and interested in this tool for learning about art. Unlike traditional media (slides and prints), she was able to interest more students in learning by using technology that creates connections to their worlds. As the teacher noted, she has discovered a new way to present art and artists, and the computer has enabled her to "find what I need and put it together the way I want."

Cyberspace Another elementary teacher used PowerPoint® with her students as a tool for learning about artists and concepts in nature. The teacher collaborated with the science, English, mathematics, and computer resource teachers to teach students about nature and artists who create environmental sculptures. Each student studied a specific artist, learned about nature (plants, weather, etc.) in science, studied graphs in math, and in English wrote stories about what they learned. Then, in art, each student designed an environmental sculpture to be placed at a selected location in Virginia Beach. When they were in the computer lab, the students learned how to search and download information about the artists and how to prepare a PowerPoint® presentation. The presentations included graphs, research, writing, and images of their environmental sculpture design. As the culminating activity, students created and delivered PowerPoint® presentations about their research and sculpture designs. To complete this project, the students were led to explore nature through art, science, English, and technology and to generate an end product that also became part of the creative process. The teacher not only used technology to teach about art, but also enabled the students to use technology to explore art and to present their findings.

The Virtual Class Technology tools have long been instructional resources for teachers, and now, through the computer, technology is slowly becoming a key learning device in art. Teachers can create a learning environment in which the students can research, create, explore, and evaluate their own learning experiences. The versatility of technology allows teachers to include digital images, video, animation, and computers in their instructional units. Using multimedia in the classroom can accommodate various learning styles and increase the students' interest and participation in the learning process. Technology allows students to work independently or in groups at all age levels. As a result, the roles of teachers and their teaching methods are changing. For teachers, technology is a powerful tool for research, planning, and assessment in the art program. Presently, the traditional methods of teaching are slowly changing to include the computer with multimedia applications such as PowerPoint®, digital images, animation, and hypertext. The versatility of these mediums requires both teachers and students to understand the creative and technical processes involved. No longer is the art class isolated from other disciplines or from other art classes; now the exchange of teaching ideas and resources has global potential. A growing number of museums, galleries, and libraries are maintaining Web sites to provide educational information about works of art and artists, exhibitions, as well as sample lessons. These resources have provided teachers and students with access to new resources and ideas which can improve learning while preparing students for the contemporary world.

Wired In today's world students are exposed to an ever-expanding body of visual information. We have become a visual culture, and visual literacy has become an important component of every student's education. It has become necessary for students to be able to examine the contexts in which imagery is produced and consumed in contemporary society. In order to

> ***By incorporating technological tools such as the computer, scanners, and digital cameras into the conventional learning processes in art, the dynamics of learning can become restructured and new ways of knowing can be developed.***

understand and process this information, students' problem-solving, creative, and critical thinking skills need to be developed. Technology in the art curriculum can facilitate the development of these skills as well as the artistic and creative processes. By incorporating technological tools such as computers, scanners, and digital cameras into the conventional learning processes in art, the dynamics of learning can become restructured and new ways of knowing can be developed. Perhaps the most important technological tool to affect the dynamics of learning in art is the integration of the computer into the art room. The computer has allowed students to explore composition, design, and technical processes more fully. Works created on computers are now recognized as an art form and more graphic representations of ideas and concepts are prevalent in galleries, museums, and school art exhibits. To be literate in our technological culture requires students to have an understanding of all technological media and the ability to communicate with new technology tools. The art room provides the optimal place to provide new ways of learning through technology. For now, teachers are becoming more confident in the high tech "wired" art classroom by embracing technology as a catalyst for improving learning in and through the arts. Through change and growth emerges a new way of knowing about art, which redefines and directs our learning in the high tech world of art.

Mona, are you smiling?

Works Cited

Matthews, J. C. "Computers and Art Education." *ERIC Digest*. Bloomington IN: ERIC Clearinghouse for Social Studies/Social Science Education, 1997.

National Standards for Arts Education. *What Every Young American Should Know and Be Able to Do in the Arts* (Consortium of National Arts Education Associations). Reston, VA: National Art Education Association, 1994.

Taylor, P. & B.S. Carpenter. "Inventively Linking: Teaching and Learning with Computer Hypertext." *Art Education* 55.4 (2001): 6-12.

Walling, D. R. *Visual and Performing Arts: A Chapter of the Curriculum Handbook*. Alexandria, VA: ASCD, 2000.

Wiggins, Grant & Jay McTighe. *Understanding by Design*. Alexandria, VA: ASCD, 1998.

About Anne Wolcott

Anne Wolcott received her Ph.D. from The Pennsylvania State University in 1991, with a dissertation on strategies for interpreting works of art in the classroom. While at Penn State, she worked for two years as an evaluator for the Getty Institute for Education in the Arts. From 1991-1994, she was an assistant professor of art education at East Carolina University. While at East Carolina University, Dr. Wolcott received a grant to spend a month in New Zealand to lecture and study their art education programs.

Dr. Wolcott has authored and co-authored numerous articles on art education and co-published a book on teaching art and interdisciplinary connections. To support and promote curriculum development in Virginia Beach City Public Schools, she has received numerous grants. Dr. Wolcott's current research is focused on teaching for understanding in an art education curriculum, specifically concept-based curriculum development. She also exhibits her photography in regional art shows.

As the Fine Arts Coordinator, she oversees curriculum development, staff development, and student and teacher citywide art exhibitions. She has taught undergraduate and graduate courses in curriculum development, art appreciation, and theory and methods courses in art education.

Manipulating a Digital Self-Portrait

by Carolyn Jo Corso

Identity Through Self-Portraits Throughout history, self-portraits have been a popular subject for many artists. Rembrandt van Rijn and Vincent Van Gogh are two who were prolific as they explored their identity through self-portraits. Often when these self-portraits are examined, the inner soul of the artist is revealed. The works are painted expressively, as in the facial expressions showing the many aspects of the personalities and emotions of the artists. This may be achieved through the look in their eyes or the use of expressive color palettes. Like many artistic works, the self-portrait paintings are manipulated to give visual clues about the lives, emotions, and the culture of the artists. Just as the famous artists from other eras explored their inner self through self-portraits, art students in Virginia Beach are able to create and manipulate self-portraits to express themselves, and they have a creative media, computer graphics, that was not available to Rembrandt and Van Gogh.

Looking in the Mirror Lewis Carroll manipulated Alice in his stories, *Alice's Adventures in Wonderland* and *Through the Looking Glass*. As the tales spun, Alice was large, small, invisible, and put into bizarre environments. Much like Alice, when students manipulate self-portraits using computer graphics, the final products are visually fascinating because they can change their images in much the same way that Lewis Carroll changed Alice. I have found that when students use the computer screen to view a portrait of themselves, they experience something akin to looking into a mirror because it is life size and at an intimate level with the student artist.

Much like Alice, when students manipulate self-portraits using computer graphics, the final products are visually fascinating because they can change their images in much the same way that Lewis Carroll changed Alice.

Using the computer to manipulate self-portraits is a stimulating lesson in art and life. Through the years during art class lessons and discussions, art teachers have helped students to reflect on themselves and their lives through self-portraits. In the past, students successfully used traditional materials to create self-portraits such as sculpture, paper, paint, and various drawing media. Technology is now opening new doors for students to visually express themselves. They are confronted with digital images daily, and it is exciting to observe students as they learn how to use digital technology in an artistic way.

The Woven Effect In Figure 1, I have included an example of a digital photo and the resulting manipulation, illustrating the before and after of the process to help make the process understandable. The picture I used is of (from top to bottom) Cindy Copperthite, me, and Anne Wolcott. Reflecting on the finished image, I find it interesting that I used the clone tool to reproduce many images of us in a collage theme pulled together with the woven effect. As a tapestry is woven, our lives have been woven together in many different ways. Like Alice's adventures, we are portrayed as large, small and in what looks like a bizarre environment. The image symbolizes the weaving together of our multi-faceted lives and personalities both professionally and socially over the last twenty-five years.

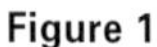

Graphic Self-Portraits The process of getting the students to create a similar work of art is professionally gratifying. The lesson of computer graphic self-portraits is used during the unit on identity which is part of the Art Foundation classes. The students are guided through a critical thinking session, analyzing self-portraits through the ages from Da Vinci, Michelangelo, Rembrandt, and Van Gogh to a contemporary artist such as Chuck Close. The students are asked to think about themselves during the class discussions, searching and reflecting on how they fit into their family, the school, the community, and the world. Several art history books and posters of artists' self-portraits are shown and discussed. Teachers ask the students to see how the different artists portray themselves as they relate to society and the world. In preparation for the time we will spend in the computer lab, I photograph groups of students in the classroom a few days ahead of our scheduled class. As part of the preparation, we review the

> *One of the major points I review here is that artists must consider the aesthetics of good balance, positive and negative space, and color.*

importance of creating good compositions along with the personal reflections. One of the major points I review here is that artists must consider the aesthetics of good balance, positive and negative space, and color. Also, we observe and discuss the elements of design (line, shape, form, space, texture, and color and value) that help orchestrate the work of art and the principles of design (movement and rhythm, unity, variety, emphasis, proportion and balance), which are essential qualities of a work of art, especially expressive pieces.

Using Paint Shop Pro™

To create the expressive self-portraits, the computer program Paint Shop Pro™ is used for the lesson. Paint Shop Pro™ is a powerful but user-friendly graphics application program by Jasc software. When we arrive in the lab, I use the InFocus® machine to project my computer screen up on the wall so they can see as I demonstrate. I have previously loaded the pictures I took of the students prior to our visit into a special folder on the school network. I show them how to access the digital picture. We review the variety of techniques they will use to manipulate their portraits. Usually among a group of twenty-eight students, there is a wide range of computer graphics skills.

> *Unfortunately, they could get lost among the infinite choices available to them when selecting effects, so I give them some requirements and boundaries.*

Unfortunately, they could get lost among the infinite choices available to them when selecting effects, so I give them some requirements and boundaries. However, before they start to manipulate the program, I ask the students to answer several self-identity questions that will lead them to think more deeply before they begin to create the self-portrait. These questions are Who am I? How am I different from others? What are my beliefs? How do I relate to my family? How do I relate to my school? How do I relate to my friends? Where have I been? Where am I going?

It is pleasing to watch them discover the tools and share them with each other. Figure 2 shows one of the several choices available to them. The one selected is the effects button on the menu bar. However, they can access several categories to change the image from across the top tool bar. These choices can be used to manipulate color and value scales. Along with these choices, students discover about eight tools with which to draw, each with many choices for size and style. The color pallet is similar to the choices an artist has when physically mixing paint colors. But, just as with someone who has been given the most expensive oil paints, brushes, and canvas, they will not be able to create a masterpiece without basic art skills such as drawing and maintaining a good composition.

Figure 2

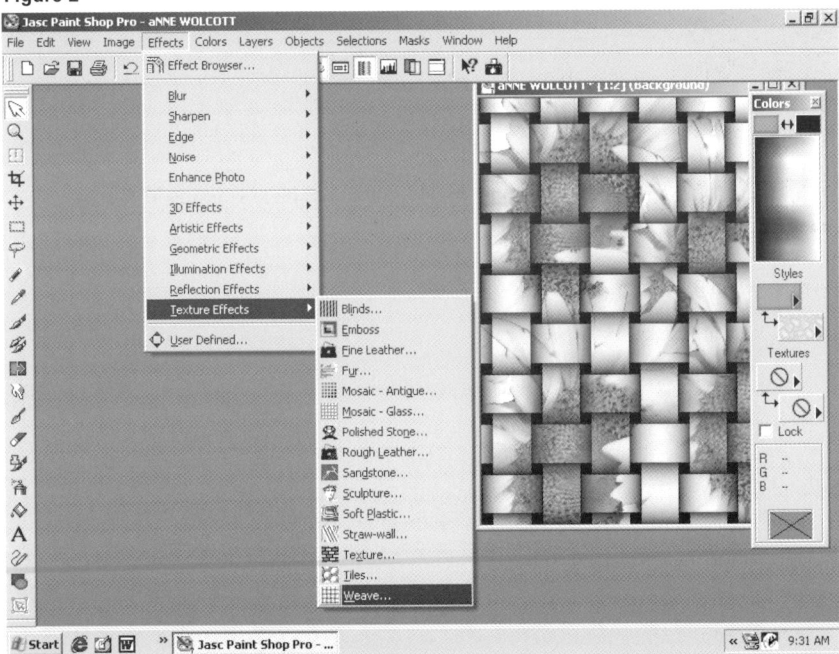

As the students work, I constantly rotate around the lab giving suggestions and helping where needed. Students are encouraged to experiment with a wide variety of techniques without losing the images of the people. Some of the varieties may include mosaic, weave, glowing edges, contours, enamel, colored pencil, neon glow, mirror image, kaleidoscope, sunburst, ripple, pinch, twirl warp, wave, wind, and many more. An example of four of them is in the illustrations included in Figure 3, A, B, C, and D. The students usually begin by tracing an image to capture it in order to copy it and then move it to a new location or add more copies such as in multiple heads. When they have cut and pasted many images, they then can apply many of the effect techniques. When they believe the composition is finished, they can print one in black and white to get the teacher's permission before they print one in color. Since color printer ink is very expensive, we have to conserve on the number of prints by the students.

Figure 3: A

Effect>Artistic>Topography

Figure 3: B

Effect>Artistic>Copperfoil

Figure 3: C

Effect>Artistic>Neon Glow

Figure 3: D

Effect>Geometric>Curly Q's

Presenting the Final Creation When the students are finished, we return to the art room and discuss the best way to present their creations. Follow-up classes include math lessons for measuring and planning a mat or a frame and demonstrating the use of the mat cutter to make a frame. Thanks to the many art galleries that donate scrap mat board, we are able to present the work professionally. Another follow-up lesson involves writing about their self-portraits. I ask them to read their responses to the self-identity questions which they used to prepare their thoughts for composing the self-portrait. Then, I ask them to state the emotion they were attempting to portray, and how they incorporated the effects they used to create the self-portrait. Using critical thinking skills and problem-solving skills, they discuss with the teacher whether or not they captured the answers they gave to the self-identity questions discussed at the start of the lesson. The self-portraits along with the writings are displayed in the school building, in the school administration building, and in local malls during the annual student art show.

> *Another follow-up lesson involves writing about their self-portraits, stating the emotion they were attempting to portray, and how they incorporated the effects they used to create the self-portrait.*

Conclusion

This has been a brief description of a very involved and creative process used in teaching the students to use computer graphics. Needless to say, computers and graphic programs are here to stay, growing and changing at an enormous speed. As an art teacher with twenty-eight years of experience, I am thrilled to be able to use technology to create art with my students.

Just as Alice sometimes found herself faced with bizarre and strange situations, using technology can sometimes result in unexpected consequences. However, by using perseverance and ingenuity, the same skills that Alice used to outwit the Queen, art teachers can work through the problems and use technology to encourage creativity in the art classroom.

About Carolyn Jo Corso

After teaching for four years in the U.S. Virgin Islands, Mrs. Carolyn Jo Corso has taught twenty-five years in the Virginia Beach City Public Schools. She has taught art on all levels, kindergarten to twelfth grade, including Advanced Placement Studio Art. She is an Adjunct Professor for Virginia Commonwealth University, where she teaches Computer Graphics.

Mrs. Corso has continued her art education since graduating from the University of Delaware in 1973. She has pursued studies at Old Dominion University, James Madison University, Virginia Polytechnic Institute of Technology, La Salle University, Manhattan College, Tidewater Community College, Virginia Wesleyan, and received a Master of Arts degree in Curriculum and Instruction from the University of Virginia in 1997. Currently, she serves as an adjunct professor for Virginia Commonwealth University in Computer Graphics.

Mrs. Corso has been very active in city, state, and national art associations. She was selected as the middle school art teacher of the year by the State of Virginia Art Education Association in 1990. She has won numerous awards including three grants from the Virginia Commission for the Arts.

In addition, she has exhibited widely in juried art shows in the Tidewater area and North Carolina. Her work can be seen in galleries, restaurants, and the permission collection of Virginia Beach City Public Schools.

Alice in Wonderland Meets Cindy in Cyberspace

by Cindy Copperthite

> *The chief difficulty Alice found at first was in managing her flamingo: she succeeded in getting its body tucked away, comfortably enough, under her arm, with its legs hanging down, but generally, just as she had got its neck nicely straightened out, and was going to give the hedgehog a blow with its head, it would twist itself round and look up in her face, with such a puzzled expression that she could not help bursting out laughing; and, when she had got its head down, and was going to begin again, it was very provoking to find that the hedgehog had unrolled itself, and was in the act of crawling away: besides all this, there was generally a ridge or a furrow in the way wherever she wanted to send the hedgehog to...Alice soon came to the conclusion that it was a very difficult game indeed* (Carroll 3).

Alice's Adventures in Wonderland, a literary example of a world of chaos, a world devoid of meaning, serves as a metaphor for my experiences with the world of technology. In many ways I not only parrot Alice, but likewise the dual role of the flamingo and hedgehog. Analogous to the tone of the passage, my journey into the world of technology seems light and comical. However, the message is wholly serious. This scene symbolizes the author's struggle and anxiety to discern meaning in a world that has reduced itself to the absurd (Chang 1) and is comparable to the struggle and anxiety I experience in my professional quest to discern meaning in the vast, inexhaustible world of technology.

Drowning in a Pool of Tears

As I journeyed at mind-boggling speed "*down the rabbit hole*," into the unfamiliar world, directly to the information super highway, I found myself getting lost, diverted, and losing focus of the big picture, parroting Alice's "*which way, which way*" mentality. I surfed the Internet for months downloading articles, jumping from link to link, not even knowing how to get back to my original quest, looking for the consummate answer to the question I was not even sure I had asked. I plummeted deeper and deeper into cyberspace; I could not stop the thrust.

"*Down, down, down. Would the fall never come to an end?*" I read. I highlighted. I took copious notes. I shuffled, arranged, and re-arranged articles and ideas. I became "*curiouser and curiouser*" as I drowned amidst pools of printed material. Like Alice, I was overwhelmed with possibilities. Both of us were not only playing a very difficult game but losing the game as well. Both of us were in a place we "*did not want to stay in any longer.*" Unlike Alice I had to "*think about stopping myself before I fell even deeper down*" the cavernous well of cyberspace. Unlike Alice, I came to a screeching halt and to the conclusion that I needed to discern meaning in this cosmic, bottomless world of technology. One way to discern meaning was not to be found in "*a little magic bottle with the words 'DRINK ME' or in very small cakes which said 'EAT ME'*" but to formulate one essential question. How do I integrate technology as a supportive tool into concept-based art education and directly relate it to the concepts and essential understandings being taught without overwhelming my students and myself? In formulating an answer to this question, I realized I must also consider the appropriateness of the technology, examine the tasks at hand, ask how technology might be used, and then decide how best to follow through (Ettinger 55). This appeared to be an overwhelming undertaking, but one I needed to embrace if I wanted to assure the use of technology as an educational tool to enhance the learning experience in concept-based art education. Otherwise, technology would serve as a meaningless ancillary source of entertainment that encompassed a glitz of gizmos and gadgets and a never-ending ride on the information superhighway. After many laborious hours and days and weeks and months of "*Which way? Which way?*" searching for the definitive macro plan, I had unwittingly committed the number one technology in education pitfall, "trying to do too much" (Pulda1).

How do I integrate technology as a supportive tool into concept-based art education and directly relate it to the concepts and essential understandings being taught without overwhelming my students and myself?

The Queen's Croquet - Ground

> *"Oh, oh, let me show you this...Did I tell you...That gives me a good idea...I'm reminded of the time...I have an example of that right over here...I didn't mean to go off on a tangent...That's a good question, let's pursue it...Quickly, pass out the books and let's try to find...Hmmmm, where were we...Did I answer your question...Oh no, the dismissal bell already...Wait, we need closure...and don't forget your homework..." These thoughts and phrases drift through my mind as I approach something new. --Coppertbite*

I am notorious for trying to do too much; this common problem plagued much of my earlier teaching. My passion for the subject matter and for motivating students often causes me to be much like Alice, a befuddled player in the Queen's chaotic and curious game of croquet. Chaos reigns! Alice would feel right at home as I lose the original focus of the unit engaging my students in well-intended activities that lack structure and cohesiveness. Alice's "*Which way? Which way?*" mentality rears its bewildered head again while I struggle to do too much, struggle to discern meaning in the still mysterious world of technology. Alice is confused. I am confused. Aren't there any rules to this game, any boundaries to the playing field, any limitations to this "*world gone mad?*"

> *Instead of searching for magic bottles, cakes, and mushrooms to solve this cyberspace predicament, I decided to heed the valuable K.I.S.S. advice offered to me by a colleague... "Keep It Simple Sweetheart."*

Instead of searching for magic bottles, cakes, and mushrooms to solve this cyberspace predicament, I decided to heed the valuable K.I.S.S. advice offered to me by a colleague..."Keep It Simple Sweetheart." "*It sounded like an excellent plan, no doubt, and very neatly and simply arranged.*" Unlike Alice I know exactly how to set about it, establishing rules to play by. I decided on Simplification Rule Number One: Implement technology into just one course, Advanced Placement Art History; Simplification Rule Number Two: Realize that the preparation and ultimate outcome has not so much to do with me, but everything to do with improving student-centered learning through the use of technology in the Advanced Placement Art History class.

The scope of what is taught in an Advanced Placement Art History class, from pre-history through the Modern era, is nothing short of daunting. The number of disciplines woven through the course embrace studio art, literary analysis, the study of philosophies and religions, and the historical, political, and social context of art and architecture within the artistic and intellectual aspects of a common culture. Cultures not only include the entire Western world but the non-European world as well. The 12 pound 1198 page textbook is, in and of itself, a frightening and intimidating tome. One would think this was more than enough for a single year course, but that is not so. Additional requirements are found on the Advanced Placement Art History exam. When they take the AP exam, students are expected to cope with the "unknown," a visual image and/or a primary source document not found in their textbook, and explain its relationship to a broader art historical context. Likewise they are asked to write from memory about Western and non-European art and culture. Whew! *"Down, down, down. Would the fall never come to an end?"*

When they take the AP exam, students are expected to cope with the "unknown," a visual image and/or a primary source document not found in their textbook, and explain its relationship to a broader art historical context.

In order to wade through a plethora of textbooks and visuals and prepare for the Advanced Placement Art History exam, it would be very easy to spoon feed or "stuff" my students with information, disjointing the big picture into fractured bits of information, via the lecture method. Even though this archaic method of teaching may have some merits, it does not engage high school students in dynamic, student-centered modes of learning. Instead of promoting passive educational experiences that alone tend to enervate and have little lasting impact (Pickering 1), I prefer to integrate meaningful hands on technology experiences that will

- engage students in gathering, organizing, manipulating, and presenting information;
- allow them an opportunity to become responsible for their own learning; and
- move them away from competitive work patterns toward collaborative ones.

Such learning experiences allow students to construct knowledge for themselves, as is expected of critical thinkers, instead of transferring information intact from the instructor. The purpose of technology then is not to replace all traditional methods of art history instruction, but to vastly expand the access to much needed information and collections of visuals. With online resources, a lack of images, particularly non-European, is no longer a limitation. Additionally, through advances in virtual tours and interactive sites, cultures and art objects produced in a given culture can be studied in context.

The Lobster Quadrille The development of constructive lessons that use online sources could find me tumbling back down the rabbit hole and succumbing to the Queen's chaotic croquet game. In order to avoid this pitfall and the consequence of needless student angst and confusion, I choose instead to dance with Alice, the Tryphon, and the Mock turtle in the "*lobster quadrille.*" This dance, the only seemingly organized rational experience in Wonderland, follows a very exact choreographed program of steps concluding in a "*delightful thing.*" As I continue to adhere to the K.I.S.S. philosophy, I must follow an exact program of steps that require the following:

- clear and reliable structure;
- specific time span, shorter is better;
- limited number of learning objectives that students can reasonably achieve in one or two classes that involve the student in active learning and not active surfing; and
- short URL list of high-quality, reliable documents, essays, and visuals (Pulda 1).

These steps are realized in the following art history lesson, which schedules online research during the 90-minute block.

Constructing Visual Imagery and Didactic File Cards That Incorporate the "Unknown" Computer networks provide powerful possibilities for student learning. The interactive capabilities of computer technology coupled with the vast amount of imagery and information available on the Internet give students a wide range of resources that they can download, print, or cut and paste into their own file (Freedman 8).

Art History students will incorporate these technology skills while creating art information file cards. Kirchner noted that this system of note-taking requires students to download two images on the back of the card. The front of the card includes information on both stylistic and contextual information. It is especially helpful to relate all work to particular "benchmark" pieces typical of the same period or style and describe similarities and differences on their information cards. By embedding technology in a concrete task, students have reason to use the application and along the way understand how the application works (Robertson 1).

The following 90-minute time schedule to engage art history students in online file card research is adapted from Arnold Pulda:

1. ten minutes to introduce the topic, set the objectives, and answer pertinent questions;
2. 55 minutes engaged in electronic research while the teacher observes students energetically, involved in creating their own scholarship and works with students one-on-one;
3. ten minutes for students to report their findings and progress to their classmates;
4. ten minutes for critique, feedback, suggestions, questions and answers; and
5. five minutes to set their personal agendas for completing the assignments (Pulda 2).

Without these concrete, choreographed steps, students like Alice and their teacher will find themselves once again playing a very difficult game indeed, a game that encourages failure instead of success. Students succeed when they are energetically involved in creating their own scholarship. They retain the content more easily because they have "lived through" the process necessary for its development (Pickering 5). Thus, assignments involving technology should require students to draw conclusions, uncover additional questions, and engage in a higher level of thinking expected of an advanced placement student. It is wise to caution the students that these sites will have numerous links to other sites, and they should not get caught up in Web surfing but remain focused on the clearly

Without these concrete, choreographed steps, students like Alice and their teacher will find themselves once again playing a very difficult game indeed, a game that encourages failure instead of success.

stated objectives. I concur with Erickson that broad, cross-cultural themes and key inquiry questions are valuable in helping students navigate through the ever-growing abundance of online information and imagery (Erickson 34).

Student-centered Primary Source Documents While traveling a tumultuous journey into cyberspace, I ultimately learned that a myriad of computer techniques exists to assist the students in constructing their own knowledge. With this in mind, I offer this piece of evidence to help jump-start the use of technology as a tool to promote student inquiry and scholarship.

Student excitement and interest peaked by having them participate in an organic formal description and analysis of Picasso's, *Guernica*. They eagerly expressed many more "What do I still want to know?" types of questions. In the past I typed these queries and during the next class meeting I handed them back along with photocopies that I made of primary source materials. Students then read the documents to answer their own questions. Inevitably many more inquiries were raised, and I either created more photocopied handouts or, because of time, I researched the answers and presented my findings to the students. However, the time for me to be the repository of all knowledge has come to an end. Instead of employing an Aristotelian approach, I can move my students to a constructivist approach (Dunn 9) by pointing them toward information that will lead to their own "meaningful and personal knowledge bases" (Gregory 8), rather than enabling them to rely on me as "the resident oracle of knowledge" (Dunn 11). A constructivist approach to electronic information allows students to collect their own original data or primary source documents from experts in the field. Students are asked to locate a single online primary source document, examine it for its meaning and relevance to the current theme, and answer three or four essential questions that lead the students into and through the document. These documents contain links to additional contextual information and a variety of other documents and images. As questions arise, answers can be found immediately online

> *Students are asked to locate a single online primary source document, examine it for its meaning and relevance to the current theme, and answer three or four essential questions that lead the students into and through the document.*

while student interest is peaking. If the abundance and quality of information available on the Internet can enrich the lesson significantly and promote students to construct understandings from a range of sources, then it should be incorporated. Through these actions, students will be more likely to learn, remember, and apply knowledge gained.

Teacher-centered Collecting and Cataloguing of Images Because the Advanced Placement national exam requirement expects students to understand architectural drawings, I am currently reformatting a very confusing architecture lesson entirely to use online resources from the beginning. This will allow me to present the lesson in a clear, concise, and summative computer-generated format. The conceptual framework of the lesson focuses on floor plans and elevation plans as they relate to building interiors and exteriors. Many electronic sources exist for collecting digital art images. Gary Kerschner, an Art History consultant, helped me simplify this process by offering his lists and guidelines.

Electronic Sources

- The World Wide Web
- CD-ROMs
- Digital photographs
- Scans from printed sources
- Scans of 35 mm film and slides
- Laser Disks
- Books using document cameras (Kirchner 1)

To catalogue digital images Kirchner recommends the core categories of the Visual Resources Association (VRA), the international organization of image media professionals. Kirchner recommends that after images are digitized and organized, one of the many presentation applications included in the following annotated list be utilized:

- Hyper Studio® (inexpensive and simple)
- Microsoft PowerPoint® (versatile but cumbersome)
- Kai Power Show® (one of the easiest and best for organizing and displaying digital images for art history slide presentations)
- Live Slide Show®
  (at http://www.totallyhip.com/Products/LiveSlideShowindex.html)
- Iview Media Pro® (my newest learning challenge)
- Pictacula® (my current favorite, very fast and very easy) (Kirchner 2)

Formatting images chronologically is but one way to demonstrate direct correlations, comparisons, and contrasts. Images can be cropped or enlarged and displayed on the same slide to illustrate progression and change. The accompanying text and ease of access allows students to view the program independently for further clarification and review. This example of electronic formatting, a difficult concept, alleviates much aggravation and waste of time as the glut of handouts, slides, additional reading assignments, and multiple texts are eliminated, thus promoting a very "*delightful thing*"... time on task for both students and teacher.

And, the Moral of the Story Is...

> ***Pandemonium continued to hold sway until I managed to tuck my flamingo's body safely under my arms, straighten out its legs, and untwist my balled up hedgehog.***

I began my professional pursuit trying to discern meaning in the vast inexhaustible world of technology by not only parroting Alice, but also the dual role of the flamingo and hedgehog. I played a very "*difficult game indeed,*" one that began devoid of meaning, of rules, of structure. Unlike Alice I could not rely on little magic bottles, or cakes, or mushrooms to assist me in this endeavor. Pandemonium continued to hold sway until I managed to tuck my flamingo's body safely under my arms, straighten out its legs, and untwist my balled up hedgehog. How was I able to pull off such an arduous accomplishment? My only way out of Alice's unruly world was to begin with a K.I.S.S. According to the duchess in Wonderland, "*Everything's got a moral, if only you can find it*" (Carroll 1). Keep It Simple Sweetheart and Remember To SAVE!

Conclusion

"Education is a dynamic field of professional inquiry and practice that regularly experiences significant trends, changing issues, and new perspectives" (Goodwin 8). If I believe these new perspectives, including technology, will be a catalyst for improving student learning and student enthusiasm for learning, then I embrace them and commit myself to acquire the knowledge necessary to incorporate them into my teaching. This has never been an easy task; however, commitment and change are not synonymous with easy. Akin to Alice, I struggle as I try to do too much.

As I journey closer to retirement, peers ask me why? Why do I push myself and often others who are unwilling? Why do I care about the latest trend, changing issues or new perspectives? Why do I muster the required energy? Why do I put so much time and effort into researching, reading, and trying to find ways to embed technology into my art education program? The answer is simple; my students are worth every bit of the effort. Technology provides me with yet another tool to

- reach all of my students,
- accommodate numerous learning styles,
- teach for understanding,
- offer more ways to relate content to a student's personal experiences, and
- open doors to active learning and new forms of creative, critical, and technical expression.

As a result of integrating technology into the Advanced Placement Art History curriculum, my students and I now have opportunities not only to improve but also to embrace meaningful learning by sharing equally in the inquiry and discovery process.

Works Cited

Carroll, Lewis. *Alice's Adventures in Wonderland.* <http://users.starpower.net/linker/wonderland/>

Chang, Annette. "The Grotesque and Chaotic in Alice in Wonderland." *The Victorian Web: Literature, History, and Culture in the Age of Victoria.* Brown University, 1993: 1-2 <http://www.victorianweb.org/authors/carroll/aiwl7.html>

Dunn, Phillip, C. "More Power: Integrated Interactive Technology and Art Education." *Art Education: The Journal of the National Art Education Association.* Nov. 1996: 6-11.

Erickson, Mary. "Images of Me: Why Broad Themes? Why Focus on Inquiry? Why Use the Internet?" *Art Education: The Journal of the National Art Education Association.* Jan. 2001: 33-40.

Ettinger, L.F. "Art Education and Computing: Building a Perspective." *Studies in Art Education.* 30(1) 1995: 53-62.

Freedman, K. "Visual Art/Virtual Art: Teaching Technology for Meaning." *Art Education: The Journal of the National Art Education Association.* July 1997: 6-12.

Goodwin, MacArthur. "Visual Arts Education: Setting an Agenda for Improving Student Learning." 2001: 1-14http://www.naea-reston.org/Agenda.pdf

Gregory, D.C. "Art Education Reform and Interactive Integrated Media." *Art Education: The Journal of the National Art Education Association*. May 1995: 8-17.

Kerschner, Gary. "Collecting and Displaying Digital Images." *AP Art History Handout LaSalle University*. Summer 2002: 1-4.

Pickering, Jane Carlson. "Teachers in Technology Initiative." *21st Century Learning Initiative: Promoting a Vision, Knowledge, Experience and a Network.* Nov. 1999: 1-18 <http://www.21learn.org/arch/articles/pickering.html>

Pulda, Arnold. "Using Technology in the Classroom." *AP Central: The College Board's Online Home for AP Professionals*. July 2002: 1-4 <http://apcentral.collegeboard.com/members/article/1,3046,184-0-0-11376,00.html>

Robertson, Bill. "Integrating Technology into Instruction." MultiMedia Schools. March/April 2000: 1-5 <http://www.infotoday.com/MMSchools/mar00/robertson.htm.>

About Cynthia Moneta Copperthite

Cynthia Moneta Copperthite holds a Bachelor of Science in Art Education from Longwood College and a Master of Art Education from Virginia Commonwealth University. Her teaching experience began in 1972 in Warren, Pennsylvania. She then moved to Virginia Beach and has taught at Kempsville Junior High School, Kellam High School, Bayside High School, Birdneck Elementary School, W.T. Cooke Elementary School, and is presently teaching art and special education at Ocean Lakes High School.

Visual Communication Rules!

by Gwen Stevens

As an art teacher who formerly worked as a graphic artist, I have maintained an interest in technology related to advertising and other commercial art fields. The advent of the graphical interface of the Internet, along with innovative advances in digital design, captured my attention in the 1990s. By 1995 our local daily newspaper was composed and printed in a digital format. Architects and other designers were forsaking the drafting table for the keyboard and mouse. In addition, illustrators and professional artists were accomplishing stunning and previously impossible works of art in the digital format. Historically, artists have always embraced newer technologies as they strove for innovation. Although my teaching assignment was on the elementary level, I felt strongly that my students should be involved with the computer as a significant art medium for both personal expression and visual communication. With this new awareness, I made a serious commitment to bring my computer skills up to par and to deliver the excitement of that learning to my students as well. Over the years I have investigated various ways of integrating computer technology into the art program of study. I have also enjoyed experimenting with the computer as a medium for my own art and as a tool for teaching.

Digital Art in the Classroom

I discovered early that drawing and erasing can occupy a student endlessly, so I structured lessons to avoid erasing.

Having only one or two computers in the art classroom created time limitations for students and forced me to design more effective lessons so that all students would learn the specific objectives in a short time period. One of the things I discovered early was that drawing and erasing can occupy a student endlessly, so I structured lessons to avoid erasing. Although technology and art objectives are met in lessons, the computer graphic is used basically as just another art medium in understanding concepts and meeting curriculum goals.

Demonstrations and presentations are enhanced by a Personal Computer (PC) attached to a TV video converter which displays the contents of the PC screen on the TV screen, whether it is a live demonstration, an Internet viewing, or a presentation. In addition, the process allows the teacher to monitor the student's progress. These converter units are much less expensive than Liquid Crystal Display (LCD) panels or video projectors and are readily available in most Virginia Beach schools.

Recommended software applications begin with KidPix®. It is already installed on most computers at the elementary level and is familiar to young students. The concept of non-objective art may be easily applied with the KidPix® lesson in Figure 1.

Figure 1

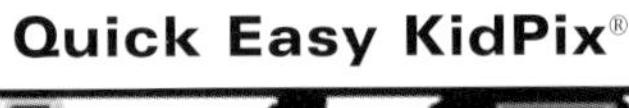

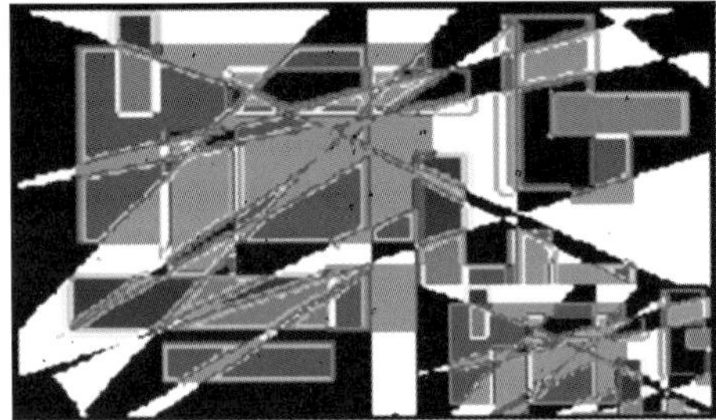

1. Use the shape tools in the solid color mode to pull out enough shapes to fill the space of the screen. No erasing allowed.
2. Limit and repeat colors.
3. Use the "Mixer" to transform the design. Two mixers are about enough for a pleasing result. (Remember the "undo guy!")

Usually, I will print directions like these and tape them to the computer. Another strategy to help students is to have a "watcher" sit next to the student who is using the computer to observe and then take the next turn. It is helpful to repeat demonstrations periodically or pull a small group to the computer for a quick review.

Other ways to utilize KidPix® include importing and manipulating visual images. Sources for visual images include clip art, photo CDs, digital cameras, scans (from hardware that copies a picture or object into the computer), and even images from the Internet that can be converted to a bitmap (PC) or pict (Mac) file. PhotoShop® and PaintShop Pro™, as well as smaller shareware programs, do this. One limitation of KidPix® is the low (72 dpi) resolution and limited colors (256). It is necessary to be sure the file is 72 dpi and horizontal in format. Images may also be copied to the clipboard and pasted into the application. Drawings may be filled with the

Paint Bucket of course, but the "Mixer" provides instant fun. The mixer tools operate like PhotoShop® filters to transform the image. Colors may be changed, images distorted, fragmented, copied, enlarged, and more. These changes are precisely those that an artist may employ in traditional media to create an abstract image. The KidPix's Keyboard® tool can be used to employ lettering as a design element or signature.

The mixer tools operate like PhotoShop® filters to transform the image. Colors may be changed, images distorted, fragmented, copied, enlarged, and more.

Art Dabbler™ and Painter™ are natural media computer art programs that can also be used in a similar fashion by importing a bitmap image and applying effects (filters) to transform it. These programs can also be used with a drawing tablet to simulate traditional drawing and painting media. Once again, a scanned student line drawing presents a time advantage over start to finish projects on the computer. A tracing paper feature can be used to trace over photos or other images and to interpret them in a new way.

Jasc's PaintShop Pro™ is a robust PC painting program similar to PhotoShop® but far less expensive. This is a professional program which allows for higher resolution or clarity. This past year I used it with a fifth-grade class to create a contemporary portrait lesson. I took a picture of each child with a digital camera and uploaded them to the computer. The students created an abstracted self-portrait by selecting from the numerous filters and effects provided by PaintShop Pro™. (See Figure 2.) Some portraits were printed and displayed in the school building and at art shows. A digital camera is an ideal source for digital art because it bypasses any copyright issues for publication or display. In this particular project students had the additional option of having their portraits posted on the Magic Internet site at www.getmagic.net.

Figure 2

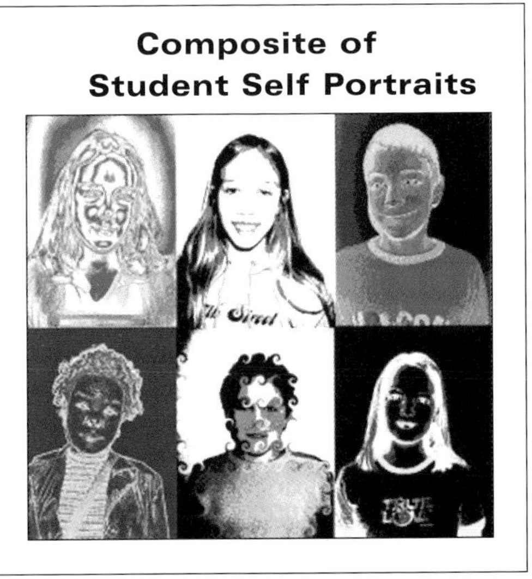

Displaying Student Art Options for displaying student art include hard copy printing for conventional exhibits, but some other choices are fun and instructive for students. KidPix® includes an easy to use slide show program as part of KidPix® Studio, in which students may insert their creations, add a zany tune or sound, or even narrate the slides themselves. Hyperstudio is another popular slide program suited to elementary age youngsters. There is a variety of slide utility programs like IrfanView which allows one to simply put a folder of files into the program and choose options to show them. Some come bundled with software for digital cameras. By using a PC to TV video converter, printing to videotape is an economical alternative to hard print copies. Students truly enjoy seeing their own and other classmates' work in slide show presentations. They can bring a videotape from home to tape the show for home viewing with family and friends, too. With the recent introduction of computers with CD burning capabilities into Virginia Beach schools, writing multimedia presentations to CD for students is another option.

Internet Art Exhibits Another way of sharing art with an audience is to post the work to Internet art exhibits. Artsonia at www.artsonia.com is an online students' art museum showcasing artwork from students around the world. One may be sent to Artsonia for scanning, and they will return it. There is no cost to teachers or students. Google.com may also be used as a search engine. Some Internet sites are devoted to particular themes.

Locally, the Magic Internet project at www.getmagic.net invites Hampton Roads students to listen to original songs and lyrics and to interpret them in an artwork for an Internet exhibit. A multi-media event is staged locally in which student art is projected onto large screens as part of a live concert. Participating students are invited to the concert which is broadcast over the Internet. This successful five-year-old program provides integrated classroom activities relating to social studies, English, math, science, music, art, and technology and is correlated to Virginia's Standards of Learning. Artwork does not need to be digital in origin but must be scanned or photographed in *jpeg* or *gif* format for Internet viewing. Posting to the Web site is amazingly easy.

> *Art teachers can work with a computer resource person to set up a great venue for the art program that is accessible to parents and the community.*

School Internet sites are an ideal location for a student gallery. Art teachers can work with a computer resource person to set up a great venue for the art program that is accessible to parents and the community. Text may accompany the work for greater understanding of the merit of the lessons. As the school Webmaster at Linkhorn Park Elementary, I used a digital camera to photograph student art and post it to a special section of our site called Student Art Online. Linkhorn's Internet address is www.linkhornparkes.vbcps.k12.va.us. Note that parent and student permission is required by the Virginia Beach City Public Schools' Internet policy, and student last names are not used to protect privacy.

Aesthetics, Criticism, and Art History

Digital technology is helpful in the art classroom in areas not directly related to art production, too. Students and teachers can access tremendous resources related to artists and works of art on the Internet and in commercially available CDs. As a user of the *html* Internet code, it has been convenient for me to cut and paste artist presentations from the Web for student viewing via the PC to TV converter, using a browser as a presentation program. Slide presentation programs such as Microsoft PowerPoint® are well suited to teacher presentations. Also, students absent at the original viewing can sit down at the computer to catch up when they return. The Web is a rich source of visual resources for classroom activities; I often print materials for use in critical thinking and assessment writing activities.

Student art reports can be brought to life by creating a group slide show; to present these, students may select an appropriate art print to combine with brief information to be enjoyed by classmates. The visual communication skills learned in art activities such as this can be applied to other areas as well in the student's future academic career and life.

Conclusion—Art, Technology, and Visual Communication

Art and computer technology are natural partners in a world where visual communication rules. The popularity of the Internet as an information source certainly lends credence to this assertion, as does the impact of visual learning and entertainment in TV and film media. The skills that students learn and apply in combining art and technology certainly

> *Art and computer technology are natural partners in a world where visual communication rules.*

will prepare them to meet the needs of a rapidly changing society. High teacher expectations, coupled with the excitement of working with newer technology, make possible powerful learning and achievement for elementary students in a "hands on" and enjoyable environment.

Note: Photographs are used with the permission of the students and parents.

About Gwen Stevens

Gwen Stevens received a Bachelor of Science in Education from Old Dominion University in 1968 and a Master of Art Education from Virginia Commonwealth University in 1980, where she was elected to the honorary fraternity, Phi Kappa Phi, for academic excellence. Her teaching career spans over thirty years and includes teaching on the elementary, middle, and high school levels. Currently, she is the art teacher at Linkhorn Park Elementary, where she is also school webmaster.

An active professional, Ms. Stevens has been involved over the years in curriculum development and has conducted numerous teacher workshops on the local, state, and national levels. She has served on the boards of Tidewater and Virginia Art Education Associations. In addition, she has written for local, state, and National Art Education Association publications.

Ms. Stevens was the 1990 recipient of the National Youth Art Month Award of Excellence for her statewide leadership in art education advocacy. She was elected Tidewater Virginia Elementary Art Educator of the Year for 1994. Her exhibit record includes works in acrylic painting and ceramic jewelry, as well as computer graphics.

A community volunteer, Ms. Stevens holds offices in both the Virginia Beach Audubon Society and in Lynnhaven Flotilla 57 of the Coast Guard Auxiliary. She initiated and has coordinated a Virginia Beach City Public School citywide student art exhibit sponsored by the Audubon Society, which is now in its eleventh year. She serves as webmaster for both groups. Her Coast Guard Auxiliary Web site was recognized as Best in the Nation for the year 2000.

Breaking the Music Box Through Technology

by Kenneth W. Smead

If you go into any school to look for uses of technology in education, I feel sure that one of your stops would not be the choral classroom. You would probably stop by the English department as well as math and science, not to mention the computer labs that are in each school. Some people might argue that the field of music has very little to do with technology; that is where they are wrong. I am a chorus director at Larkspur Middle School, and I use technology in my classroom every day to complete administrative tasks, to enhance the musical classroom experience, and to allow my students to become part of the active learning process.

> *I have kept my head above water by using the computer to organize and complete assigned tasks.*

Administrative Tasks and Lesson Plans

Administrative tasks can quickly overwhelm the most experienced teacher. I have kept my head above water by using the computer to organize and complete assigned tasks. As a choral director, I have the same tasks that most teachers have: lesson plans, grades, activity worksheets, and tests. Additionally I need to create concert programs and musical examples for my students to sing. Most of this can be accomplished by using a word processor.

Using Microsoft Word®, I created a basic template for my chorus lesson plans that can be easily filled in each day. The template cuts down on the amount of time spent formatting my lesson plan, so I can spend additional time on lesson content. When an administrator visits my classroom and wants to see the Virginia Standards of Learning (SOL) objectives on which I am working that day, it is easy to oblige. I have a list of all the standards in one document, and I have copied and pasted them into my lesson plan. I am also required to keep an SOL task list for each semester, listing the objectives taught and class progress toward completion. Using my SOL document, I can copy and paste objectives into my task list and note student progress. Using the copy and paste technique, I have the ability to carry objectives and music from one day to the next without writing and rewriting them.

Creating professional looking music handouts and worksheets is extremely easy using a word processor and music notation software. Notation software

Creating professional looking music handouts and worksheets is extremely easy using a word processor and music notation software.

is designed to create a printed sheet of music. It is a word processor for music. Musical examples can be created using the "music processor." Then these are inserted into a document. Figure 1 was created using a software program called Sibelius™. After the musical example was created, I turned it into a simple graphic file to insert into this document.

Figure 1 – C major scale

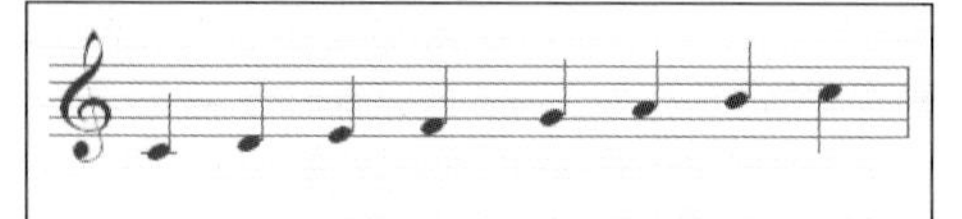

Singing handouts can be created using notation software to reinforce the comprehension of reading music. I can create my own examples that stress the SOL objective on which I am currently working. After creating the handout, I make copies for all my students, and we sing using the handout at the beginning of class. Our school has a wonderful machine which can take a normal sheet of paper and enlarge it to poster size. This allows me to create a poster of musical examples for class that I laminate at various times for reuse.

I am currently creating a database in Microsoft Access® to house our entire music department's library: choral, band and orchestra. This database will be placed on our school network so that all music teachers will have access to our inventory. Not only will we have instant access to performance notes and composer information, but we will also be able to track when the selection was last performed in our school. For choral music, a special field will be created to store musical accompaniment files.

Enhancing the Musical Classroom Experience

As a choir director, one of the most difficult problems is being able to perform several complicated tasks at the same time. It is extremely demanding to listen to the students' performance, read all six to eight parts of the music, and worry that my fingers will strike the correct keys on the piano. I realized that about forty percent of my energy was not focused on what the students were doing, but on what I was doing at the keyboard. This is not how things should be; my students should have one hundred percent of my attention. Technology came to the rescue in the form of the Musical Instrument Digital Interface (MIDI).

To me, one of the greatest advances in the field of music was the creation and standardization of the MIDI computer language. The MIDI language allows musical instruments to talk to computers and computers to talk back. Many would compare this to a digital player piano. Using MIDI software, I can sit down at my electronic keyboard at home, play a piece of music, and have the computer record my performance. I then take the recorded performance and use it as accompaniment for my choir. I use two types of music software in my choir class daily, music notation software and music sequencing software.

> *The MIDI language allows musical instruments to talk to computers and computers to talk back.*

Music notation software also presents me with a computerized sheet of staff paper on which to write music. Using the mouse and keyboard, I can enter a piece of music into the computer to give to a student. At the same time that I am creating a printed piece of music, I am also creating a MIDI file that can be used for playback. This year our music department combined our classes for the Music in Our Schools Month Concert. We scoured countless catalogs and quickly realized that there is very little music written for middle school bands, orchestras, and choirs. With the aid of notation software, I was able to take two of the choir selections on which I had worked and orchestrate the accompaniment for band and orchestra. Because notation software is designed to create a printed page, and I wanted a piece of music I could give to all the band and orchestra students, I began to work with a program called Sibelius™. The first task was to create a score for the conductor which has all the parts printed on it. Sibelius™ allowed me to input the list of instruments with which I had to work and create a blank piece of staff paper to begin the accompaniment. Several instruments play notes that do not sound as they are written; these are known as transposing instruments. To create a score for these instruments, a composer must be able to read the score and mentally make the transposition to know what note an instrument is playing. Sibelius™ allows the computer to create a score in concert key, or sounding key, so that each note shown is the actual note that will be sounded by the instrument. With the push of a button, Sibelius™ automatically shifts all instrumental parts to where they should be written. After making this shift, the program extracts each instrument part individually so that these can be printed for the band and orchestra. Creating the accompaniment for each selection would have taken me two weeks using pen and paper. It would have involved creating a score for the

Using notation software, I was able to accomplish each accompaniment in two days with zero errors in the transposed instrumental parts.

conductor, then individually copying each part for the instruments. Using notation software, I was able to accomplish each accompaniment in two days with zero errors in the transposed instrumental parts.

Whereas music notation software is designed for creating a printed piece of music that students read, music sequencing software is designed to create performance music or sound files. This software works with the sound of the music. Music sequencing software is the workhorse in my classroom. Sequencing software allows me to bring the musical focus back to where it should be, one hundred percent on the students and their performance. I am able to take each musical selection we perform and, through the use of sequencing software, enter it into the computer. This creates the accompaniment for the choir. Using sequencing software and my computer, I can not only play the accompaniment for all my choir music, but also have the students' parts play at the same time. When I am working on a specific section of the music, I can mute all parts except the section on which I am working, so only that part is played by the computer. After students learn their respective parts in the music, I can mute those parts, and the students will hear only the accompaniment. I can also add additional instrument parts if needed. For our holiday concert, we performed a selection that included optional drum parts. I was able to sequence the drum parts into the computer allowing students to practice with the drums prior to the concert. Simply adding a Hip Hop beat to *Deck the Halls* can easily liven up a holiday concert.

On one occasion this year, I selected a piece of music for a performance and after listening to it, the choir was extremely excited and ready to begin work. Two days before the concert several of my sopranos came down with sinus problems, so severe that many of them temporarily lost a few notes at the top of their singing range. Instead of removing the selection from the concert, I was able to quickly move the entire selection to a key that was easier to perform. During the concert, I hooked my computer to the auditorium sound system for the accompaniment. It was fantastic!

Technology has also given musicians the ability to create practice Compact Discs (CDs). During auditions for All-district Chorus, I created an audition CD for each of my students. Using sequencing software, I was able to enter the music and set the music so the accompaniment played in the right ear and their part played in the left ear. As the students learned the music, they would only listen mainly to the right ear, using the left ear to occasionally correct pitch errors. Soprano, alto, and bass were given separate CDs that contained each one's own part and accompaniment so they did not have to listen to the other voices. Also, on occasion, I have created special CDs for students who were having a particularly tough time learning a song or who were learning a solo for a concert.

The Active Learning Process Active learning has become one of the "buzz" phrases that administrators love to hear, and music lends itself very easily to this process. Coda Music® has a free piece of notation software called Finale Notepad™ that can be downloaded from the Internet and installed in a computer lab. This software allows every student the opportunity to create his or her own composition and be able to hear how it sounds. Students enter the program using the mouse and can then immediately listen to their creation. When the students come to a section they do not like, they can use the computer to make changes and then listen to the revised music. This gives the students immediate feedback on their work. We began this year with simple rhythmic examples and worked our way up to eight-measure compositions using three instruments. When we were working on note names, each student was required to spell seventeen words using the lines and spaces on a staff. Each word had to fill an entire measure, so students were forced to think about rhythmic values as well. The Computer Resource Specialist (CRS) was very helpful in installing the software and setting up a day each week, so I could bring my students to the computer lab. This was the first year we used music software in the computer lab, and I hope that by the time my current sixth graders move into the eighth grade they will be creating music with lyrics to be performed on a concert. For our spring concert, I took compositions from each class and placed them on a computer in the lobby of the auditorium. The computer was set to play the compositions as parents were entering the school for our performance. Two students from each class were assigned to the lobby prior to the concert to answer any questions parents might have about how the music was created.

> *This software will allow every student the ability to create his or her own composition and be able to hear how it sounds.*

Financing Your Program Someone asked me how I could afford to use technology in my classroom, and my reply was, "How can I not afford to use it?" Music software runs the gamut in pricing from Finale Notepad™, which is free, to Cakewalk Sonar 2.0™, which runs approximately $500.00; there is software available for everyone. The more expensive software definitely has more bells and whistles, but, for what classroom teachers need, many software packages under $75.00 will suffice. The least expensive programs that I have used in my classroom are Finale Notepad Plus™ ($24.95), a simple notation program, and the Cakewalk PC Music Pack™ ($49.00), a simple sequencing program. Finale Notepad Plus™ is a notation program for writing vocal warm-up exercises for students to sing in class. The main difference between the free version of Finale Notepad™ and the $24.95 version is the ability to create standard MIDI files. For me, spending $24.95 to add this ability is worth the extra cost. The Cakewalk PC Music Pack™ comes with the sequencing program Cakewalk Express™ and a set of cables to connect a computer with an electronic keyboard. The main difference that one would notice as a teacher is that Cakewalk Express™ limits the number of MIDI tracks a student can create to eight, which should be more than enough for most choral music. With the use of music software I can enhance many core academic classroom objectives like spelling, fractions, and poetry. What is more innovative than that?

Enhancing Classroom Objectives I like to have my students write a short report on a famous musician. This can be someone who was a classical composer or who is a current popular singer. The first time I assigned this, I came to the conclusion that many of my students had trouble spelling correctly. I quickly developed two lessons using Finale Notepad™ that would help my students become better spellers. Music uses the first seven letters of the alphabet, A – G. If the teacher includes an R for rests, the students now have eight letters to use to spell words. For lesson one I gave each student access to a dictionary and told them to make as many words as possible using these eight letters. The students not only had to write the word, but also had to use the correct pitches on the staff. Each word could fill only one measure. This caused students to think about how the word was spelled and concentrate on correct rhythmic values as shown in Figure 2.

Figure 2 – Spelling Lesson One

Figure 3 – Spelling Lesson Two

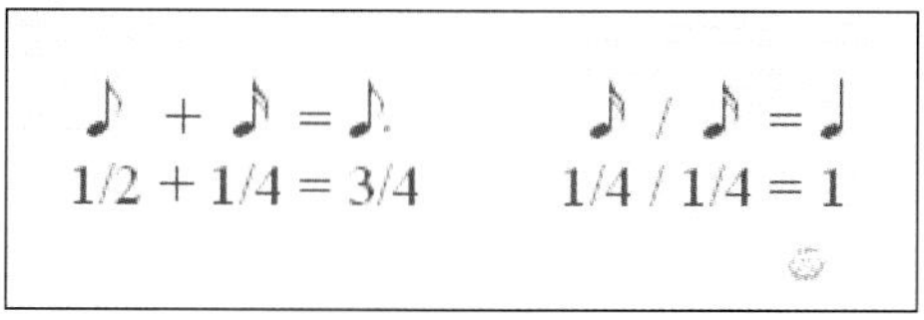

For the second lesson, I created a sheet of words spelled out in simple musical notation. I then scrambled the letters for each word. The students had to write the correct pitch name on the space below the word. In the second set of spaces they had to unscramble the words as shown in Figure 3.

Figure 4 – Fractions

1/2 + 1/4 = 3/4   1/4 / 1/4 = 1

When I discovered that the math teachers were working on fractions with their students, I created a worksheet that used note values instead of numbers. On the worksheet the students had to take each note value and convert it to a number. Eighth notes became ½ while sixteenth notes became ¼ because there are two eighth notes in a quarter note and four sixteenth notes in a quarter note. Once the answer was obtained, the student took the answer and converted it back into rhythmic notation as shown in Figure 4.

When I discovered that the math teachers were working on fractions with their students, I created a worksheet that used note values instead of numbers.

Poetry was a simple unit to prepare because most songs written today have a set of lyrics that read like poetry. In class we talk about simple poetic meter such as iambic pentameter and trochaic pentameter and notice if any of the songs written today use these meters. I then try to take a verse from a poem they are currently studying in English and put simple rhythmic notation to the words. In my advanced class, once we have put a rhythmic value to the words, we use Finale Notepad™ and create melodies to accompany the poem.

Conclusion Technology implementation is a daunting task, but the rewards for the students and for me are immeasurable. I found that using technology in my classroom has not only enhanced my students' musical experience, but also has enhanced mine as well. With the time saved by using the computer, I can work on my own musicianship by creating new arrangements and compositions for my choirs to perform. I am able to focus more on the content of my music, rather than making sure it looks correct. From completing administrative tasks to refocusing a teacher's energy in the classroom, technology has come a long way. In education we are always looking for a new way to introduce information to our students, and our supervisors are often asking us to "Think outside the box." With the advances technology has made in the field of music, the "box" has been broken and a whole new and innovative way to work awaits those who wish to take the journey.

About Kenneth Smead Kenneth Smead is a second-year chorus director at Larkspur Middle School. Mr. Smead retired from the United States Navy as a Chief Musician where he performed and taught as a vocalist. He has given lectures at the school level and traveled throughout the Commonwealth of Virginia giving lectures on the implementation of Music Technology. Ken recently made a presentation on Music Technology at the State Conference of the Virginia Society for Technology in Education.

Section Two

From Elephants to Odysseys: English Teachers Entwine Technology *With* Reading and Writing

Gwen S. Stevens

Rose in Water: Inner Secrets

Description: I began this artwork by selecting a rose from my garden, which I scanned directly into Photoshop® for image manipulation. In exploring computer graphics, I am constantly delighted with its capacity for magical transformations, which refresh, refine, and intensify the perceptual experience. The experimental aspect of investigating newer media is engaging, exciting, and it has expanded horizons for me in teaching as well in personal art production.

Medium Used: Computer Graphics

Educational Background: Gwen S. Stevens received a Bachelor of Science degree in Education from Old Dominion University in 1968 and a Master of Arts in Education from Virginia Commonwealth University in 1980, where she was elected to the honorary fraternity, Phi Kappa Phi, for academic excellence.

Teaching Experience: Ms. Stevens' teaching career spans over thirty years, and includes teaching on the elementary, middle, and high school levels. She is currently the art teacher at Linkhorn Park Elementary School, where she is also the school Webmaster.

Awards: Ms. Stevens was the 1990 recipient of the National Youth Art Month Award of Excellence for her statewide leadership in art education advocacy. She was elected Tidewater Virginia Elementary Art Educator of the Year for 1994. Her exhibit record includes works in acrylic painting and ceramic jewelry, as well as computer graphics. Her Coast Guard Auxiliary web site was recognized as "Best in the Nation" for the year 2000.

From Elephants to Odysseys: English Teachers Entwine Technology With Reading and Writing

The appropriate use of technology in the English/language arts classroom goes far beyond seating a child in front of a computer to react to programmed learning situations. English/language arts teachers are using computer programs, digital portfolios, Web sites, online academic communities, and digital cameras not only to deal with the ever increasing administrative paperwork that is demanded more and more of classroom teachers, but to improve instruction.

Just as Hannibal used elephants to conquer the Alps, Rhonda Green used an elephant named Elliott to introduce a computer reading program to kindergarten students. In addition, this program enabled her to reach Chen, a student who entered her classroom with very little understanding of English. As she guided Chen through individualized learning experiences coupled with lessons on the computer from the *Breakthrough to Literacy*™ program, Chen changed from a withdrawn and hesitant student into a confident writer and reader of English. By the end of the year, he was giggling with excitement as he quickly typed sentences on his computer.

Throughout the 90s and the early years of the twenty-first century English teachers were bombarded with articles from the news media about the deplorable writing skills displayed by high school graduates. Many solutions to this problem were written about in journals and experimented with in English High School classrooms across the country. In Virginia Beach, English teachers explored the use of writing portfolios to encourage students to become more involved in the improvement of their writing. In this section, two English teachers who have used writing portfolios to assess their students' writing progress describe how they have moved from using the paper portfolio to the digital portfolio. Each of the teachers is in a different place on this academic journey. Lisette Piccillo, a twelfth-grade English teacher, explains how she began using portfolios with her students and discusses how that experience led her to evaluate and change several aspects

Left to Right: Lisette Piccillo, Donna Spence, Patricia Sears, Rhonda Green, and Susan Motley

of her instruction that finally led her to using the digital portfolio in her classroom. On the other hand, Elizabeth Beagle, an English teacher at Landstown High School, jumped feet first into digital portfolios with her students. As she describes this sink or swim experience, she relates how her students have improved their writing skills and their attitudes toward writing through the use of this technological tool.

Experiencing a lesson that failed is every teacher's nightmare. When this happened to Susan Motley during a lesson focusing on the poets of the first world war, she turned to Oxford University's "Virtual Seminars for Teaching Literature," a Web site rich in information about British writers. The site provided the students with primary sources that would have been unavailable to her and her students before the advent of the Internet. Through this technology, Susan was able to turn an unsuccessful experience into a positive one for herself and her students.

Overwhelming piles of administrative paperwork and multiple sets of students' papers caused Jennifer Baise-Fisher to create an online academic community that not only enabled her to communicate more effectively with parents, but also led to students participating in discussions online after school hours. She concludes in her article that, ironically, she spent far more time maintaining her online community than she spent in former years shuffling papers and answering parent phone calls, but her attitude has changed. She states, "It is the difference between managing and creating." And in her case, she would rather create!

In "Child's Odyssey—A Journey of Imagination," a high school English teacher teams with a geography teacher and an office systems teacher to demonstrate how learning outcomes in each of their classes are connected. By using the computer, a digital camera, a scanner, and a printer, the students in all three classes were able to use the skills learned in each class to create instructional stories and games for elementary students that would entertain and increase the knowledge of literature and geography for both the high school students and the elementary students.

As described in these articles, instruction in the English classroom is fraught with changes in technology and instructional strategies. English/language arts teachers are constantly searching for tools that will allow students to connect to the content and that will make learning a richer experience for their students and themselves. These teachers have all begun an educational Odyssey that will extend far into the future.

Transforming the English Classroom Through Audience and Technology

by Lisette C. Piccillo

Hyperlinking

Twenty-eight expectant faces looked up at me from their computers and waited for my instructions. My choices were to plunge head first into the newest phase of my involvement with portfolio assessment or to scrap the day's lesson plan completely and retreat into the safety of simple word processing. As I handed out the instructions for hyperlinking which I had prepared for the students, I knew that I was taking an instructional risk. I took a deep breath and began. "The first step is to highlight the title of the piece." When no questions came from the students, I felt a little better! I continued, taking the students through all the steps. Most of the students were able to follow my directions, and those who had difficulty were quickly helped by their neighbors who had successfully hyperlinked their work.

> *For the rest of the class, my twelfth-grade English students typed, copied, pasted, hyperlinked, and completed the first day of work on electronic portfolios.*

My students were able to hyperlink with absolutely no difficulty, and I felt as though I could finally relax! For the rest of the class, my twelfth-grade English students typed, copied, pasted, hyperlinked, and completed the first day of work on electronic portfolios. I was exhausted from the worry of making mistakes, but I found when I did make mistakes, the students worked with me to find ways of correcting them and moving forward! As is typical in a high school classroom, the students caught on quickly or already knew something about our new lesson. Through the hyperlinking process their items in the Annotated Table of Contents were effectively linked to the documents themselves, and we all left the room knowing much more about where we were headed with portfolios this year. They begged to know when we were coming back to the lab to work on using software programs to enhance the graphics aspect of the portfolios. I promised them that as soon as I learned, I would bring them back; they were sure that we could all learn together.

Diving Into the Digital World At a workshop in the fall of 2002, our first meeting of the fourth year of the Virginia Beach portfolio assessment project, Dr. Kathleen Yancey, professor at Clemson University and an expert in the field of writing portfolios, had challenged us to expand our commitment to and work with portfolio assessment to include trying digital portfolios. Because I had committed to the portfolio project in 1999 and participated first as a beginner and later as a mentor, I willingly, yet cautiously, agreed to continue to grow as an educator and continue my participation using a model different from the paper portfolios my students had completed for the first three years of the project.

It All Began When... What first intrigued me about the portfolio process was the level of the students' involvement which ultimately led to ownership of their work. I had been dissatisfied for a while with the level of commitment on the part of my students to all of their work, especially their writing, and found the portfolio concept to be a way for me to feel more confident about my teaching as well as my students' progress. My department chairperson asked me to take the place of another teacher who had dropped out of the Virginia Beach portfolio assessment project at the last minute. Little did I know how intrigued I would become with what the portfolio can do for student writing and achievement.

The first summer of the project, we gathered at First Colonial High School for two days of intensive workshops with Dr. Kathleen Yancey. These days involved spending time writing, talking, planning, and sharing our understandings and misunderstandings about using the portfolio as part of the secondary classroom. Our learning focused on how to make portfolios work without making more work for us! We worked in grade-level groups to generate a plan for involving parents and administrators, as well as the students, surmising what strategies we could use to begin implementing portfolios, deciding what types of writing would be included in them, and determining how that writing was to be selected.

By the end of the two days, I had a plan for how I would use portfolios in my classroom the following school year, including a letter to parents, an outline of what to include in the finished portfolio, many strategies for improving student writing, and a desire to make portfolios a dynamic strategy in my classroom. I learned about philosophies surrounding their success and what types of portfolio models had been used within various disciplines, but most of all I caught Dr. Yancey's enthusiasm; she promised that this practice is something that works. On the second day of the workshop, Dr. Yancey made a reference to the possibility of a broader audience for the portfolios, explaining the value of having some sort of outside reader. At that moment, the idea of working with members of the Rotary Club of South Hampton Roads as outside readers for my students came to mind.

As one of our Partners in Education for the Virginia Beach City Public Schools, this group of professionals had expressed a desire in the previous spring to be more closely involved with students and their educational success and to have more opportunities to work directly with students to make a positive difference in their lives. As soon as I left the workshop the second day, I went to school and spoke to one of my assistant principals about the possibility of using the volunteers in this way. He sounded enthusiastic and as soon as school started in the fall, I contacted a representative of the Rotary Club by telephone and then later in the school year by letter. They agreed most heartily to my request, and the relationship between my twelfth-grade students and representatives from the Rotary Club began. My students knew from then on that each writing assignment had the potential to be read by one of these professionals from the community, and many of the students kept this idea in mind as they wrote. I believe that teaching students about audience is one of the most difficult aspects of the writing process because most often the only reader of their work is the teacher. As a consequence of using the Rotary Club as readers for the portfolios, I found that the term "audience" held more meaning and significance for my students than ever before. By the spring, my students were clearly excited about their readers and asked many questions about how the reading would go. Their questioning meant that I needed a workable plan for the readers.

My students knew from then on that each writing assignment had the potential to be read by one of these professionals from the community, and many of the students kept this idea in mind as they wrote.

My Rotary Club contact person and I decided that I would deliver packets of finished portfolios to his office on a Thursday afternoon, and he would take them to the Friday morning meeting to be distributed to the readers. He surprised me when he told me that more than twice the number of readers expected had volunteered to participate. I had hoped that the portfolios would be read by the following week because I still had to evaluate them before the end of the term, but two weeks went by before I saw the first one! However, when I received the portfolios, I found it was worth the wait. The comments made by the members of the Rotary Club were both thoughtful and personal. I was thrilled! One reader even went so far as to write a personal letter to each student about the portfolios she read. The students were full of suspense the day I came to class to return their portfolios. They had been asking every class period when they would get them back. Their eagerness for a response other than a grade on a piece of written work was another confirmation of the value of this relationship between adults in the "real world" of work and students. The students felt connected to the outside world of professionals and adults in a way that could not have happened without this project.

The Process

This project allowed the students to be involved with their community in a meaningful way. They felt grown up and important because these people cared about their academic lives and their achievement. Seniors in high school yearn to have people other than teachers and parents show interest in them as individuals and adults. For this reason, many of my students use their employers as sounding boards and role models. For the members of the Rotary Club to agree to read the students' portfolios gave my students one more positive experience with adults in the outside "real" world.

In order to connect with the Rotary Club members, the students had to decide what they wanted their readers to know about them as students and writers, and what they wanted the readers to respond to in their portfolios. Each student submitted three questions for response, and as a class we discussed their suggestions, selecting five questions for the readers. (See Appendix A.) This element turned out to be more important than I had imagined because it became another aspect of student ownership of their work. They wanted to know which of their pieces was most effective for the assignment, trying to move themselves from the value judgment of "the best," to what strengths and weaknesses were evident, and what could be improved. I was pleased with the final list of questions because it addressed many aspects of the writing process that I had been emphasizing all year!

Putting the portfolios together proved to be another aspect of student ownership in the assessment project. They were given the task of decorating a folder with pictures and phrases which represented themselves as writers – a metaphorical representation was recommended. Some of them used the metaphor of a roller coaster; another showed a road with potholes, speed limits, and interesting sights along the way to a final destination; another showed her growth as a writer by showing baby feet and adult feet on one side and on the other side, kitchen utensils to show how she had collected all the tools of good writing. Then they had to select which pieces they would include for each of the required categories. These included personal or college essays, an in-class essay, a literary analysis, a writer's choice, and a reflection piece on the whole portfolio. The most important element in this phase of the process was their annotated table of contents; it was a way for them to realize what they had written, when it was written, and to describe the writing task to a new audience by including their feelings about their accomplishment. Including the date of each piece enabled them to see at what point in the school year they were doing their best writing thus providing their readers with a framework for gauging student progress and growth.

When the portfolios were all returned and the students had read the comments and suggestions of their respective readers, it was time for me to evaluate them in their entirety. I used the rubric that my group had developed in a spring workshop. The rubric consisted of a paragraph description of the features of a portfolio on a 1 – 4 scale to judge the effectiveness of the individual pieces and the growth of the writer over the course of the school year. Because I had not seen two of the portfolio pieces that were sent to the Rotary Club members, I was surprised when I read them by some of the comments the students made about the process of putting their work together. These two pieces (the annotated table of contents and the portfolio reflection) revealed a sense of ownership about their work that the students had not expressed to me in class or in conferences. In addition, many of the reflection pieces revealed an excitement about the outside readers of which I had been unaware. The students were amazingly (or not so amazingly) honest about their strengths and weaknesses, enough so that I felt frustrated that we had not accomplished more in the way of instruction on some of those issues during the school year.

From the readers' comments, I learned that they were expecting more precision on the part of the students (or perhaps the teacher) in their use of all of the conventions of meticulous writing. They were disappointed, as a whole, about such things as spelling errors, punctuation mistakes, etc. But even with those concerns, they expressed an enthusiasm for their task and an appreciation for being able to see into the lives, minds, and classrooms of these young people. They were intrigued by the variety of writing tasks and expressed interest in specific topics presented by the students. One reader's epiphany about his high school English class concluded with, "I'm beginning to think Mrs. Englehart wasn't the enemy after all! (It has taken forty years!)" Another, in response to a group of five portfolios from students of widely varying abilities, was "astounded at how much a skillful writer leads one to want to read his work." One of them noted, "All of the students... are interested in participating in your assignments to improve their writing. All show an interest in writing. All are willing to express their ideas."

Adding Research to the Mix

In the second year of the project, Dr. Yancey challenged me to add some aspect of teacher research to my implementation of portfolios. I chose to survey my second group of readers more specifically about what they could glean about my classroom and my students from reading the portfolios. Their responses were thorough and thoughtful, and they even made suggestions, as they had the year before, about the type of writing that they felt most important for students to practice while in high school.

My annual letter to the Rotary Club usually includes whatever new aspect of the process on which I have been working with my students, as well as an invitation to visit the classroom, especially on a day during which we are working on writing. I anticipate that both groups of people will benefit and the future of this project will include the input of those who make it work – the students and the community members. Their comments, while recognizing "the different skill levels" with which a teacher must work in a typical classroom, suggested that students be able "to think, organize, and synthesize as demonstrated" in their assignments, and also concentrate on "business letters... and any kind of writing that teaches communication skills." Many of them complimented the curriculum as well as the portfolio model, and several concluded with "I couldn't do your job."

Conclusion After several years of working on this project and learning from both my students and their readers, I am energized by each new phase. To those better versed in computer use than I am, teaching my students to hyperlink may seem like a small step on the journey of using technology to enhance classroom instruction. For one who has long been comfortable with paper and pencil, I found the road frightening at first. I realized I was a rookie in this business, but each small step generated excitement and motivation to learn more as I saw the impact technology has on my students, and I noted their improvement in writing. Creating an annotated and hyperlinked table of contents will lead to other electronic tasks, until someday, entire portfolios will be electronic.

As I continue to work with my students on a digital version of their portfolios, I realize that I need to alter my grading rubrics in order to reflect elements such as color and graphics, in addition to the elements of composition. I need to make decisions and respond to handwritten drafts and reflections. Will the scanner reproduce their cover collages accurately and richly? Will the use of engaging software enhance or detract from their written work? A new portfolio model with a new set of challenges for them and for me! And then I remember that from the beginning of this project my goal was to try new strategies to involve my students deeply in the writing process and to grow with them.

As I continue to work with them on a digital version of their portfolios, I realize that I need to alter my grading rubrics in order to reflect elements such as color and graphics, in addition to the elements of composition.

Each year I am amazed by the difference that portfolios can make for the students. Their high level of ownership in their work, their willingness to try new approaches to writing, and their delight in their discovery of their voices as writers with an audience of community professionals reminds me how much the students are the focus of this type of assessment. One of my students discovered through reflection that "looking back on how we've grown as writers and students helps us have a better understanding of how important the process is."

OK, they get it, and I can breathe.

Appendix A

Outside Reader Questions

English 12 Portfolio Reader Questions

Please respond to the following questions written by the students.

❶ Which piece of writing do you see as the student's best? What are its positive features?

❷ Which piece of writing best shows the student's individuality and personal voice?

❸ What suggestions for improvement do you have for this writer?

❹ What strengths in writing are evident in this student's work?

❺ From what you have read in these portfolios, what similarities and/or differences do you note with regard to your senior English class? (You may answer this question once.)

Portfolio Reader Survey

For my research purposes, please take a moment to respond to the following statements. Check as many blanks as appropriate.

1. After reading these high school portfolios, I have a better understanding of

_________ the type of writing required in an English 12 class.
_________ the interests and ideas of high school seniors.
_________ the value of the portfolio concept.
_________ the benefit of reflection in the development of writing skills.
_________ other, please specify ______________________________

2. What skills do you see represented in student work?

_________ to synthesize information and draw conclusions
_________ to communicate effectively in writing
_________ to share ideas with an outside audience
_________ to use the writing process: prewriting, drafting, revising, editing
_________ other, please specify ______________________________

3. What type of writing, either represented in this portfolio or not, would be most useful for high school students to practice?

____

____

____

____

Appendix B

Student English 12 Portfolio Survey

In order for me to learn from my students what aspects of the portfolio to keep and what to change, please respond as thoughtfully and thoroughly as possible to the following questions.

1. Did you change anything in your papers or portfolio expressly because of having outside readers? If so, what?

2. What do you see as the role of reflection in the learning and writing process?

3. What changes in the reflection aspect of the portfolio would you recommend?

4. What changes in the portfolio process would you recommend?

5. What was the most difficult aspect of putting this portfolio together?

6. What recommendations do you have for future students?

Appendix C

Student Reflections on Reflection

At the end of the year, when all portfolios had been submitted, I gave my students the survey reprinted on the previous page. The responses which follow are samples from questions two and three.

"Reflection is to realize and recognize the actual process of learning and getting better in writing. When it is written you have to think exactly how you changed as a writer."

"It helps you to realize how much you've grown over the last year. At the beginning of the year, you were more juvenile than you are today."

"I believe you learn from mistakes. Looking back on how we've grown as writers and students helps us have a better understanding of how important the process is. Thus our learning and ideas increase and expand."

"Reflecting on our work helps us look back on our assignments and helps us evaluate our own work. It lets us look at our own work like we are reading someone else's as something out of our literature book."

"The whole idea of being able to reflect and realize how you've grown as a writer and an individual is great. It helps to know that in a school year you do actual growing."

Appendix D

DATE:

Dear Rotary Club Member,

On behalf of my twelfth grade students, I thank you for agreeing to read the enclosed portfolios. These projects are a culmination of their year in English 12 and include selected works which demonstrate their practice with a variety of writing assignments. My students are enthusiastic about having a new, professional audience for their work. You will find a variety of skills evident in their writing, as is expected in a core level English class at Kempsville High School.

As you read each portfolio, please respond to the questions attached to the inside cover of each portfolio. The students created the questions in a class discussion in order to show you what they value in their writing. In addition, please complete the reader survey for my research purposes; you will only have one of these in your packet. Your contribution of time and your involvement in the Partners in Education program at our school makes a difference for my students, their parents, and me. I hope you enjoy this opportunity!

Sincerely,

Lisette C. Piccillo

About Lisette C. Piccillo Ms. Piccillo graduated from The University of Virginia in 1980 with a Bachelor of Science in English Education and was granted a Master of Arts in English from Old Dominion University in 1986. She has taught at Kempsville High School since the fall of 1980. There she has taught English 10 and Honors English 10, as well at English 12 and 12 Advanced Placement: Literature and Composition.

Bravely Go Where Few Have Gone Before With the Digital Portfolio

by Elizabeth Beagle

Our Age of Anxiety is, in great part, the result of trying to do today's job with yesterday's tools. — Marshall McLuhen

Technology is here. It's in our homes, at our job sites, and in our cars. Even with this abundance of technology in our everyday lives there are still many people who fear technology. I remember when I first learned that if I wanted to be a teacher I would have to become computer literate. It was 1990. I was a junior in college, and I was terrified! I was still using an old portable typewriter. I did not even own a computer! How was I going to become adept with the computer? When I look back on that time in my life, I laugh because now I integrate a great deal of technology into my classroom. Although I am nowhere near proficient, I have overcome the fear and discovered it is easier to use technology than I thought.

How did I get here? I made the transition by immersing myself in everything about the computer. Then I began taking my English classes to the computer lab to use the word processor. Next, I used the Internet to aid the students in completing research projects. Recently, I have been experimenting with the digital portfolio.

I have found success in using that which they know best—technology—and using it to teach and access that which they know least—writing.

It seems fitting that the writing portfolio should step into the twenty-first century. The students are inundated with technology on a daily basis—cell phones, pagers, computers, video games, etc.—why not use their world to enhance and evaluate their writing? Writing does not have to be dull. It can be fun with the use of technology. For some reason, the students I teach believe that writing on the computer is fun; according to some of my students it is not writing at all. It seems that the student's perception of writing changes when a computer is involved. I have found success in using that which they know best—

technology—and using it to teach and access that which they know least—writing. I have succeeded by using digital portfolios to meet my goals and the objectives of the curriculum and the Standards of Learning.

Evolution of the Portfolio

To clearly understand the evolution of portfolios one must first have a basic understanding of writing pedagogy over the last 40 years. In 1966 English teachers from all over the United States met in Dartmouth, New Hampshire, to discuss the state of English education in America. The title of the conference was "The Language of Failure," and the aim was to define the teaching of English and to brainstorm ways to improve teaching methods (Adams 3). This was the beginning of many such meetings sponsored by the International Federation of Teachers of English. Although the first conference did not bring about immediate change, it did begin the dialogue and provided the foundation for a new age of pedagogy in the teaching of English.

Prior to the 1960s, the main emphasis in the teaching of composition was on the final product (Gleason 3). However, in 1965 Gordon Rohman and Albert Wleche introduced the writing process in three stages—pre-writing, drafting, and editing. In 1973, Peter Elbow published *Writing Without Teachers* in which he emphasized the stage of invention, specifically free-writing, as a means of searching for personal style and growth ("Writing Process" 3). Rooted in the 1960s with the support of such leading theorists as James Britton and James Moffett and established in the 1970s with the works of Peter Elbow, the writing process is now widely acknowledged as the best way to teach composition (Gleason 3).

Writing folders became a byproduct of this process. Teachers were encouraged to have their students place their works in folders (Pirie 1). One reason for this was to include the student in the assessment evaluation processes. In some school districts students were asked to select pieces of their writing which they considered their best for evaluation and explain why they selected these pieces (Dyson & Freedman 4). The emphasis remained on single pieces of writing housed in a folder. Unfortunately, these folders often became storehouses for writing that were shoved in a drawer and forgotten.

Primitive portfolios began in the mid 1980s. Peter Elbow and Pat Belanoff served as administrators for a writing program that required a written exit exam. Elbow and Belanoff were dissatisfied with the written exit exam and the holistic scoring method used to evaluate the exam because it did not mimic what they taught in the classroom; Elbow and Belanoff experimented with portfolios by having their students submit folders with a variety of genres instead of a single piece of writing (Yancey 4). In the late 1980s and early 1990s other models for portfolios emerged such as the portfolio-based basic writing program at Purdue University, the exemption program at Miami University, the placement program at the University of Michigan, and the rising junior portfolio at Washington State University (Yancey 4).

As the age of accountability dawned, teachers were looking for alternate means of assessing student writing based on the "whole picture." The trend in assessment moved toward an emphasis on evaluating the student's writing ability based on many pieces of work and not just on individual ambiguous assignments. In the twenty-first century, writing folders have blossomed into writing portfolios in which the emphasis is on the whole collection of work, not on single pieces of writing.

The trend in assessment moved toward an emphasis on evaluating the student's writing ability based on many pieces of work and not just on individual ambiguous assignments.

What Is a Writing Portfolio?

The Northwest Evaluation Association defines a portfolio as "a purposeful collection of student work that exhibits the student's efforts, progress, and achievements" (Lankes 5). Furthermore, a writing portfolio is a collection of student writing in various stages. The purpose, or model, is largely teacher or student defined. It can be a collection of all the student's best work, it can be a sampling of the student's writing that indicates growth, or it can be a compilation of writing that demonstrates the various stages of the writing process. There are four strategies that are used when compiling a portfolio: collection, selection, reflection, and evaluation. Students collect different writing assignments (in various stages of the process), then begin the selection process (selecting those items that best meet the model chosen by the teacher or student), reflect (students reflect on the individual assignments or the portfolio itself) (See Appendix A), and finally evaluate (students submit their portfolios to their teachers/audiences for assessment).

What Is a Works in Progress (WIP) Folder? In the Virginia Beach City Public School division, students use Works in Progress (WIP) folders and portfolios. The Works in Progress folder contains all the student writings in various stages and modes. The student selects from the WIP folder any pieces that he or she would like to revise to include in the portfolio. The portfolio is the showcase for student growth in writing. It should demonstrate the student's progress during a year or during several years. Also, it should demonstrate the variety of types or forms of writing that the student has attempted during a certain period of time.

What Is a Digital Portfolio? The digital portfolio is very similar to a standard print portfolio in purpose and strategy. The purpose remains to showcase student writing, indicate growth, or demonstrate the writing process in action. The students continue to collect, select, and reflect. The difference lies in the mode of publication. The digital portfolio can be defined in many ways. Again, teacher leadership is key. It can be simplistic or complicated depending on the teacher's desire and resources. It can be as simple as using a word processing program such as Microsoft Word® (See Appendix B) to create hyperlinks to documents (See Appendix C), or it can be as complicated as using Front Page® to create sophisticated Web designs (See Appendix D or view an example at http://members.tripod.com/cook.mark/). The possibilities are endless. The digital nature of the digital portfolio offers many advantages over the traditional portfolio.

What Are the Advantages of the Digital Portfolio? There are several benefits. They include advantages for the teacher as well as the student:

Teacher

- Storage
- Ease of reading
- Option of alternative assessment
- Variety
- Integration of state technology standards

Student

- Easy management
- Faster revision and editing
- More creativity
- Skill acquisition
- Audience concerns

Teacher Benefits

- **Storage**

  One challenge for teachers connected with the portfolio and WIP folders is storage. This issue arises every year. Schools typically have very little storage space, and writing folders and portfolios are bulky. Digital portfolios solve the storage dilemma because they can be stored in several ways. Students can save their documents on a floppy disk, on a CD, or on a network server. They can also publish their portfolio on the World Wide Web (www). The digital portfolio negates the storage problem.

- **Ease of Reading**

  Digital portfolios are easy to read because all the entries are typed. I cannot tell you how many times I have wanted to scream because I could not read a student's handwriting. The digital portfolio eliminates the need for students to spend tedious hours rewriting their papers as well as the frustration experienced by the teacher when he or she cannot read the paper.

- **Option of Alternative Assessment**

  Teachers of writing continue to emphasize the importance of the writing process. The portfolio process affords an excellent opportunity to work with different pieces of writing in various stages. The nature of the portfolios requires students to incorporate writing in all stages of the process so that later they may go back and revise some of these pieces. The emphasis again is on the fact that the writing process is continual and recursive. Consequently, the teacher is able to evaluate the student's writing as a whole and not just on a single ambiguous piece of writing.

- **Variety**

  Thanks to the diversity of software available (PowerPoint®, Front Page®, Microsoft Publisher®, Microsoft Word®, etc.) the students are given many possibilities for publication in the digital portfolio. This is a major plus when facing the evaluation of 120 portfolios.

- **Integration of Virginia Technology Standards**

  The digital portfolio is one way to integrate technology into instruction in order to satisfy the Virginia Technology Standards of Learning. Students begin using computers in elementary school; then in middle school students begin to refine the skills they learned in previous years. By the time they reach high school, most students are quite knowledgeable about computers, so more time can be spent on using the computer to create products rather than concentrating on how to use the computer.

Student Advantages

- **Easy Management**

  One great plus for students is that the digital portfolio allows the student to manage his or her portfolio with ease. Hyperlinking (See Appendix C) offers an easy way for students to move from one piece to another with the click of the mouse. This is a great advantage especially for those students who have trouble with organizational skills. It is less likely that they will lose pieces if they only have to be responsible for keeping a disk or a CD.

- **Faster Revision and Editing**

  A second advantage for students is that it is easier to revise and edit with digital portfolios. Because the entries are all digital, the revisions are done rather quickly. Not only will editing and revising be quicker, but students will not have to write the whole essay over and over again. They will just make the revisions. Thomas commented, "…I didn't have to rewrite the material by hand… I type much faster than I write. This allowed me to finish my entire rewrite in about twenty minutes as opposed to a full hour and a half."

- **More Creativity**

  A third advantage for students is that they have a chance to showcase their creativity. The digital portfolio will allow students to incorporate pictures, graphs, charts, colors, hyperlinks, etc. For many of the students surveyed, the ability to be creative was a big plus. Elizabeth said, "It's more fun to type! We get to pick our font, colors, background colors, and nifty little pictures!" The students really get a chance to dazzle the teacher, and the teacher is given the opportunity to see another side of the student. Many times I have been amazed at how creative my students really are.

- **Skill Acquisition**

  The most obvious benefit for students is that the digital portfolio is a great opportunity to learn new skills. As a teacher, I am always looking for ways to teach my students life skills. The digital portfolio offers the perfect opportunity. Not only do the students have to practice their typing skills, but also they have to learn how to use and create hyperlinks. Some portfolio models teach the students how to use different kinds of software such as Hyperstudio®, Front Page®, and PowerPoint®. Learning these skills will help students later in life when they are in the work place and in college.

- **Audience Concerns**

  A final advantage for the students is that the digital portfolio allows for the possibility of a wider audience. If students are using a network server to save their work, other students can access it and offer suggestions which not only encourages peer editing, but also helps to instill a sense of community within the classroom. Furthermore, if the students publish their portfolios on the Web, then an even wider audience is available. Publishing on the Web allows for more feedback which will lead to better revision.

Getting Started

To begin, the teacher will need to decide on a model. It can be one of many or a combination of several. Some consideration should be given to the experiences of other teachers with digital portfolios and the dictates of the local curriculum. I have found that the best model is one that combines all these possibilities (See Appendix E).

A unique component of the digital portfolio is that one has to consider the resources that are available. Will the data be stored on a floppy disk or on a CD? Who will purchase the disk or the CD? Will the server be the sole place to save the portfolios, or will the server be used as a back up? In my experience, I have discovered that floppy disks are not large enough nor are they reliable. A CD is the best choice; however, will the students have access to CD burners? The server is a great place to use as a back up, but I would not recommend it be used as the primary place for storage. Many servers are open to everyone. It is very easy for portfolios to disappear. I recommend having the students use floppy disks which they purchase and the server as a back up.

Once a model has been selected, a decision needs to be made on how to present this information to the students and their parents. I recommend sending a letter home to the parents explaining the teacher's expectations and the portfolio model that has been chosen. This is a good time to enlist the help of the students with the process (See Appendix E).

The Digital Portfolio Process

As mentioned before, the process is unchanged from that used in a traditional portfolio. The students will continue to collect writing in various stages of development. These pieces will be stored on a disk or server instead of in a WIP folder. The students will continue to select pieces to reshape and revise and place in their portfolios. I recommend that the students receive help in making these selections. The teacher, of course, should be the first line of defense, but why not enlist the help of the parents and friends? (See Appendix F)

Reflection plays a key role in the selection process for either a paper portfolio or a digital portfolio. After the student has selected the pieces that will go into the portfolio, the student should reread the pieces and reflect on the changes he or she wishes to make to improve the work or works. It can be very difficult to include process pieces in a digital portfolio unless the students have been taught to insert text boxes or use the spilt screen (See Appendix G).

After reflection, students rework their pieces of writing and submit the portfolio for evaluation, and the teacher will need to decide how to assess it. There are several ways to evaluate the digital portfolio. I recommend the use of a rubric, either holistic or analytical (See Appendix H). I have tried both types of rubrics and have discovered that I prefer the analytical form. It gives the students a clear idea of expectations, and it is easy to convert into a grade.

The Final Product

In the end, the students will have something of which to be proud. The students will not only experience a sense of achievement for having completed the process, but also they will have writing portfolios that can be given to potential colleges, to universities, and to future employers. In addition, they will have proof of the new computer skills they have learned. In addition, the instructor will have the satisfaction of knowing that he or she has helped the students meet their goals. Further, the instructor will have a variety of writing to use to evaluate their writing skills.

The Critics and Beyond

Critics will argue that the paper portfolio offers the same advantages as a digital portfolio without all the work. I would have to disagree and so did my students. After my students completed their first digital portfolios, I surveyed them to gain their insights. I was pleased to discover that many of their responses supported what I thought and hoped that the digital portfolio offers many benefits for teachers and students. One item on the survey was whether or not they would rather create a paper portfolio or a digital portfolio. Seventy-five percent of the students said that they would rather compile the digital portfolio. Also, when asked, many of the students responded that the digital portfolio was more stimulating than

> *The digital portfolio is a means by which the minds and fingers of a student are unlocked. The student who hates to write will invariably try to write if a computer is involved.*

the paper portfolio. The digital portfolio is a means by which the minds and fingers of a student are unlocked. The student who hates to write will invariably try to write if a computer is involved. It goes back to the student's perception of writing discussed earlier in this article. The messiness and tedium of writing and rewriting are eliminated when students use the computer to compose. Moreover, many of the student responses indicated that the technology aspect of the digital portfolio allowed them many ways in which to demonstrate their creativity, and that this was a major reason for their preference for the digital portfolio. Susan responded, "It's more exciting when we can experiment with colors, buttons, and pictures. It appeals to more of our creative side..." As demonstrated earlier the digital portfolio offers a myriad of advantages for teachers and students, but I believe the best advantage is that it makes writing creative and enjoyable.

Conclusion

Each day, technology is changing and with these changes the unimaginable or impossible is now possible. Are we as educators ready to meet the challenge, or do we want to remain in our comfort zone and miss the opportunities to get to know our students better and help them unlock their potential? The choice is ours; as for myself, I am awaiting the chance to seek out new forms of technology to use in my classroom, hoping to unlock more minds and fingers. Won't you join me?

Works Cited

Adams, Anthony. "From Dartmouth to New York: 1966-1995." *International Digest.* Cambridge University, 6 July 2002. <http://www.nyu.edu/education/teachlearn/ifte/adams.html>

Dyson, Anne Haas and Sarah Warshauer Freedman. "On Teaching Writing: A Review of the Literature." (July 1990). *National Center for the Study of Writing.* 6 July 2002. <http://www.writingproject.org/downloads/csw/op20.pdf>

Gleason, Barabara. "Teaching at the Crossroads: Choice and Challenges in College Composition." *The Writing Instructor.* 2001. 7 July 2002. <http://www.writinginstructo.com/reflection/gleason.html>

Lankes, Anna Maria D. "Electronic Portfolios: A New Idea in Assessment." *Eric Digest.* (Dec. 1995). <http://www.ed.gov/databases/ERIC_Digests/ed390377.html>

Pirie, Bruce. *Reshaping High School English.* Urbana, IL: NCTE, 1997.

"Writing Process." UVM. 7 July 2002. <http://www.dana.ucc.nau.edu/~sga5/guide11.html>

Yancey, Kathleen Blake. "Looking Back as We Look Forward: Historicizing Writing Assessment as a Rhetorical Act." (Feb. 1999). NCTE. 7 July 2002 <http://www.ncte.org/pdfs/members-only/ccc/0503-feb99/08Yancey.pdf>

Notes

- All student names mentioned in the article have been changed, and all student work has been used with permission.
- Much of the information and worksheets seen in this article are a result of my involvement in several portfolio activities in which, I along with others, created tools to use in the portfolio process including the following:
  - The Federal Improvement Plan for Secondary Education (FIPSE) project with Tidewater Community College (TCC) and Salem High School and Landstown High School (2000-2001). This project is going into its fifth year. Its aim is to decrease the number of freshmen going into remedial English. Over the last four years, the program has been extremely successful in lowering the number of students entering remedial English.
  - Virginia Beach City Public Schools Cohort 3 Portfolios Assessment Project (2001-2002). This project was designed to help implement the use of portfolios across the city. Members of all the cohorts were trained in the use and assessment of portfolios. The project is in its fourth year.

Appendix A

Digital Reflection

❶ Which piece do you like the best and why?

❷ Which piece did you find the most difficult to write and why?

❸ Look back at your opening reflective letter; of the weaknesses you mentioned, have any improved? If so, what is the reason for the improvement?

❹ Select one or two of your remaining weaknesses and outline a plan for improvement.

❺ Of the pieces you have written thus far, which one best represents your strengths as a writer?

❻ What tools of revision, such as peer editing, teacher conferencing, tri-editing, etc. have worked the best for you and why? Do you have any suggestions for editing tools?

❼ Explain how the pictures, colors, hyperlinks, etc. have affected your portfolio.

❽ What do you like and dislike about the digital portfolio?

Appendix B

Table of Contents

Dear Reader Letter

In this chapter it shows me talking about my strengths and weaknesses. It also shows what I wish to learn about in the future and what I should practice on more in English.

Fairytale Rough Draft

In this chapter it shows my first fairytale. It's a story about princesses, a knight, and a prince. This story also includes an evil scheme with a romantic twist. Will it end happily ever after? Read and you'll find out!

Fairytale Remake

This chapter is another love story. It's about a young girl who has a spell cast upon her, and when she thinks everything's over something surprises her.

I'm Really in Love This Time

This is my second entry for the essays. It's about my crush, bestfriend, and ex-boyfriend.

Portfolio Reflections

This is the conclusion to my project. It talks about my writing skills and certain papers.

The end!

Appendix C

Hyperlinking

The first step in hyperlinking is to highlight the text you want to link (the title of the piece).

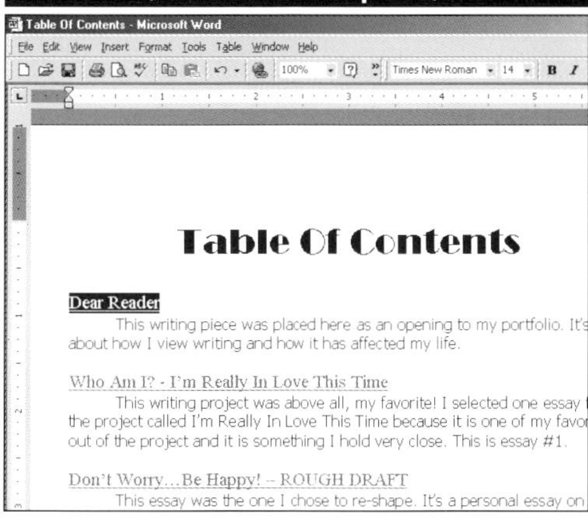

Step 2 in hyperlinking is to click on INSERT on the menu bar at the top of the screen.

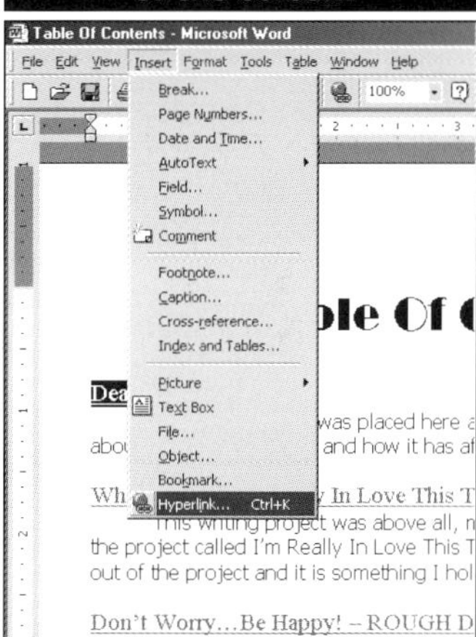

Step 3 is to click on HYPERLINK

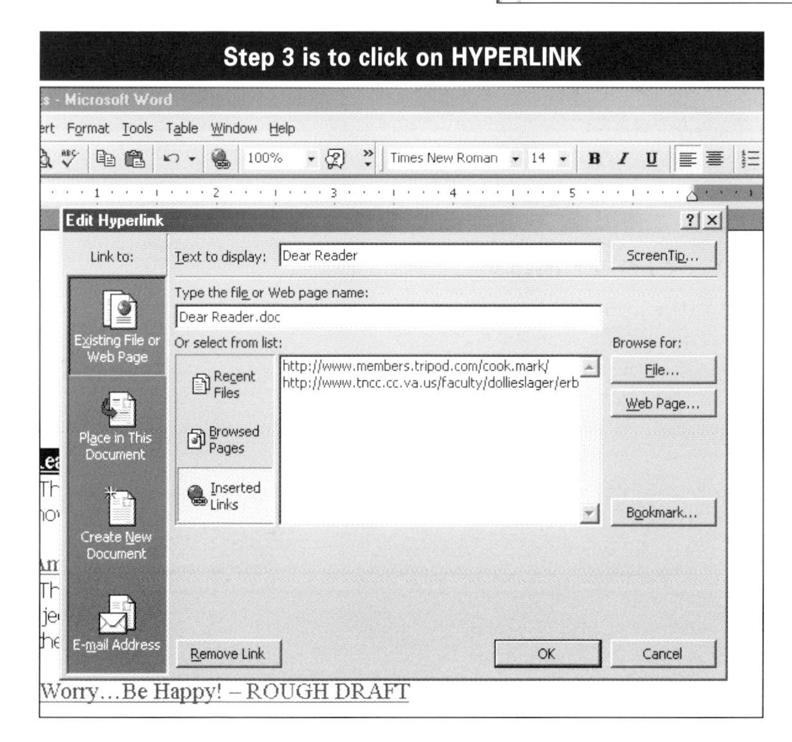

Step 4 is to click on BROWSE FOR FILE

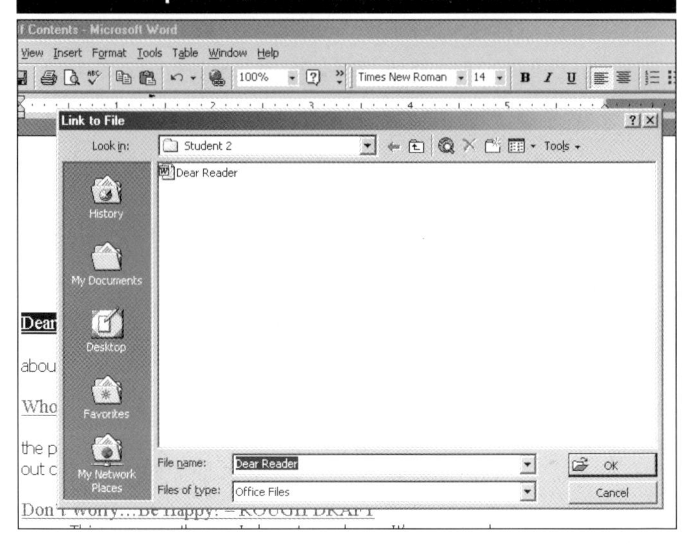

Step 5 is to select the correct file to be linked (title of the piece) then click OKAY.

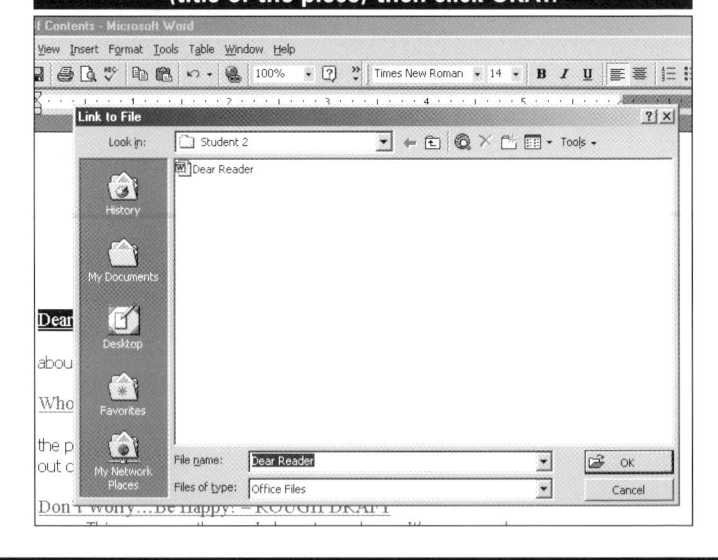

Step 6 is to check your hyperlink. Go to your table of contents and see if the title is linked correctly by clicking on the title. If you did it correctly, it should appear in blue font and the link should take you to the correct file (paper).

Step 7 is to repeat steps 1-6 until all your entries have been properly linked. Good Luck!

Appendix D

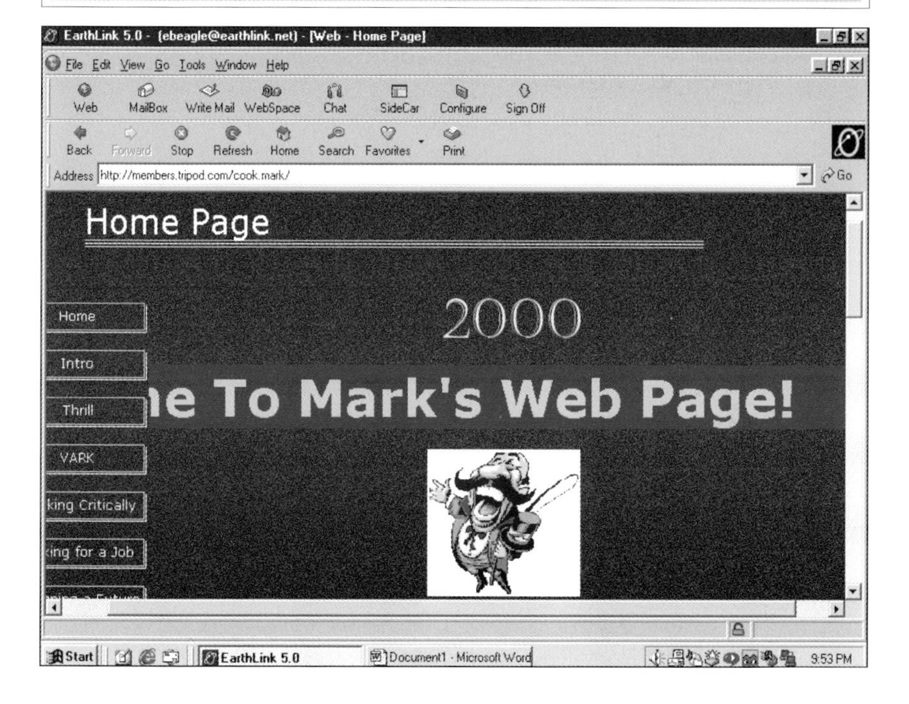
EarthLink 5.0 - (ebeagle@earthlink.net) - [Web - Home Page]
File Edit View Go Tools Window Help
Web MailBox Write Mail WebSpace Chat SideCar Configure Sign Off
Back Forward Stop Refresh Home Search Favorites Print
Address http://members.tripod.com/cook.mark/
Go
Home Page
2000
e To Mark's Web Page!
Home
Intro
Thrill
VARK
king Critically
king for a Job
Start
EarthLink 5.0
Document1 - Microsoft Word
9:53 PM

Appendix E

September, 2002

Dear Parents/Guardians,

This year we will be compiling a digital writing portfolio. The purpose is for the student to select pieces of writing that showcase his or her growth as a writer. The portfolio will be collected several times this year including at mid-term and the final exam. The portfolio will be used to evaluate student writing and to assess his or her improvement. We will be calling on you to help us in this process. I look forward to working with you in an effort to improve your child's writing. The portfolio will contain the following:

- ❍ Annotated table of contents
- ❍ Opening reflective piece
- ❍ Two pieces of writing completed in this class and a reflection, for each piece
- ❍ Writer's choice
- ❍ Closing reflection letter

The students will be asked to supply 2 floppy disks (3.5 HD). If you have any questions or concerns, please feel free to contact me at 468-3800 (2010) or via e-mail at ehbeagle@vbcps.k12.va.us.

Sincerely,

Elizabeth H. Beagle

❖ ❖

I have read and understand the attached letter about the digital portfolio expectations.

____

Student:

____

Parent/Guardian:

____

Comments:

____

____

Appendix F

May 20, 2002

Dear Parents/Friends,

Once again we need your help. We are getting ready to add the finishing touches to our writing portfolio. We need your advice in order to make the final selections. Please review the pieces in the portfolio and select two pieces that you feel reflect the writing strengths of the author. You do not have to grade them; just select two pieces that you feel are good and fill in the bottom of this page. Thanks again for your help!

Sincerely,

Elizabeth H. Beagle

◈ ◈

Parent:

Title of piece you like:

Reason(s) you liked it:

Title of piece you like:

Reason(s) you liked it:

Signature:

◈ ◈

Friend:

Title of piece you like:

Reason(s) you liked it:

Title of piece you like:

Reason(s) you liked it:

Signature:

Appendix G

Process Reflection Letter

The purpose of this letter is to elaborate on the process you used in order to write the final draft of your letter. Follow the steps below:

1. Address your informal letter to "Dear Reader".

2. Your letter should be thorough and cover the following areas:

   - Explain in detail the steps you took in creating the final draft of your essay. "Walk" your reader through each step. Where did you begin (pre-writing)? Comment on your drafts. How many drafts did you make? Did you have any teacher or peer conferencing, etc.?

   - Explain the changes you made from draft to draft. It is important to give examples here because you will not be submitting your drafts with your portfolio.

     - For example, instead of writing, "I included more detail." You should write, "I included more detail in my first paragraph as a result of my trip to the writing center. The original said, 'I felt sad when my grandmother died.' I changed it to read, 'On the day my grandmother died, I experienced the worst kind of pain and sadness imaginable. It felt as if someone had stabbed me with a knife and had taken away my best friend.'"

     - These examples will enable me to better assess your revision.

3. Lastly, you should comment on any help you received while writing this paper. Did you have a teacher conference? Peer review? Make a trip to the writing center? If so, how did these activities help you complete your final draft? Be specific!

4. Don't forget to sign your letter.

Appendix H

Scoring Guide for Digital Portfolio

Name:______________________________

	5-A Excellent	4-B Above Avg	3-C Average	2-D Below Avg	1-E Poor
Completion					
Shows a mastery of a variety of tasks (4 or more)					
Includes an annotated table of contents					
Includes hyperlinks					
Revision					
Shows evidence of significant revision					
Exhibits evidence of coachability					
Reflection					
Used as a means of self-reflection					
Addresses strengths & weaknesses					
Indicates growth in writing					
Demonstrates and explains the writing process					
Style					
Voice is evident					
Variety of sentence structures					
Shows an awareness of purpose and audience					
Texts are relatively free of errors					
Presentation					
Effectively used the chosen medium					
Includes hyperlinks, graphs, pictures, etc.					
Total					

About Elizabeth H. Beagle Elizabeth H. Beagle has been teaching for nine years. She has a Bachelor of Arts in Education from Old Dominion University. Her experience ranges from at risk students (Open Campus High School) to the private sector (Ryan Academy). Currently she teaches at Landstown High School. She has been involved in numerous professional activities including curriculum writing, Federal Improvement Plan for Secondary Education (FIPSE) project (Salem and Landstown High Schools), and Summer Professional Development Academy (SPDA) and Applying Practical Principles with the Learning Environment (APPLE) training. She is eager to integrate technology into her classroom and is continuously seeking new ways to do so.

Into the Trenches Through the Virtual Classroom

by Susan A. Motley

It was 7:25 A.M. on a spring morning in my senior English class. I had planned a brief study of Wilfred Owen's "Dulce et Decorum Est" and Siegfried Sassoon's "The Rear Guard" as a transition from the structured grace of the Romantics and Victorians to the often startling realism of the Moderns. The poems portray the horrors of the poison gas and the trenches identified with World War I combat. In past years, my high school seniors had expressed some appreciation for this poetry, but this year they seemed alarmingly detached and they were laughing. That's right. Laughing.

Unable to detect the source of the humor or to imagine what could possibly be funny about coughing up blistered lungs, I forged on.

Unsuccessfully suppressed giggles were erupting around the classroom during a preliminary silent reading of Owen's depiction of a mustard gas attack and the death of one soldier who didn't get his mask on in time. The sniggering intensified through the oral reading and our efforts at discussion. Unable to detect the source of the humor or to imagine what could possibly be funny about coughing up blistered lungs, I forged on. Hoping for a connection, I queried, "Have you seen *Legends of the Fall*? Do you remember that horrible scene where Brad Pitt's brother is trapped in the barbed wire when the gas canisters hit?"

"Ooooh! Brad Pitt," the girls swooned, but those unexplainable sniggers persisted. Beginning to feel this lesson was a lost cause, I decided to move on for one last try. "OK, let's read a poem about the complex system of tunnels used in this war." Together we turned the pages of our textbooks to Sassoon's "The Rear Guard," and the class utterly disintegrated into fits of laughter. Owen's "Gas! GAS! Quick boys! –an ecstasy of fumbling..." had tickled that part of the funny bone reserved for the lowest form of humor; and when the "gas" was juxtaposed with "The Rear Guard," it was more than my students could hold in. Finally, I was in on the joke.

At home that evening, I reflected on the day and had an unsettling vision of one of my students advising a future college classmate that "Dulce et Decorum Est" is hilarious. I had not planned to make the Trench Poets of

World War I a significant part of the unit, but I could not leave the study of this literature with the students having such an unsatisfactory understanding of the message of the poets.

What did my students need to know, I wondered, to ensure a meaningful experience with this literature? How could I help them arrive at a better understanding of the plight of the soldiers so that they might go on to appreciate the poets' craft—their artistry? Hoping to find an answer, I went online and chanced upon Oxford University's "Virtual Seminars for Teaching Literature." This is an extensive and information-rich Web site dedicated to preserving the works of the Trench Poets by providing the background necessary for modern readers to understand the motivations behind their work. After only a cursory review of the site, I knew that I could not simply tell my students about it—they had to see for themselves.

I reviewed the site more thoroughly and created a worksheet (Appendix A) that includes directions for navigating the site as well as brief activities for the sections I wanted them to experience. I left for school early the next morning hopeful that the computer lab would be available for us but armed with an alternate lesson plan just in case.

Fortunately, the computer lab was open for my classes. That morning I told my students that we were going to have the opportunity to pay a virtual visit to Oxford University in England where actual Oxford scholars would be enlightening us on the literature of the Trench Poets. We reviewed the worksheet and moved to the computer lab. After the hubbub of assigning seats, reassigning seats, and responding to students' questions, I realized that the normal hum of classroom activity had faded to an unfamiliar hush.

I began to move quietly about the lab. Students had been able to access the site quickly, and they were as intrigued as I had hoped they would be. My students began by reading and taking notes on the definition of war poetry found in Tutorial 1: "An Introduction to War Poetry." Here they began to comprehend the staggering number of casualties and the seeming futility of these losses.

With a mouse click on "Proceed to Poems" and another on "Wilfred Owen," my students began reading his biography. Here they learned of his early interest in writing. Students found that he had not been accepted to the school he had most wanted to attend, that youthful patriotism had prompted him to enlist, that he had been hospitalized with shell shock and had been returned to the Front. With another mouse click students viewed photos of Craiglockhart Hospital, the site of Owen's rehabilitation from shell shock and his inspiring meeting with Siegfried Sassoon. With some quick figuring, students calculated that Owen had been only twenty-four when he died in combat.

Next the students read two lengthy letters written by Owen to his mother. The first, dated January 4, 1917, describes his uncomfortable living conditions, his duty as a letter censor, and his desire to hire a servant who was good with a bayonet. The second letter, dated April 25 of the same year, describes twelve consecutive days at the Front that concluded with his being blown into the air by enemy shelling and then waiting "a terribly long time" for relief.

In a letter to Leslie Gunston, Owen describes his first meeting with Siegfried Sassoon at Craiglockhart—a perfect segue into the research on Sassoon.

Students moved back to "Poems," and clicked on "Sassoon." His biography reveals the privileged life into which he was born and his anti-war sentiments which surfaced following the deaths of two fellow officers. In two diary extracts, Sassoon articulates these sentiments—views which would ultimately lead to his being placed at Craiglockhart for treatment for shell shock in order to avoid court-martial.

Next, students clicked on "Survivors," a poem Sassoon wrote at Craiglockhart about the victims and the symptoms of shell shock. By clicking on underlined sections in each line of the poem, students are able to access close interpretations by Oxford scholars and make connections to other poetry. The portion of the poem which follows is presented as it appears on the site:

Survivors

No doubt they'll soon get well; the shock and strain
Have caused their *stammering, disconnected talk.*
Of course they're *'longing to go out again,'*---

When students click on the third line, they learn that the poet is not writing about simply taking a stroll on the hospital grounds. Using a flat tone, he is referring to the victims' half-hearted claims that they are willing to go back to the front.

The second tutorial, a look at Isaac Rosenberg's "Break of Day in the Trenches," affords students the opportunity to participate in their own preliminary poetry interpretation followed by an in-depth study that includes interpretations of lines with connections to other British poetry. My students and I bypassed this excellent tutorial, however, and moved on to "Tutorial 3: An Introduction to Manuscript Studies" where we worked with Wilfred Owen's "Dulce et Decorum Est."

Here students viewed four different drafts of Owen's poem, each in his own handwriting. The site employs two frames in which students can display sections of two drafts simultaneously.

Here students viewed four different drafts of Owen's poem, each in his own handwriting. The site employs two frames in which students can display sections of two drafts simultaneously. After the tutorial participants have examined all four drafts and identified preferred lines, they can compile their own versions by adding to and deleting from an edition of the poem provided by the site. Finally students can compare their new editions to Jon Stallworthy's edition that most typically appears in high school anthologies.

I had calculated correctly that we would not have enough time in the lab to complete the "Manuscript Studies," so it was offered to students as an extra credit assignment. My goal, after all, had been simply to assist students in developing an understanding of the poets' motivations so that they could talk about the poetry without laughing.

This is the part of the story where my students redeemed themselves. Having actually participated in the "Manuscript Studies," they recognized more clearly than I that this is a vital culminating activity, and they were so engrossed in the project that all but one of them completed it outside class. These student-edited versions of the poem powerfully reveal their complete understanding of the pathos that the work of Owen and Sassoon and all of the Trench Poets should evoke.

Although their renderings varied, students nearly unanimously selected four revisions to the version typically presented to readers. Ashley Allen's editing of "Dulce et Decorum Est" incorporates these four changes, and others, that in turn reflect the degree of her compassion for the poets and her involvement with the subject and the text. Ashley's edition with her revisions in italics follows. It parallels the poem as it appears in Holt, Rinehart and Winston's *Elements of Literature Sixth Course*, *Literature of Britain with World Classics*. (See Figure 1.)

Figure 1

Dulce et Decorum Est
By Wilfred Owen

Bent double, like old beggars under sacks,
Knock-kneed, coughing like hags, we cursed through sludge,
Till on the haunting flares we turned our backs
And toward our distant rest began to trudge.
Men marched asleep. Many had lost their boots
But limped on, blood-shod. All went lame; all blind;
Drunk with fatigue; deaf even to the hoots
Of tired, outstripped Five-Nines that dropped behind.

GAS! GAS! Quick, boys! --- An ecstasy of fumbling,
Fitting the clumsy helmets just in time;
But someone still was yelling out and stumbling
And flound'ring like a man in fire or lime ...
Dim, through the misty panes and thick green light,
As under a green sea, I saw him drowning.

In all my dreams, before my helpless sight,
He plunges at me, guttering, choking, drowning.

If in some smothering dreams you too could pace
Behind the wagon that we flung him in,
And watch the white eyes writhing in his face,
His hanging face, like a devil's sick of sin;
If you could hear, at every jolt, the blood
Come gargling from the froth-corrupted lungs,
Obscene as cancer, bitter as the cud
Of vile, incurable sores on innocent tongues, ---
My friend, you would not tell with such high zest
To children ardent for some desperate glory,
The old Lie: Dulce et decorum est
Pro patria mori. (929)

Dulce et Decorum Est
By Wilfred Owen
Edited by Ashley Allen

Bent double, like old beggars under sacks,
Knock-kneed, coughing like hags, we cursed through sludge.
Till on the *glimmering* flares we turned our backs
And toward our distant rest began to trudge.
Dead slow we moved. Many had lost their boots,
But limped on, blood-shod. All went lame; all blind;
Drunk with fatigue; deaf even to the hoots
Of *disappointed shells* that dropped behind.

Then somewhere near the front:
Whew…fup…fop…fup…
Gas-shells or duds? We loosened masks, in case---
And listened…Nothing…Far guns grumbled Krupp…
Then stinging poison hit us in the face.
GAS! GAS! Quick, boys! --- An ecstasy of fumbling,
Fitting the clumsy helmets just in time;
But someone still was yelling out, and stumbling
And flound'ring like a man in fire or lime.
There, through the misty panes and thick green light,
As under a green sea, I saw him drowning..

In all my dreams *I hear him choking, drowning.*
In all your dreams if you could slowly pace
Behind the wagon that we *lay* him in
And watch the white eyes writhing in his face,
His hanging face, *tortured for your own sin.*
If you could hear, at every jolt, the blood
Come gargling from the lung,
And think how once his face was like a bud,
Fresh as a country rose, and keen and young,
My friend, you would not go *telling* with such high zest
To *small boys* ardent for some desperate glory,
The old Lie: Dulce et decorum est
Pro patria mori.

Ashley, as most students, likes the onomatopoeia: the Five-Nines sounding, "Whew…fup…fop…fup" and machine gun fire, "Krupp." In the last stanza, most students emphasized the nightmarish quality of the scene by mentioning tormented dreams twice. Most students chose to respectfully "lay" the body in the cart rather than to "fling" it. The comparison of the victim's face to a country rosebud "keen and young" perhaps most profoundly demonstrates the student's connection to the millions of young men who sacrificed everything.

At the next class meeting, my students shared their editions of the poem and their enthusiasm about their experience with the Trench Poets and this Web site. While they agreed that the Stallworthy version is better poetry, they were enthusiastic about their own work, and they recognized the high quality of Oxford's Seminars:

- They were impressed. The "Virtual Seminars for Teaching Literature" have been developed by a prestigious educational institution for purposeful instruction.
- They recognized the quality. The site is well constructed. It is easy to use and features arresting graphics, photographs, art, and sound.
- They realized that they had utilized rare materials. The site allows access to primary sources. These include letters, diaries, and drafts of poems from the Oxford archives.
- They were involved. The site provides scholarly insights from resident instructors along with links to their email addresses so that students can communicate with them from home or school if it is allowed.
- They could see the value. Enriching activities have been developed for participants.
- Additionally, I now know that the site is a work in progress. Nearly every time I return to the site something new has been added.

Conclusion

On a spring morning, my students and I sat in on a virtual seminar on the Trench Poets conducted by scholars from Oxford University, and we accomplished real-life learning. We utilized primary sources that would have been unavailable to us otherwise. The virtual instructors shared historical background and insights into the culture and literature coupled with compelling activities that enabled my students to demonstrate their mastery of the subject. We experienced the Trench Poets in meaningful ways, and I came to understand more fully than ever the Web's potential for powerful educational opportunities.

On a spring morning, my students and I sat in on a virtual seminar on the Trench Poets conducted by scholars from Oxford University, and we accomplished real-life learning. We utilized primary sources that would have been unavailable to us otherwise.

Appendix A

COMPUTER LAB ASSIGNMENT SHEET
Developed by Susan A. Motley

The Virtual Seminars for Teaching Literature

THE TRENCH POETS OF WORLD WAR I

We will work together to get everyone to this site:
<http://info.ox.ac.uk/jtap/tutorials>

This is a site developed by Oxford University.

After we are at the site:

Click on Tutorial 1: "An Introduction to War Poetry."
Click on the Seminar Introduction.
Click on "What Is War Poetry?" Read this and write a definition of war poetry.

Click on "Proceed to the Poems" at the bottom of this page.
Click on Wilfred Owen.
Take notes on his biography. What seems important to you in light of the poetry?

Read Owen's letters to Susan Owen and Leslie Gunston.

From the letter of 4 January 1917, describe the conditions under which Owen was living.

What was Owen's criteria for selecting his ideal servant?

To what duty has Owen been assigned?

What are Owen's impressions of Sassoon?

Go back to "Poems" and click on Sassoon.

Appendix A

Read his biography and take notes.

Click on "Diary Extracts." What views does he reveal?

Read "Survivors" and the analysis provided by clicking on the underlined portions of each line. Write responses to the following questions.

Where was Sassoon when he wrote the poem?

How does the poem seem to reflect Sassoon's condition while at Craiglockhart?

Based on your reading of "Survivor," describe the symptoms of shell shock.

For Extra Credit: Complete Tutorial 3: "An Introduction to Manuscript Study." This requires that you examine four actual drafts of Owen"s "Dulce et Decorum Est." You are supposed to decide how you would like the poem to read. Be ready to share your revisions next time and to defend your choices.

Works Cited

Owen, Wilfred. "Dulce et Decorum Est." *Elements of Literature Sixth Course, Literature of Britain with World Classics*. Ed. Richard Sime and Bill Wahlgren. Austin: Holt, Rhinehart and Winston, 2000.

Virtual Seminars for Teaching Literature. Project Manager Dr. Stuart Lee. 17 August 2000. Oxford University. 04 June 2002 <http://info.ox.ac.uk/jtap/tutorials/>.

About Susan Motley Ms. Motley received her undergraduate degree from Lincoln Memorial University in Harrogate, Tennessee. She completed her Masters Degree in Administration at The George Washington University. Ms. Motley's teaching career began in Smithfield, Virginia in 1971. She has taught Adult Education classes in Hawaii, Kentucky, and Virginia. For the last fourteen years, she has taught in Virginia Beach, first at the Adult Learning Center, then at Kempsville Junior High School, and at Tallwood High School since its opening in 1992.

Sessions in Cyberspace: Establishing an Online Academic Community

by Jennifer Baise-Fischer

Rationale for Creating an Online Academic Community

Huge sheaves of paper, including a multitude of phone messages, progress reports, and late student work shifted about my desk in sinister heaps. For three years, I engaged in a daily battle with the forces of chaos. If I attempted to discard or otherwise address my textile antagonists, I would find myself facing an academic Hydra. It seemed that each piece of paper of which I disposed would spawn two or three additional missives, all of which were "urgent." But perhaps my paper muddle would not have seemed so insurmountable had I not been confronted with more than a hundred and thirty students, each of whom possessed a singular obsession with his or her current grade point average in my English class.

Although I loved the act of teaching, I wondered if the secretarial functions were wedded implacably to the pedagogy. Was the love of the profession worth the bureaucratic drudgery

I must confess that I began to have unpleasant thoughts about those mounds of paper, those phone message slips, and those morose expressions of dismay on the faces of students newly informed that I could not provide them with their current average (to the decimal point) on command. Although I loved the act of teaching, I wondered if the secretarial functions were wedded implacably to the pedagogy. Was the love of the profession worth the bureaucratic drudgery?

For me, the answer to this question is complex. Yes, the pleasure of teaching is worth all sorts of inconvenience. However, I do not have to relegate myself to a Kafkaesque existence consumed by secretarial functions. This is, after all, the information age.

Last summer, I decided to establish an online academic community because I knew my students would benefit from it and because I thought it would be possible for me to eliminate some of the clutter from my professional life if I chose to employ available technology. Although I had enjoyed the Internet for years, I knew (and know) nothing about computer programming. I am a technological dilettante. I cannot discern Java from HTML, nor do I wish to do so. Nevertheless, I was determined to alleviate at least one of my annoying clerical duties, namely, keeping parents and students apprised of each student's current academic progress.

Getting Started In my mind, I envisioned a home page with a list of grade point averages updated on a weekly basis. Students and parents could access the list at any time. At the end of the nine weeks, neither students nor parents would be able to claim ignorance of poor student performance, especially ignorance for which I was to blame. I also decided to include a list of missing assignments next to each student's average. No more would I continually have to remind students to make up tests and quizzes; they would simply go to my Web site, check the list, and then schedule a make-up date with me. I even discovered that I could include a link to my email address so that students and parents could ask questions immediately after viewing the student's status.

I could list some of the components I wanted to include on my home page, but before I could actually design the site, I first had to obtain some server space, that is, space for my home page to live on the World Wide Web. Google, the metasearch engine, provided me with a multiplicity of Web hits offering free server space and free Web design software. Google searched through more than two billion URLs (Universal Resource Locators) and selected over two thousand sites with my search criteria, "free server space" (Google Inc.). The three most user-friendly sites to my inexperienced eyes were GeoCities, Tripod, and Angelfire, all of which offer similar free services. GeoCities, which is affiliated with Yahoo!, offered me fifteen megabytes of free disk space, access to Yahoo! PageWizards and Yahoo! PageBuilder Web-building software, site statistics capability, professional templates, options for add-ons such as a guestbook, an upload tool, and a file manager (Yahoo! Inc., "Membership Brochure").

In exchange for space on their server, GeoCities required me to allow a promotional banner at the top of my home page. I would have no control over the content of the banner, nor could I remove it from view (Yahoo! Inc., "Terms of Service"). Before I began to develop my site using GeoCities software and server space, I visited a few consumer-created GeoCities, Tripod, and Angelfire sites. Each of these sites displayed an advertisement in the top fifth of the page. While these advertisements were not objectionable in content, the pages did lack a professional appearance because of them. I decided to examine other Internet options, one of which was Blackboard.

Using Blackboard Blackboard Incorporated provides both a free and a fee-for-service Web-based "e-Education Infrastructure" to teachers and to schools (Blackboard Inc.). My first encounter with Blackboard occurred in a graduate course at the College of William and Mary. Upon registration for any undergraduate or graduate course, students gain access to CourseInfo, an interactive academic Internet community at the college that allows students and professors to communicate with one another through email, posted documents and announcements, and group and class discussion boards. Through CourseInfo, which is accessible to students both on campus and at home, professors can add links to germane Web sites and display current student academic performance. Students can also send electronic files to professors or classmates for evaluation.

As a student, I loved CourseInfo. Frequently, my classmates and I would engage in lively discussions of class content on the discussion board. The professor employed the announcement page as well, both to let us know when class was canceled and to remind us of important conferences or speakers on campus. When the professor assigned a group project, he also established closed group discussion boards for each team, allowing us to communicate privately with other members in the group.

The effects of my professor's use of CourseInfo moved beyond the realm of classroom content; he successfully established an online academic community. As students, we developed a collegial respect for one another and for the diverse perspectives each of us brought to the group. Because much of our activity on CourseInfo occurred as posted messages, we learned to consider the unseen writer as we read. We attended to each other, even to the soft-spoken individuals, an act that is difficult in the frenetic pace of the "real time" classroom. I discovered that it is possible to use "e-mail and threaded discussions as a conduit rather than an impediment to conversation" (Richards 39). I still regard participation in that course as one of the most valuable educational experiences of my career, primarily because my professor was unafraid of using new and unfamiliar technology.

I investigated Blackboard's teacher information site at the beginning of the summer of 2001. To my surprise, Blackboard makes a two-month-long trial version of its interactive educational software available to teachers at no cost, along with five megabytes of free server space (Blackboard Inc.). Furthermore, Blackboard does not require clients to allow advertisements in banner or pop-up form to appear when students view pages. Blackboard funds itself by offering enhanced site capabilities and additional server space on a fee-for-service basis. Teachers who wish to extend Blackboard's services beyond the trial period have two options: they can pay a $295 fee for a one-year contract, or they can request a reduced rate from Blackboard (Blackboard Inc.). The free two-month trial package for educators includes the five megabytes of server space, communication capabilities for class emails, discussion boards, and real-time chats, student performance software, course statistics calculators, and numerous page editors that can be tailored to match course needs. The page editors function with templates, an aspect of Blackboard that I find essential. The templates allow Web neophytes without any knowledge of Java or HTML Web programming languages to create attractive home pages. In other words, Blackboard enables educators to type or to paste in text, as well as to insert photographs or other graphics. Blackboard's templates then organize course content into a palatable and visually appealing form. Although critics of Blackboard's templates may find the service's structures stifling to page designer creativity, those of us who number ourselves among the computer illiterate will be grateful for Blackboard's guiding hand. After I viewed Blackboard's educator information pages, I quickly registered for a Blackboard account and began developing two home pages, one for my Advanced Placement English class and another for my Honors English 10 classes.

One of the advantages of Blackboard is its ability to customize client accounts to the specific needs of each course. As a public schoolteacher, I realize I have certain responsibilities to my students and their parents, not the least of which is my responsibility to keep students in a safe environment. The World Wide Web in its uncensored form is not a safe environment. I was initially concerned about the interactive portion of Blackboard because I was afraid of exposing my students to outsiders masquerading as classmates. Blackboard's structure alleviated my fears; when I began building my first Web site, the Blackboard set-up software asked me if I wished to have an open or closed course (Blackboard Inc.). Closed courses require instructors to register a student before that student can access the site. Upon registration, a student obtains a unique user sign-on and a password. Because it is password protected, a closed course is protected from most interlopers. For a secondary school teacher attempting to create an online academic community, the closed course option is the only option; minor children need to be protected from cyber-predators. I did, however, create a generic user sign-on and password for parental access.

> *This generic sign-on allows me to achieve one of my primary technological goals, namely, keeping parents informed about current student academic progress.*

This generic sign-on allows me to achieve one of my primary technological goals, namely, keeping parents informed about current student academic progress.

Most Virginia Beach City Public School teachers, including myself, use InteGrade Pro to calculate student grades and to create periodic progress reports. Although Blackboard makes its grading software available to clients, I was too deeply entrenched with InteGrade Pro to switch to a new program. This left me with a dilemma: how was I to display student grades without violating student confidentiality?

I found my solution in the back of a textbook. Most statistics textbooks include a table of random numbers for use in double-blind experiments. I assigned each of my students a confidential number from one of these tables, thereby ensuring that their grades would remain a private matter for themselves and for their parents. When I post grades on my Blackboard page, I sort students according to their random numbers rather than by alphabetical order. (See Figure 1.)

Figure 1

Sample Current Academic Progress Display
Current Academic Progress
Student Number: Current Grade/Missing Work

Block 2A

- 1767: 81%/Vocabulary Cards #19
- 2266: 91%/None
- 3740: 84%/Vocabulary Quiz #18
- 4075: 65%/Chapter Nine Final, Vocabulary Quiz #18, Vocabulary Cards #19
- 5282: 86%/None
- 6415: 96%/None
- 6944: 91%/None
- 8161: 86%/Epic Test
- 8482: 62%/Chapter Nine Final, Vocabulary Cards #18
- 8520: 87%/None
- 8804: 92%/None
- 9407: 57%/Epic Test, Chapter Nine Final, Vocabulary Cards #18 & #19
- 9832: 75%/Chapter Nine Final

Random numbers were derived from Gay, L. R. *Educational Research: Competencies for Analysis and Application,* Fifth Edition. Upper Saddle River, New Jersey: Merrill, 1996.

My grade posting system is quite popular with my students. Blackboard allows me to track "hits" to my home pages by user and by date. By April of 2002, my Advanced Placement English Web site had attracted 4483 hits. Although the Honors English 10 page draws less traffic per student, Blackboard statistics calculate total hits to that site at 4361. My students tell me they love being able to check their grades online, and they always remind me to update the site regularly.

Parents also appreciate the availability of online student grades, especially parents who are anxious about student performance and who would tend to call frequently "just to check on things." During open house night at our

Figure 2

Blackboard Instructions for Parents
Honors English 10—Mrs. Fischer

Parents may now access the course Web site to monitor their child's current academic progress. I will post each student's class average and missing work. I will update these statistics weekly.

Directions:

1. I will give you your child's confidential class number. This number was randomly assigned to your child from a list of computer-generated random numbers. I will not reveal your child's confidential number to anyone except you and your child.
2. Go to www.blackboard.com/courses/Baise-Fischer. This site is password-protected to prevent outsiders from having contact with our class. Parents may access this Web site by using the generic sign-on and password. The generic sign-on ID is *******. The password is *******.
3. Once you have accessed the site, go to "Course Information." The list of confidential class numbers and corresponding averages will appear. Find your student's class block. Then find your child's random number and view his or her current academic progress. This list is not in alphabetical order. The students have been sorted in ascending order according to their random number. Your child's privacy is protected.
4. I encourage parents to explore the Web site. Major assignments, syllabi, and course expectations will be posted periodically; students are discussing literature, composition, and academic experiences on the "Discussion Board" page.
5. My e-mail address is ************. Please e-mail me if you have any questions, comments, or concerns. I believe children will always be more successful when teachers and parents work together.
6. I look forward to a great year with your student!

school, I distributed a preprinted instruction list for accessing my home page on Blackboard. (See Figure 2.) I also provided parents with their child's confidential number. Of course, some parents were unable to attend open house, and for these parents I made alternate arrangements, including emailing instructions, explaining instructions by phone, and delivering instructions during parent-teacher conferences. Ultimately, my goal to improve communication with stakeholders while simultaneously assuaging my own workload is achieved through my use of Blackboard.

Creating a Community While I am grateful for the success of my online academic status page, I am thrilled by the online community my students established this year, particularly in my Advanced Placement English class. Many students check the site daily and participate in sophisticated online discussions of literature and rhetoric. They also spend a great deal of time commiserating with one another about the stresses of their course loads. As the Advanced Placement and Standards of Learning exams approached, students shared strategies and encouraged one another to do well and to study. Learning and thinking, I noticed, are valued on the discussion boards. Students seem to enjoy being able to dialogue with one another about literary texts and about issues that matter to them. (See Figures 3 and 4.)

Figure 3

Sample Student Post to the Discussion Board
(Unedited Student Response)

From: Tracy Green
Sent: 2001-07-21
Subject: Re: The Scarlet Letter

Message: Okay here are my ideas.

First has anyone noticed how Hester Prynne is always touching the Scarlet Letter which is over her heart and one sees that this placement of the hands is also shadowed by Reverend Mr. Dimmesdale. I think that he is the father of Pearl and this action of the hand over the heart signifies different things to each of them.

Also, I think that the jail symbolizes the Puritan way of life. How old and harsh yet strong and stable it is.

As well, the rosebush is a reoccurring object in the novel. This must have a meaning yet I can not at this time figure out what it is.

Well that is it for now. Maybe others will see what I have seen and can reply with their observations.

Thanks, Tracy Green

Figure 4

Sample Student Post to the Discussion Board
(Unedited Student Response)

From: John Williams
Sent: 2001-07-27
Subject: Re: Re: The Scarlet Letter

Message: Of course he is the father, I find this book very interesting. In the time this story was occurring people were very tight about this thing. The thing I was wondering is what will happen to Mr. Dimmensdale once the town finds out what he did. IF something like this actually happened in that time nothing short of a rebellion would have occurred. He was church official and trusted as the word god. If the people find out, it's going to be bad.

But enough about that. Has anyone noticed the way Pearl acts, Or the way people, after seven years are treating Hester. I think that this is the true story. This book isn't a mystery. It's a drama. Were not trying to find out who had Hester's Child. This text is, in my opinion about the struggles a single mother has in taking care of a child and about how societal _on't of a single mother can effect how to take care of their children. I think that hawthorne had Liberal _on't on this subject because of the way he tries to find good in Hester. The one thing that is distracting about this book is the fact that pearl seems to smart for her age. We haven't so far seen Hester tell pearl about what the letter means but she seem to have a clear understanding all ready.

I sure do hope that in AP _on't_i we still have time for _on't_ic seminars. Also I saw that the chat isn't up. I think that if we _on't have time in class, then that chat room would be a great place for it.

Sorry for the long reply but there are two more things. This Web site is the best thing that happend to schools since i can remember, Thank you Ms Fischer it is very useful. Oh and check out my Page!

My course's online academic community fulfills many of my own personal and professional needs, as well. I believe that all students are entitled to a challenging and rewarding education and that a valuable education is one that moves beyond simply dispensing information to cooperative students; an education of worth helps students to develop the rigorous habits of mind necessary for their future achievement and happiness. As a teacher, I try to provide students with opportunities to establish their own connections with content, to discover their own passions, and to create their own meanings. In a cyber-community, the teacher is invisible. I am not the "sage on the stage" because there is no stage.

In a cyber-community, the teacher is invisible. I am not the "sage on the stage" because there is no stage.

Students construct their own learning experiences. My hope is that a child-centered, constructivist learning environment will allow my students to develop the scholarship, creativity, and intellectual courage they will need to succeed outside the classroom. If the content of our online discussions is an indicator of intellectual growth, my aspirations for my students are not unrealistic.

Although the students' grammar and mechanics in the sample posts are not anywhere close to perfect, the posts do represent the sort of dialogue about literature about which English teachers dream. The authors were engaged in a struggle with a complicated text. Their enthusiasm for the analysis is tangible, and this enthusiasm was later transported into the actual classroom.

Employing Caution The trial-version of Blackboard includes discussion board, email, and real time chat capabilities. The service also allows students to create their own home pages within the larger scope of my site. While I was creating my site, I decided to disable the real-time chat capabilities because I wanted to maintain a high level of control over page content. It was and is my fear that high school students might use an online academic community for purposes that are far from academic. By disabling the instant chat function of Blackboard, I can closely monitor student posts, both on the discussion boards and on the personal Web pages. At the beginning of the year, I told students I would be checking the site daily for inappropriate posts; thus far, no one has tested my resolve. The ability to disable functions on Blackboard is typical of the service's level of customization. While chatting online about course content unmonitored is entirely appropriate for graduate students, high school students have not yet attained the requisite maturity for such freedom in a teacher-sponsored venue.

Conclusion

Ironically, I think if I were to calculate the number of hours I spent maintaining my online academic community this year and then compare the figure to the number of hours I spent fielding phone calls and shuffling papers last year, I would find that I spent far more time developing and caring for my Web site. However, my attitude toward my labor is utterly different. I do not resent the time I spend updating my pages; I am excited by what my students and I have accomplished. It is the difference between managing and creating. I would rather create.

My hours this year were dedicated to helping my students learn and to communicating with parents. One attentive parent in particular checked the site almost every day to keep a close watch on her son; I know there were times when he wished I had never touched a computer, but he is ending the year with a passing grade.

Yet there are some things less tangible that come from participation in an online academic community. My students respect my willingness to learn new things about technology, even at my advanced age of twenty-eight. They interpret my interest in the World Wide Web as an interest in their world. More importantly, however, is the notion that learning does not begin and end at the classroom door. Learning keeps on happening at night and on the weekends, with friends and even with classmates with whom students never interact in the real world. The Internet is an equalizer, and I enjoy theorizing that the closeness of my Advanced Placement class is due in part to our online community, a community that embraces rather than dismisses individual differences among students.

My online academic community is a work-in-progress. I am already planning next year's sites. I would like to try an electronic peer review, with students submitting papers online to others students for evaluation. Additionally, students will be posting on the discussion board for homework. As the technology develops, opportunities for enhancement will present themselves. I like to imagine what my pages will look like in five years, or in ten.

Notes: All student names are pseudonyms. All student work has been used with permission.

Works Cited

Blackboard Inc. "About Blackboard." *Blackboard.* 2002.16 April 2002 <http://company.blackboard.com/index.cgi>.

Gay, L. R. Educational Research: *Competencies for Analysis and Application*, Fifth Edition. Upper Saddle River, New Jersey: Merrill, 1996.

Google Inc. "Press Center." Google. 2001. 18 April 2002 <http://www.google.com/press/facts.html>.

Richards, Geraldine A. "Why Use Computer Technology?" *English Journal* 90.2 (2000): 38-41.

Yahoo! Inc. "Yahoo! GeoCities: Membership Brochure." *Yahoo!GeoCities*. 2002. 18 April 2002 <http://us.geocities.yahoo.com/v/info. html>

---. "Yahoo! GeoCities: Terms of Service." *Yahoo!GeoCities*. 2002. 30 April 2002 <http://docs.yahoo.com/info/terms/geoterms.html>

About Jennifer Baise-Fischer

Jennifer Baise-Fischer taught English at Bayside High School for four years. She graduated from Old Dominion University in 1998 with a Bachelor of Arts degree in English with an emphasis in Secondary Education. She is currently pursuing a Master of Arts in Educational Policy, Planning, and Leadership at the College of William and Mary, where she was recently named a Hanny Scholar.

A Child's Odyssey—A Journey of Imagination

by Donna Spence and Sandra Starkey

"Wow! What a neat orange pencil," exclaimed one third grader. "Cool. My own map," another third grader commented excitedly. The class listened intently and traced the travels of the characters with colored pencils and handmade maps. Although this was usually story time with the teachers, on this day the storytellers were ninth-grade high school students who shared their compositions with the classes at a local elementary school in order to experience real life application of writing skills.

The class listened intently and traced the travels of the characters with colored pencils and handmade maps.

The project involved three high school teachers, a third-grade supervising teacher and her team members, and a librarian from a local public library. With the intention of creating an effective integrated lesson, an English teacher and a Computer Information Systems (CIS) teacher who frequently worked together devised the initial plan, then approached a World Geography teacher for her participation. The three high school teachers developed a collaborative lesson involving students in World Geography, Computer Information Systems, and English 9 with the objective of designing a child's adventure story.

The collaboration began after the ninth-grade English students read literature chronicling heroes and their adventures. Upon completing a study of Homer's Odyssey, all five classes collaboratively wrote an adventure story for third graders. Each class selected a theme, title and characters. Then each class was divided into five groups, each group charged with writing one chapter of the adventure. As each chapter's draft was completed, one member of each group sat with the group in charge of the following chapter, and adjustments were made to tie one chapter to another so that the story flowed from beginning to end. Rough drafts were peer edited by the CIS classes and returned to the English classes for revision. In addition to the stories, English students designed story-related board games, which the children could play after the stories were read.

While the English students were developing their stories, the CIS students were trained in the use of the digital camera as they recorded the progress of the compositions and the development of the board games. In addition, these students photographed all high school groups so that their pictures could be included in each publication.

Once the English 9 students jig-sawed the basic outline of the adventures, the travels of each set of characters were given to each of the five World Geography classes. The students in those classes created hand-drawn maps, which the elementary children would use to trace the adventures with their colored pencils while they listened to the stories being read. After the World Geography students voted on which maps to include, they were duplicated for the elementary classes to use.

English and CIS classes worked together to design and select appropriate designs and artwork to illustrate the stories. Classes were matched according to class periods. Some of the artwork included original drawings by English students, which the computer students scanned into the documents, thus increasing their knowledge of available technology. CIS students then keyed the stories. At this point the stories were returned to the students in the English classes for needed revisions. Final copies of the adventure were duplicated and bound by the computer students. Copies were provided for all high school students involved in the project as well as a copy for each third grade class. In addition, copies were put on public display for over a month in the Great Neck branch of the Virginia Beach Public Library.

In order to determine which students would represent the English classes on the field trip to the elementary school, each class voted for one representative for each chapter written. The teams of five students carried the stories and selected board games to share with the elementary school students. The CIS students accompanied the English representative on a field trip to videotape the activities. A mini-grant from the High Schools That Work program paid for a school bus and substitutes for the high school teachers. Students were given field trip permission forms which were returned to the respective teachers. After the teachers and students arrived at the elementary school and were introduced to their respective third grade classes, the maps and colored pencils were distributed. The elementary students listened intently as the adventure unfolded while the teacher in each classroom helped them trace the path of the adventure on their maps.

To further delight the third graders, the high school students then sat down and played the games with small groups of elementary students.

The third graders said they were happy to have shared the experience with the older students, and they were equally pleased to have the stories and games left with them for further enjoyment. Students were reminded that their parents could take them to the Great Neck branch of the Virginia Beach Public Library in order to share the stories with their families. The stories were also made available to any young child coming into the library.

They realized that what was done in one class actually related to what was done in other classes as well as there being a genuine correlation to real world experiences.

Those high school classes involved in the project had the opportunity to view the videotapes that the CIS students had recorded so that the fruits of their labors could be enjoyed. The older students remarked that writing was so much more rewarding because of the excitement of the small children! They realized that what was done in one class actually related to what was done in other classes as well as there being a genuine correlation to real world experiences. They also commented about how much fun it was to go back and be an elementary school student again, even if just for an hour or two.

By combining the lessons and materials from three different courses, we were able to demonstrate to the students that the skills learned in all their classes are related and not to be used in isolation. We were also able to meet many objectives from each of our courses. (See Figure 1.)

Conclusion

At the end of the project we were proud of the way we had worked together to make learning a more meaningful experience for our students. Our students had combined "old world" technology (the pencil, paper, and textbooks) with "new technology" (the computer, digital camera, scanner, and printer). From this all of us had learned to find connections between courses and technologies.

Figure 1

English: **The student will**

- 9.2 make planned oral presentations.
- 9.3 participate in planned discussion.
- 9.4 demonstrate responsibility for individual and group learning activities.
- 9.7 apply problem solving and critical thinking to literature study.
- 9.8 read and analyze a variety of literature, including works of classical and contemporary authors from other countries and various ethnic backgrounds.
- 9.12 using the writing process: pre-writing, writing, reviewing, editing, and publishing.
- 9.13 develop narrative, literary, expository, and technical writings to inform, explain, analyze, or entertain.
- 9.14 communicate ideas in writing, using correct grammar, usage, and mechanics.

Geography: The student will

- 10.1 use maps to apply concepts of scale, orientation, latitude and longitude; create political, physical, and thematic maps.
- 10.7 create maps of countries and regions.

Office Systems: The student will

- 1.7 prepare camera-ready copy.
- 1.8 reproduce and distribute documents and information using the computer, digital camera, scanner, and printer.
- 1.9 create and maintain effective and productive work relationships.
- 2.5 maintain printer.
- 5.5 enhance formatting of documents.
- 6.1 demonstrate time-management skills.
- 6.9 follow written/oral directions.
- 7.4 provide feedback to teams and individuals.
- 7.8 maintain production records.

About Sandra Starkey Having received her Bachelor of Science in English Education from the University of New Jersey in 1963 and a Master of Science in Administration and Supervision from Chicago State University in 1976, Sandra Starkey returned to the East Coast where she has been teaching English in the Virginia Beach City Public Schools since 1981. She served on the First Colonial High School Planning Council and as a member of citywide curriculum committees. Before her retirement, she was the Coordinator of the High Schools that Work program and the Career and Academic Preparation Center (CAP) Lab at First Colonial High School.

About Donna Spence A native of Virginia Beach, Donna Spence received her Bachelor of Science in Secondary Education at Old Dominion University in 1969. She is completing her eighteenth year as a Business Education teacher in the city of Virginia Beach. Currently, she is the Chairman of the Business Education Department at First Colonial High School and the sponsor of the Future Business Leaders of America.

Elliott's Magic Gift

by Rhonda Green and Patricia Sears

Elliott the Elephant It was a Monday afternoon, and the children had just returned to the classroom, hot and sweaty from a thirty-minute physical education lesson with my teacher assistant. The only thing on their minds was a cold box of juice and the anticipation of the story they would hear me read that day. To my students' surprise, however, our school secretary called our classroom at the precise moment the children were comfortably sitting on the carpet. She announced that someone had left an enormous gift for us in the school office and requested that two of my best behaved students walk down to get it. Naturally, fifteen hands eagerly began waving in the air to reassure me that they were all the best behaved. I glanced at each of my students, relishing the looks on their small faces, a look I simply adore. I then chose two children and gave them explicit directions to walk directly to the office, to retrieve the package without peeking, and then to return to our classroom. Little did the children know that I had planned the entire event. The office staff was closely monitoring their every step on security cameras.

As the classroom door closed behind my two students, I took the opportunity to begin a shared writing activity with the single purpose of keeping the remainder of my class occupied until the surprise gift arrived. I began filling my students' heads with thoughts of what the gift could be. They predicted everything from a new puppy to a box of tasty chocolate cupcakes. I wrote each of the responses as quickly as I could, trying not to miss a single word. As luck would have it, just as I finished writing the last student response, my classroom door opened, and the students began squirming and giggling with excitement. The surprise gift was brought to my rocking chair, and I immediately began commenting on how beautifully it was wrapped. "Open it, Mrs. Green." "Open it, please!" I slowly opened the gift and peered inside, then removed a neatly folded letter and a small stuffed toy elephant. I passed the elephant around so each of the students could hold it and look at it carefully. I then read the letter aloud. It said:

> *Dear Boys and Girls,*
>
> *Hi! I'm going to be your special friend this year. As we get to know each other, I am going to need your help! I do not have a name. Would you please help me decide on a name? Perhaps your teacher can help you do this.*

In the bag are some special books that you can take home to read to your parents. I have also sent you many books for your classroom and will be reading those stories to you on the computers. Please help your teacher keep them in their special containers.

Thank you for taking special care of me. Do not forget to think of a name for me and write it on the poster. Good-bye for now.

Love,
Your new friend

Once I finished reading the letter, the students and I began brainstorming various names that we could give to our new friend. We chose the name Elliott. All of the students seemed pleased and proud, as if each of them were a new parent.

The Program Elliott was in fact the mascot for a research-based technology program that uses childrens' familiarity with computers to bridge the gap from the computer being used as entertainment to being used as a teaching tool to help students become successful beginning readers in kindergarten. To use this program, I selected a book each week that I could combine with the daily shared reading and writing. On Mondays, I introduced a "Book of the Week" to my class by putting the book inside a large blue canvas bag and placing the bag with Elliott on my rocking chair. As my students returned from recess, they looked for Elliott sitting with the big blue bag and immediately knew that they had a wonderful new story waiting for them. Together we looked inside the bag and removed a small letter from Elliott. The letter included three different clues for guessing the title of the book. I read each clue, pausing to allow students to think of what the title could be. The students were always very excited after I read the first clue. They frequently knew the title before I finished reading the second clue. The children guessed the title so quickly because of their experiences with listening to the stories over and over through the computer component: *Listen to Stories*.

The literacy lessons are designed by the classroom teacher to help children build upon and extend their individual knowledge and strengths. Each day of the week has a special emphasis. On Mondays the "Book of the Week" story is introduced; the focus of the lesson is on predicting and reading. On Tuesdays the lesson centers around remembering, retelling, and reading. On Wednesdays the emphasis is reading, personalizing, and reading again. On

Thursdays the focus is reading and creating, and on Fridays the lesson culminates with rereading, summarizing, analyzing, and celebrating. The children are encouraged to read each story independently also, both in individual student books and on the computer. The classroom teacher provides both whole group and small group instruction that relates to story structure and meaning.

Research Proven The research-based program that I was using develops a strong foundation for reading success. Carolyn Brown, Ph.D., developed the program while she was a research scientist in the Department of Speech Pathology and Audiology at the University of Iowa. The program builds a strong conceptual framework that combines behavior predictors of language and literacy with the environmental predictors of reading success. One of the major research findings that is a basis for this program suggests that certain home and environmental factors play determining roles in reading development. Young children who grew up in homes rich in language and reading material, where parents talked with their children and read to them often, were far more likely to develop the perceptual/behavioral predictors of reading achievement and go on to become successful readers. Conversely, children who were raised in environments where such experiences were not available were much more likely to fail when they attempted to learn to read. Research in school districts throughout the United States indicated that children who used this program achieved significant and lasting improvement in their reading skills. The program creates experiences that develop the structure of language and print, phonemic awareness, and the foundations for beginning readers. It facilitates a developmentally appropriate transition from speaking to reading.

> *Ready, set, go! A child puts on headphones, positions the mouse, clicks on an assigned color icon and name, and chooses one of the five program components: Listen to Stories, Tell Stories, Explore Words, Explore Alphabet, and Paint.*

Ready, Set, Go! Ready, set, go! A child puts on headphones, positions the mouse, clicks on an assigned color icon and name, and chooses one of the five program components: Listen to Stories, Tell Stories, Explore Words, Explore Alphabet, and Paint. Through these components children naturally discover the relationship between spoken and written language at their own level and pace.

A Teacher's Perspective: Rhonda Green As I reflect upon this school year and my first year using this technology program, I am reminded of the vast changes that I have seen occur with the children in my classroom. The children have become focused, quite independent, and more excited about learning now than they were on the first day of school. More importantly, though, the children have acquired new skills and strategies in reading on which they will continue to build for the remainder of their lives.

I believe that all of the children in my classroom are successful due in part to using the technology program. One child that quickly comes to mind as having grown the most is Chen. Chen is a very young English as a Second Language student who began the school year understanding some English and speaking even less. Initially, Chen cried for the majority of the first two weeks in my classroom. He appeared to be confused, frightened, and perhaps slightly isolated. He was placed in an environment that was strange and new to him with people whose language he could not completely understand. Everything was different for Chen, the children, the books, the letters of the alphabet, and even the food. Many times, I too, would cry in private for Chen. I wanted so much to be able to teach this young child and wanted even more for him to learn like the other boys and girls in my classroom.

Soon after Chen was placed in my class, I began working individually with him, trying to establish an element of trust. Slowly I began teaching him the words for unfamiliar items, similar to the way I teach my son. Together Chen and I sang songs, looked at picture books, played various games, and worked with an alphabet book that I had made. Often, while I would be working with the other students in my class, my assistant would also work with Chen. To a stranger, some of the things that my assistant and I were doing with Chen would more than likely seem silly or a waste of time, but with him they were valuable learning experiences. Gradually, Chen began to trust me, and I knew that I could begin to close his gap between the unfamiliar and learning.

After approximately two weeks in my classroom, Chen began using the *Breakthrough to Literacy*™ program. I enrolled him at the lowest possible level, "Language Acquisition." With reinforcement and support, Chen began making progress. He began learning letters, followed by sounds and rhymes. Before long, he knew enough letters and sounds to decode some simple words and read short books. This allowed him to practice his decoding skills. When he first began to apply his letter sound knowledge, Chen seemed to go more slowly than most and was quite unsure of himself. The more that he read, though, the more skilled and confident he became. I supported him as he practiced by using different books at his instructional level. Soon, Chen began learning how to recognize errors in his reading and how to correct them. He was now making progress faster than most of the children in my classroom. Before long, Chen was working on the level of "Upper Emerging" in the program.

All of the work and progress that Chen had made was in a literacy rich environment. At every opportunity, I modeled purposeful reading and writing so that not only Chen, but all of my students could see and hear how readers looked and sounded. Soon my students began to make the connection that good readers read all of the time.

Chen was reading more and more. It was as if he could not get enough books to read. One day, he even brought his own personal books to school to read to me. He was so proud to show them to me. To my surprise, however, the books were written in Chinese instead of English. I could not help but think how ironic this was. I was now the student and Chen the teacher. He was attempting to bridge my gap of the unfamiliar with items that are most familiar to him. Chen truly enjoyed that experience.

By the time that spring break arrived, Chen was writing as much as he was reading. He wrote about everything and used a variety of media. He really seemed to like using a keyboard. For him, using a keyboard was a level of comfort that the other students did not seem to have. Each week when we would visit our school computer lab, I would hear Chen giggling with excitement as he quickly typed a sentence on his computer. He would always want to read it to me immediately and then go on to create another.

Each week when we would visit our school computer lab, I would hear Chen giggling with excitement as he quickly typed a sentence on his computer.

As Chen continued to make progress, he was also building self-confidence. He began assisting other students with their reading and writing. The students, in turn, began to see him differently. They were looking to him for help now instead of helping him. Before too long, Chen became more independent. He continued to improve weekly until he was placed in the level of "Fluency" in the *Breakthrough to Literacy*™ program. Chen was the only child in my classroom to reach that level during this school year.

On Chen's report card during the final grading period I wrote these comments, "Words cannot begin to express how proud I am of Chen and of all the progress he has made during this school year. I am honored to have been his teacher and wish Chen nothing but success as he embarks on a lifetime of learning." In my previous years of teaching kindergarten, I have encountered several students who have had tremendous impact on me. These students helped shape the way I teach, the way I think, and even the way I approach learning. None of my previous students, however, had an impact on me quite like Chen. I know now that I am in some ways changed forever. I was given a student that I did not completely know how to teach, but with the help of the program I was not only able to teach him, but also I was able to help him to achieve success and to become a reader for life.

Does Technology Bridge the Gap?

At the beginning of this school year, my question was, "Could a teacher use technology to bridge the gap between what students know and what they did not know?" Based on student observations, student work, and individual test results, it is my professional opinion that technology does help to bridge the gap. I have learned that I can use computers to help students bridge the gap, becoming successful beginning readers in kindergarten armed with the necessary tools and strategies they need.

At the beginning of this school year, my question was, "Could a teacher use technology to bridge the gap between what students know and what they did not know?" Based on student observations, student work, and individual test results, it is my professional opinion that technology does help to bridge the gap.

Planning for Future Instruction

As I plan for the next school year, I am armed with data to support my confidence in the program. Student observations, student work, and test results paint the picture of achievement. A comparative study was designed with the first year implementation data to discover the validity of *Breakthrough to Literacy*™ in a kindergarten program with student reading achievement. Two full-day kindergarten classes at Bettie F. Williams Elementary, each with fifteen students, were selected.

Both classes participated in the Phonemic Awareness Literacy Screening (PALS) early intervention program and followed all VBCPS curricula. Teacher A's class used the *Breakthrough to Literacy*™ program as a supplement, and Teacher B's class did not.

The following data was collected from Teacher A and Teacher B. (See Figure 1.) It included the Extended Day Kindergarten Assessment (EDK) given in September, the Phonemic Awareness Literacy Screening (PALS) given in October, report card assessments given in October, and the Developmental Reading Assessment (DRA) given in November. All of the assessments were combined for the fifteen students to reach a total of 120 assessments, or 60 assessments per class. Each of the students was then ranked as performing "Below grade level standards," "Meeting grade level standards," or "Above grade level standards."

Figure 1

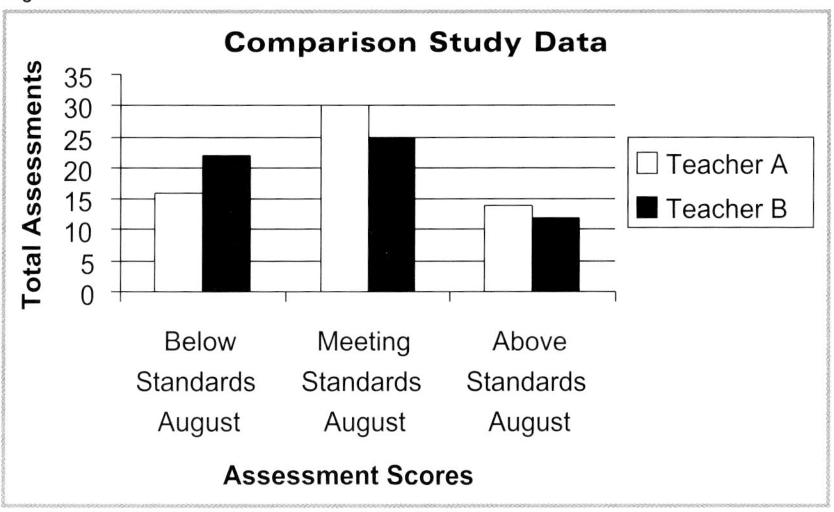

The results of the initial comparison show that both of the classes were relatively equal in student achievement. Both classes had the highest majority of students performing at "Meeting grade level standards," and the lowest number of students achieving "Above grade level standards."

At the conclusion of the school year, the same data was collected from the two classes and the results are shown in Figure 2.

The results of the final comparison show that overall both classes are relatively equal in two of the three categories of student achievement; students achieving "Above grade level standards" and students "Meeting

Figure 2

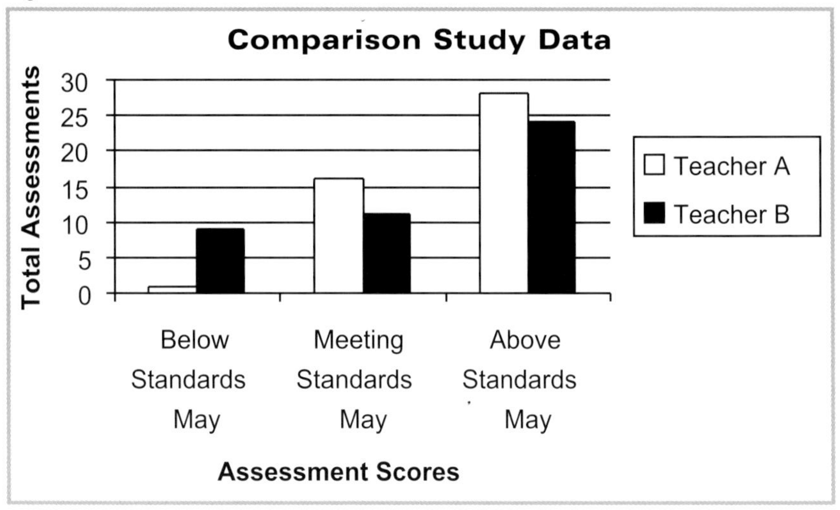

grade level standards." The largest increase for both classes was the number of students that achieved "Above grade level standards." Teacher A again had the highest percentage. The category with the most significant outcome, however, is the one with the number of students performing "Below grade level standards." Teacher A had only one of fifteen students placed in this category, whereas teacher B had several more. Could this be a direct end result of having used *Breakthrough to Literacy*™ in teacher A's classroom? I believe so.

Conclusion

A Child's Perspective

If you want an honest answer, you can always depend on children to tell you exactly what they think. Children were asked one on one to tell what their favorite part of *Breakthrough to Literacy*™ was. The following are some of their responses:

Student quotes about "*Breakthrough to Literacy*"™

Chen – "I like the stories. They're good."

Sarah – "I like reading books because its fun, and I know how to read now."

Ruby – "I like when Elliott tells me I can paint and when to hang up my headphones."

Tommy – "I like listening to stories because they have more reading than I have at home."

Dion – "I like painting because I can make the picture look how I want."

Michael – "I like story time because you can listen to good stories."

Mary – "I like getting yellow stars!"

Sheila – "I like exploring and doing the ABCs because I know them."

Wendy – "I like hearing my voice, going to the green box, alphabet, and just everything on the computer. It's really cool!"

Alyssa – "I like the green box and the ABCs. Telling stories is fun, too."

Ready or Not, there they go...

When the school year ended and the children walked out to board the big yellow bus, ready for first grade, I heard them saying, "I know my letters." "Mrs. Green taught me my sounds." "My first grade teacher won't believe how well I can read." These positive comments make me realize that my students have the necessary skills and confidence to be successful first graders.

Note: `All student names are pseudonyms and all student work has been used with permission.

Works Cited

Breakthrough to Literacy™: The New Three Rs Research Reading and Results. Bothwell, WA: The Wright Group, 1999.

Breakthrough to Literacy™: Teacher Guide. Bothwell, WA: The Wright Group. 1999.

About Rhonda Green

Rhonda Green is a third-year kindergarten teacher at Bettie F. Williams Elementary School. Prior to teaching kindergarten, Mrs. Green was a Phonemic Awareness Literacy Screening (PALS) early intervention teacher for Virginia Beach City Public Schools. She has a Bachelor of Science in Education.

About Patricia Sears

Patricia Sears is the Early Childhood Coordinator for Virginia Beach City Public Schools. Ms. Sears works closely with kindergarten teachers in each of the 54 elementary schools. She is always looking for new ways to help children become successful in school. She has a Master of Science in Education.

Section Three

Spinning Lessons From the Web *to* Enhance Student Improvement

Anne G. Wolcott

Flower Fusion

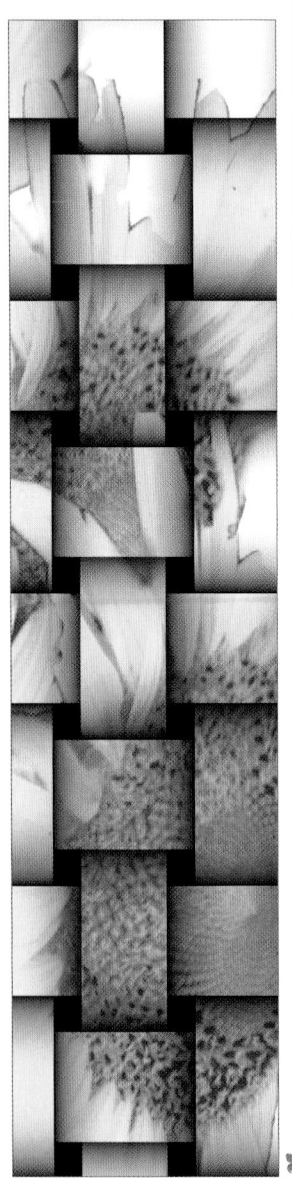

Description: The artwork originated from a cibrachrome photograph of a sunflower taken in my garden. The photograph was scanned and manipulated on the computer using a computer graphics program.

Medium Used: Computer-generated cibrachrome photograph

Educational Background: Dr. Anne Wolcott received a Bachelor of Arts in 1973 from Stratford College, a Master of Arts in Art Education from Virginia Commonwealth University in 1986, and a Doctor of Philosophy in Art Education from The Pennsylvania State University in 1991.

Teaching Experience: Dr. Wolcott taught art at the middle and high school levels in North Carolina and Virginia Beach from 1975-1984. She was an Assistant Professor of Art Education at East Carolina University from 1991-1994. Currently, she is the Fine Arts Coordinator in the Office of Instructional Services with Virginia Beach City Public Schools.

Awards: Dr. Wolcott was recognized as the Virginia Art Education Association Art Supervisor of the Year for 2000-2001. Her artwork has been exhibited in regional art shows and most recently exhibited in the 2003 Waves Exhibit at the Contemporary Art Center of Virginia.

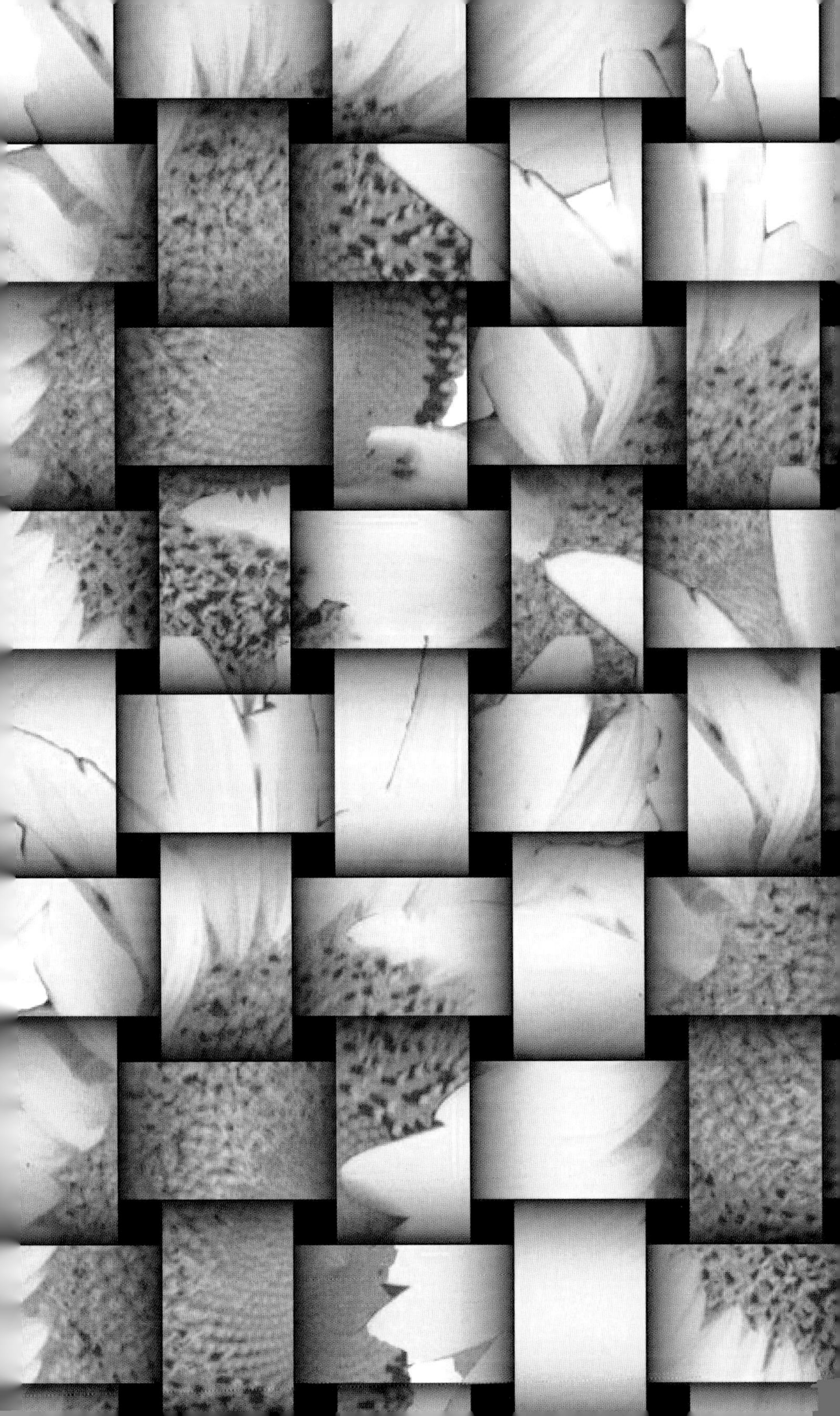

Spinning Lessons From the Web to Enhance Student Involvement

How do teachers motivate students to learn a foreign language? Even though most students are excited about learning a foreign language at first, they lose much of that enthusiasm when they experience the struggle to master the vocabulary, sounds, and grammatical structures of the selected language. Maria Nuzzo, a Spanish teacher at Corporate Landing Middle School, noticed that the joy of learning a new language seemed to disappear by the end of the first quarter. When she surveyed her students to evaluate the quality of instruction, they responded that Spanish was either too hard, boring, or just not as rewarding as they had anticipated.

Nuzzo wondered if using technology to replace some of the rote-learning activities she used to evaluate learning would help the students regain some of their original enthusiasm. After reading David Jonassen's book, *Computers in the Classroom*, she knew that she wanted to avoid using traditional computer-assisted instruction which relies on tutorials or drill-and-practice software. Rather, she wanted to create tasks that forced the students to construct their own knowledge instead of just recalling information. To accomplish this, Nuzzo began to replace such customary activities as skits, dialogues, tests, and quizzes by having the students create multimedia presentations, participate in teacher-created WebQuests, and design their own Web pages. She found that not only did the students enjoy the computer activities, they seemed to learn and retain the material more easily. As well as describing this change in attitude, Nuzzo's article includes step-by-step instructions that other teachers may use to design these exciting tasks.

Maria Nuzzo

Technology: No Longer "Foreign" to the Classroom

by Maria Nuzzo

I clearly remember the makeup of my classroom when I was my students' age: a bare room with a blackboard, a teacher's desk, and a number of perfectly aligned students' desks and chairs. No features of technology such as televisions, video recorders, or computers were at hand. In fact, not even an overhead projector adorned the lackluster and dull looking room. What instructional tools or materials were available to teachers in those days? For the most part, textbooks, sticks of chalk, and blackboards were the tools that helped teachers instill knowledge and thinking skills into the minds of thirty or so teenagers.

Today's classrooms are considerably different from the ones I remember and yet are still quite similar. These are the places where teachers instruct and where pupils, not always willing recipients of instruction, learn academics, and life skills. However, while the instructional and learning dynamics have not changed significantly, teachers now have many options in the choice of tools and materials to aid them in the instructional process. Technology is one of these tools.

However, while the instructional and learning dynamics have not changed significantly, teachers now have many options in the choice of tools and materials to aid them in the instructional process. Technology is one of these tools.

I Thought it Would Be Fun!

As a middle school foreign language teacher, I had been teaching Spanish in a fairly traditional way. I utilized conventional instructional methods and tools such as vocabulary drills, audiotapes, flash cards, and transparencies. For cultural enrichment, I relied on videos of Hispanic countries and visits to Mexican restaurants. Even the assessments I used to evaluate my students' learning were fairly customary: skits, dialogues, tests, quizzes, and rather uninspiring projects that had students draw family trees on poster boards and label family members in the target language.

As I watched my students struggle to master the Spanish vocabulary, sounds, and grammatical structures, I saw something gradually drift away from my

I wished to resurrect the enthusiasm and excitement about learning a new language that inspired my students at the beginning of the school year.

classroom: the students' desire and joy to learn a new language. By the end of the first quarter, I rarely heard my students talking about how important or gratifying learning a second language would be. In fact, when I periodically surveyed my classes to evaluate the quality of instruction and learning environment, I sometimes received statements such as, "It's too hard," "It's boring," or even, "I don't like Spanish." Since my students were for the most part fairly disciplined learners, they continued to tackle the new language and strove to do their best. However, my students' rote compliance to their academic obligations did not satisfy me. I wished to resurrect the enthusiasm and excitement about learning a new language that inspired my students at the beginning of the school year.

Finding Novel Ways Finding ways to make learning Spanish more meaningful and enjoyable to my students became a new focus for my teaching. While pursuing a Master of Science degree in Secondary Education, I completed several courses that explored the use of technology to help students learn. The more I studied and researched the topic, the more I became fascinated by the incredible instructional possibilities that technology, and computers in particular, offer. I came to understand that I did not need to know electronics to use a computer, and, most importantly, I could use computers to help my students learn Spanish. Then I began to search for ways to use technology to motivate my students and facilitate their learning.

Computer Applications to Enhance Learning Several books enhanced my ability to create tasks that integrate technology into the learning environment. One that I found most enlightening was *Computers in the Classroom* by David Jonassen. I learned in Jonassen's book that a more innovative and effective approach to using computers in the classroom is to use computer applications that make the learner think about the content studied. Hence, one learns with computers rather than from or about computers (Jonassen 4).

In fact, several of today's computer applications (i.e., databases, spreadsheets, multimedia applications, etc.) require learners to think in "meaningful ways" and to represent what they know. This enhances thinking and learning, unlike traditional computer-assisted instruction which relies mainly on the use of tutorials or drill-and-practice software. The learners must think critically in order to use these applications and must construct their own knowledge rather than recall the information. The learners reflect on what they know, on what they still need to know, and on personal goals of learning (Jonassen 11). These processes are necessary steps in the learning dynamics to create self-directed and life-long learners.

Motivated by Jonassen's writing and other related studies, I began to develop tasks for my students that required the use of computer applications. In doing so, I discovered another advantage of technology.

An Additional Rationale to Use Technology: Motivating Students

Many of today's students are proficient in the use of computers. They own digital cameras, navigate the Internet, chat on line, play computer games, or communicate via electronic mail. Using technology to help students learn academic subjects adds an element of realism and authenticity to the learning. Learning is more student-centered and cooperative because technology-based tasks lend themselves to working in pairs or groups. At the same time, the students' self-esteem is enhanced by the completion of challenging and novel tasks while hands-on activities make learning more exciting. Whether students are kinesthetic, auditory, or visual learners, technology engages all learning modalities and styles. For these reasons, technology is a powerful tool to motivate students.

Using technology to help students learn academic subjects adds an element of realism and authenticity to the learning.

Caveats: Teachers' Time and Training

Despite these advantages and benefits, technology is not yet fully or widely used in many classrooms. Teachers' inadequate technical preparation is viewed by some as a major hindrance to the use of technology in schools. After all, "it is difficult for students to do sophisticated Internet projects if the teacher struggles to differentiate the hard drive from the floppy" (Grabe 302). While I concede that this argument has some truth, I believe teachers can successfully use technology in the classroom if given more planning time and training.

Educators must have additional time to preview programs and software, to carry out Internet searches for materials and activities, to create handouts and worksheets, and to design appropriate lesson plans. They also need training in the use of both software and hardware. Models and guidelines must be provided to novice users of technology in the classroom. Increasingly, school systems are recognizing these needs and are offering technical preparation and support to teachers willing to overcome their hesitancy and to learn how to use technology as an instructional tool.

Meeting Educational Needs

Becoming trained in the use of technology requires more than computer literacy. Educators need to find ways to use technology to "meet educational needs" (Grabe 34). The task at hand for teachers is to determine how to use technology to enhance the students' learning while meeting curricular objectives. In fact, I found integrating technology into the curriculum in meaningful ways the toughest challenge.

The general goal of a foreign language curriculum is to help students achieve certain levels of proficiency in the target language in both oral and written skills. To achieve this goal, foreign language teachers have to provide as much immersion in the target language as possible. While commercially prepared computer applications can be used, I have found that a better approach is for a foreign language teacher to design appropriate activities in which students use technology to meet instructional objectives in the target language.

While commercially prepared computer applications can be used, I have found that a better approach is for a foreign language teacher to design appropriate activities in which students use technology to meet instructional objectives in the target language.

I teach beginning levels of Spanish, and my students have limited oral and written proficiency in the target language. For instance, after nine weeks of instruction, the Spanish I students have a Spanish vocabulary of approximately 100 words and knowledge of two to three verbs (i.e., the verbs *to be*, *to have*, and *to like*). Certainly, students can easily perform Web searches or quests, but the teacher must ensure that whatever knowledge the students acquire in such activities should transfer to using the target language in potentially authentic tasks.

Creating Tasks

The following are some tasks and appropriate rubrics that I have created, used, or plan to use in my classroom. I believe these tasks meet the foreign language instructional criteria mentioned above through the use of technology. In addition, the tasks can be adapted for use in other academic subjects. (See Appendix for rubrics and a detailed description of each task.)

Task # 1

This first task has the students create a multimedia presentation in Spanish in which they describe themselves and state their likes and dislikes. Students work individually on their presentations and then share them with the class.

For this activity, I created detailed and extensive directions on how to use Microsoft PowerPoint®, but I discovered that many of my students were already familiar with this application because they had learned about it in computer technology classes or had used it in presentations for other academic subjects. Still, some less confident students benefited from having detailed directions at hand. I allowed my students to choose the layout of their presentations as long as they included the required content.

Overall, this task, which students could complete even in the first few weeks of Spanish instruction, was especially successful. The presentations were creative and, for the most part, the students used the target language correctly and appropriately. When surveyed about the activity, they expressed their beliefs that it had enhanced their knowledge of the grammar and vocabulary of the specific unit of study and that their confidence to communicate in the target language had increased.

Task # 2

The second task is an example of a tele-computing activity in which students are asked to use the Internet to search for weather conditions in a city of a Spanish-speaking country of their choice. Following the search, they make an oral presentation to the class about their findings. The presentation also includes statements about appropriate clothing to wear and possible activities to enjoy according to the weather conditions. Students can work individually or in pairs for this task.

I found this task, which can be performed by first year Spanish students, to be very effective. It provides an authentic context for the practice of the content studied. Students must use a variety of vocabulary and grammatical structures to describe weather, clothing, and leisure activities. Moreover, students indirectly make connections to other disciplines such as geography and science (i.e., Celsius measurement system for temperature versus Fahrenheit).

As an additional instructional activity, students could be asked to compare and contrast the weather in their community with that of the Spanish-speaking city. Clothing and leisure or work related activities can also be compared or contrasted.

Task # 3

This third task, created for a unit of study on foods and meals, is a WebQuest that has the students explore Mexican cuisine. I have not yet used this task in my classroom, but my students have performed some of the activities included in the quest.

A WebQuest is a document, usually designed as a Web page, which guides students in the completion of an investigative activity. It provides scaffolding by supplying background information and resources to help the students complete their tasks. Although WebQuests are extremely time-consuming to construct, they are a wonderful way to use computers to help students learn. They can be designed for a variety of topics and activities, and even though they provide the students with resources and guidelines, students use their creativity and thinking skills to complete the quest. In fact, an even more effective way to use WebQuests in the classroom is to have the students create them.

> *Although WebQuests are extremely time-consuming to construct, they are a wonderful way to use computers to help students learn.*

I designed my WebQuest using Microsoft Word® (document saved as html file) so that it can be accessed with any Internet browser. The WebQuest is totally navigable: students can navigate from page to page and task to task. All the Internet sites are hyperlinked. Background colors, pictures, sounds, and Web art are added to make the quest more visually appealing. In addition, I differentiated tasks according to their degree of difficulty. Level 1 and 2 Spanish students can perform the first two tasks of the quest. Spanish 2 students will employ a greater variety of vocabulary in their presentations. The third task, if completed in Spanish, is appropriate for upper level Spanish students. In any case, the WebQuest offers choices to students of different abilities and interests. My students thoroughly enjoyed performing some of the tasks in the WebQuest. They were fascinated by the various foods and customs they encountered while searching the sites.

Task # 4

I was inspired to create this task by one of my students who had designed a Web page about himself. I realized that having students create Web pages in Spanish could be an additional and effective way to use computer applications to help them learn, requiring them to use a variety of Spanish vocabulary and grammatical structures while allowing them to demonstrate their creativity. This fourth task, which first-year Spanish students can perform, has students create a Web site about their school in Spanish. I have not yet used it in my classroom because it requires students to spend a considerable amount of time in the computer lab. However, I look forward to using this task in the future.

The Four Tasks: Differences and Similarities

In the above tasks, I attempted to integrate various forms of technology into instruction to facilitate learning. The tasks are similar in that they use computer applications; however, they differ in the choice of applications and levels of difficulty. Nevertheless, they require the students to use all communicative skills in the target language and computers in a variety of ways. Computers are used for word processing, Internet searches, multimedia presentations, and the creation of Web sites. In addition, the tasks are suitable for foreign language students of all levels since each task can be completed using basic Spanish vocabulary and grammar or more complex features of the target language.

Finally, by offering various samples of tasks, I hope to give foreign language teachers a choice of tasks according to their students' interests, needs, abilities, and the teachers' own preferences and comfort levels.

Conclusion: Designing computer-assisted tasks in which students are able to put to work their fairly limited Spanish skills has not been an easy experience; however, it has been especially rewarding. My students not only enjoy the computer activities tremendously, but also they seem to learn and retain the material under study more easily. I, on the other hand, enjoy watching them work attentively and conscientiously using their creativity, imagination, and skills.

Yet, as I write this article, my students and I are still at the threshold of using technology to aid and assess learning. The use of technology in my classroom to this day has been limited and not as pervasive as I would like it to be, mainly due to time constraints. However, while I still rely on traditional methods of instruction and assessment, I try to include for each unit of study at least one task that integrates technology. Further, a problem that I have encountered is that Web sites often change or disappear altogether. It is necessary to check often to make sure that the site is still good.

However, while I still rely on traditional methods of instruction and assessment, I try to include for each unit of study at least one task that integrates technology.

Using technology in instruction will make my students better Spanish learners and most importantly, life-long learners. The process of weaving technology into instruction to improve learning has proven challenging for my students and me, but I continue to persevere because I believe that the outcome is certainly worth the effort.

Appendix

- The format for the following tasks is modeled on the template for performance-based assessments in the Virginia Beach City Public Schools Spanish curriculum guide from the Department of Curriculum and Instruction.

Task 1

Title: El nuevo trabajo

Topic: Biographical Information, Likes and Dislikes

Level: Novice (Spanish 1)

Goals: Communication Comparisons Connections

VBCPS Progress Indicators: P.I.1.1 P.I.1.3 P.I.3.2 IR.I.4.4

Time Frame: 2 to 3 class periods (50 minutes each period)

Materials Needed: computer lab, diskettes, digital camera

Teacher Notes: Teacher's guidance in the use of Microsoft PowerPoint® is strongly recommended. Students should go to the computer lab one or two times to practice using the software prior to creating the presentations. It is best to take pictures with the digital camera on a separate day and have students write and edit the content of their presentations before actually creating them. This will save time in the computer lab.

Description of Task:
You are applying for a summer job at one of the establishments frequented by tourists in your city. The company for which you wish to work has asked job applicants to send, via e-mail, a picture of themselves and some autobiographical information to speed up the interviewing process. To make your presentation as attractive as possible, you should use the multimedia presentation software Microsoft PowerPoint®. Since the company to which you are applying for work is expecting many Spanish-speaking tourists to visit your city, you will write your presentation in Spanish to demonstrate your ability to use the language. The following format will help you create an effective presentation.

Content of Slides:

1. **First slide:** a greeting.
2. **Second slide:** state your name and insert your picture previously taken with a digital camera and saved on your diskette.
3. **Third slide:** biographical information on the bulleted list such as your age, place of origin, birthday, and phone number (not your real phone number).
4. **Fourth slide:** at least three activities you like to do on the bulleted list; include a picture from clip art.
5. **Fifth slide:** at least three activities you do not like to do on the bulleted list; include a picture from clip art.
6. **Sixth slide:** at least three adjectives that describe yourself on the bulleted list (I am...); insert clip art if you like.
7. **Seventh slide:** at least three adjectives that do not describe yourself on the bulleted list (I am not…); insert clip art if you like.
8. **Eighth slide:** a good-bye.
   - In your text, include vocabulary studied (preliminary chapter and chapter 1) and expressions such as a veces, pero, también, ni...ni, mucho, nada.
   - Remember that while you wish your presentation to be attractive, you want it to be easily read and viewed. Choose background colors, fonts, and slide transitions wisely.

Evaluation:
Refer to the multimedia presentation rubric to understand how your presentation will be evaluated.

Appendix

Task 2

Title: ¿Qué tiempo hace?

Topic: Weather

Level: Novice (Spanish I)

Goals: Communication Connections Comparisons

VBCPS Progress Indicators: P.I.1.1 P.I.1.3 IR.I.1.4 IR.I.3.1 P.I.3.2 IR.I.4.4

Time Frame: 2 class periods (50 minutes each period)

Materials Needed: computer lab, handouts

Teacher Notes: The teacher should guide students in the Internet search. Practice of appropriate vocabulary and modeling of reports is recommended prior to the actual presentations

Description of Task:

Your school is celebrating Foreign Languages Week. You are asked to give a weather report in Spanish during the morning announcements for a city in a Spanish-speaking country. To prepare your report, you should do the following:

- In the computer lab access an appropriate Web site. In the site, click on tiempo; choose a Spanish-speaking country from the list given and a city from that country. On the weather table, record the weather conditions for five consecutive days. Log temperatures for each day (Fahrenheit and Celsius).
- Your oral report will include the following information: name of the city and country, weather conditions for each day, two to three statements about possible activities for each day (i.e., swimming, riding a bike, listening to music), and appropriate attire.
- Include the table used by students to record the information gathered on the Internet.

Appendix

Nombre ______

Timbre ______

Fecha ______

Continente: ______

País: ______

Ciudad: ______

Día	Temperatura		Tiempo
	Fahrenheit	Celsius	
Lunes			
Martes			
Miércoles			
Jueves			
Viernes			
Sábado			
Domingo			

Evaluation:
Refer to the oral presentation rubric to understand how you will be evaluated.

Appendix

Task 3

Title: ¿Qué comemos?

Topic: Foods/Mexican Cuisine

Level: Novice and Intermediate (Spanish I and above)

Goals: Communication Cultures Connections Comparisons

VBCPS Progress Indicators: P.I.1.1 P.I.1.3 IR.I.2.2 IR.I.3.1 P.I.3.2 IR.I.4.4

Time Frame: four to five class periods (50 minutes each period

Materials Needed: computer lab, media center, and props chosen by students for their presentations

Teacher Notes: Teacher's guidance and advice in the choice of tasks and organization of the presentations are recommended. Students need to rehearse presentations thoroughly. Internet sites need to be checked beforehand for availability and content

Description of Task:
You have entered a cooking contest and wish to prepare a Mexican dish. To better prepare yourself, you decided to investigate Mexico's cuisine and eating customs. Your Spanish teacher made available to you a WebQuest that can help you in preparing for the contest. Explore it carefully, and attempt to complete at least one of the tasks indicated.

Evaluation:
Refer to the oral and written performance rubrics to understand how you will be evaluated.

Appendix

México: Una experiencia culinaria

Introduction Tasks Process Resources Evaluation Conclusion

Introduction

This WebQuest will take you on a tour of the Mexican cuisine. You will become acquainted with some of the best Mexican recipes and dishes as well as some of Mexico's finest restaurants. This is a chance for you to apply the Spanish language skills acquired in school to explore the Mexican culture and traditions through cuisine.

Tasks

① **Task – Recetas deliciosas**

Investigate, explore, and sample authentic Mexican dishes.

② **Task – ¿Adónde vamos a comer?**

Visit top Mexican restaurants and choose your favorites.

③ **Task – La cocina mexicana**

Learn about the history and tradition of the Mexican cuisine

Process

Read carefully the process for the completion of each of the three tasks. Reflect on which task will better prepare you to meet your learning goals and choose it. You are required to complete only one task. Talk to your teacher if you would like to complete more than one task.

- Task 1
- Task 2
- Task 3

Appendix

Resources

❑ Listed below are the resources you will need to carry out your task.

- **Web sites**
- **Your textbook**
- **Spanish/English dictionary**
- **Media center**

Access Web sites for recipes

Recipes 

Access Web sites for restaurants 

Conclusion

❖ During this WebQuest, you have the opportunity to explore Mexico's cuisine, culture, and traditions. I would like you to make the following reflections on this experience:

- How was this experience valuable for you?
- How did this WebQuest improve your ability to use the Spanish language?
- What did you like best or least about the WebQuest?
- Are there any similarities between the Mexican cuisine/culture and your own? Are there any differences?

★ We will discuss these questions in class. I hope you enjoyed being a part of **"México: Una Experiencia Culinaria."**

¡Adiós!

Top

WebQuest - Task One

Recetas Deliciosas

- **Process:**
  - ➢ Browse the Web sites for recipes (Main Page).
  - ➢ Choose one recipe of your liking.
  - ➢ Use a dictionary (or ask your teacher) to find any words you do not know.
  - ➢ Prepare yourself to present the recipe to the class.
- **Class presentation:**
  - ➢ Describe the recipe that you chose to your classmates.
  - ➢ Tell about its ingredients and preparation.
  - ➢ Tell why you chose this particular recipe.
  - ➢ Tell when you are going to prepare this recipe and mention people you may invite to sample it.

❖ Present all information in Spanish.

- **Optional Activity:**
  Prepare the recipe for your classmates to view or sample.

Main Page

WebQuest - Task Two

¿Adónde Vamos a Comer?

- **Process:**
  - You may choose to do this task individually or with a classmate.
  - Browse the Web sites listed for restaurants (Main Page).
  - Choose 2 restaurants that appeal to you.
- **Class presentation:**
  - Tell your classmates about these restaurants.Provide the following information:
    - Name
    - Location, address, and phone number
    - Hours of operation
    - Menu
    - Available entertainment
  - Make sure that you:
    - Give geographical information about the location of the restaurants (i.e., city and region of Mexico).
    - Describe the menu: appetizers, first and second courses, side dishes, desserts, beverages, and specialties of the house.
    - Tell why you chose the restaurants.
    - Use visuals: i.e., pictures of the restaurants printed from the Web sites, or transparencies to describe the menus

❖ Presentation must be in Spanish

Main Page

WebQuest - Task Three

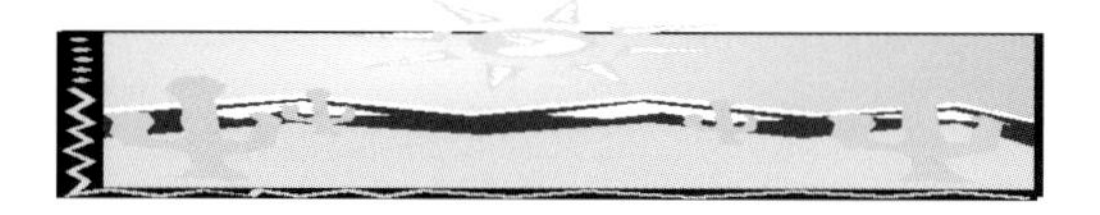

La Cocina Mexicana

- **Process:**
  - ➢ You may choose to do this task individually or with a classmate.
  - ➢ Go to a Web site that relates to food.
  - ➢ Read carefully the information provided on the history of the Mexican cuisine.
  - ➢ Supplement your reading with other sources from the media center or the Internet, if necessary.
  - ➢ Write an essay, one to two pages in length, describing what you learned about the history of Mexico's cuisine. Cite additional sources from the media center or Internet, if used.
- **Presentation:**
  - ➢ A written essay to be given to your teacher
  - ➢ An oral presentation to your classmates about what you have learned
  - ➢ Visuals of your choice for your oral presentation, i.e., pictures, transparencies, videos
  - ➢ Oral presentation and written essay in Spanish

Main Page

Task 4

Title: Mi escuela

Topic: School/School Subjects/Extra-curricular Activities

Level: Novice (Spanish I)

Goals: Communication Connections Comparisons

VBCPS Progress Indicators: P.I.1.1 P.I.1.3 P.I.3.2 IR.I.4.4

Time Frame: At least five class periods (50 minutes each period)

Materials Needed: computer lab, diskettes, digital camera

Teacher Notes: Teacher's guidance in the design of the Web site is strongly recommended. Detailed instructions on how to create hyperlinks, insert pictures, etc. may be necessary. In forming students' groups, it is best to include at least one student in each group with good computer skills if possible.

Students should practice generating html documents in Microsoft Word® before actually creating the site. In addition, they should take pictures with the digital camera, design the Web pages, and edit their content beforehand. This will save time in the computer lab.

Even if the site is not actually linked to the school's Web site, permission from students, parents, and teachers is needed if their pictures are used. It is preferable to limit pictures to those of the students working on the task. Clip art, drawings, or digital pictures can also be used.

It is best to save all pages on the same disk drive or on the school server. This will make linking the pages easier.

*Many other software programs in addition to Microsoft Word® are available to create Web pages easily (i.e., Microsoft Front Page®, Macromedia Dreamweaver®, Geocities®).

Description of Task:
Since your community has a considerable Spanish-speaking population, you were asked to create a Web site about your school in Spanish. Follow the directions given to create an effective site.

- You will work in groups and each group will create one page of the site.
- The Web site will contain the following pages:
  Page 1: Home Page
  Page 2: School
  Page 3: Classes
  Page 4: Sports
  Page 5: Clubs
  Page 6: Teachers
  Page 7: Spanish Class

— Content of the Home Page

1. Title (i.e., school's name)
2. Picture of the school
3. Links to the next pages (i.e., students, classes, sports, etc.)
4. Link to the city of Virginia Beach Web site
5. Link to the Virginia Beach school system Web site
6. Link to the school Web site (if allowed)

— Content of page 2: The School

1. Description of the school
   (i.e., size, color, location, time the school day starts and ends)
2. Pictures and descriptions of three to four locations in the school such as the cafeteria, auditorium, gym, computer lab (i.e., the cafeteria is big, there are many tables and chairs)
3. Link to the home page and next page

— Content of page 3: The Classes

1. Pictures and description of at least 4 classes
   (i.e., the math class, the art class, etc.)
2. List type or amount of homework for the classes
3. List items found in the classrooms
   (i.e., desks, chairs, computers, chalkboard)
4. Link to the home page and next page

— Content of page 4: The Sports

1. List the sports (at least three) played at the school
2. Pictures of teams or playing fields, if available, or clip art
3. Link to the home page and next page

Appendix

— **Content of page 5: The Clubs**

1. Mention of the various clubs (at least three) at the school
2. Pictures of the clubs, if available, or clip art
3. Link to the home page and next page

— **Content of page 6: The Teachers**

1. Mention of at least four teachers (i.e., the math teacher, the science teacher, etc.)
2. What they teach and what they are like (i.e., tall, dark hair, nice)
3. Picture of the teachers, with permission, or clip art
4. Link to the home page and next page

— **Content of page 7: Your Spanish Class**

1. Picture and a description of your classroom
2. Name and a description of your teacher
3. Number of the students: how many boys and how many girls. Another bullet with general description of the students (i.e., smart, nice, tall, dark hair, etc.)
4. List at least four topics you are studying (i.e., numbers, foods, clothes, colors, etc.)
5. Link to the home page and next page

— **Design for all pages:**

1. Work in groups: each group is responsible for the creation of one of the site pages. Your Spanish teacher will help you and guide you in the completion of your task. You may wish to ask the computer club for advice and suggestions.
2. Create the Web site with Microsoft Word® (document saved as html file).
3. The site will have a total of seven pages. Each page must have background color, title, horizontal dividers or banners, links to the home page and to the next page, various fonts, and pictures or images.
4. Use a digital camera to take pictures of places or students. Ask for students', parents', and teachers' permission before including their pictures in your project. (A form may be obtained from the Department of Media and Communications Development.)
5. Include sound in your Web site if you like.

— **Remember that the site should:**

1. Be informative.
2. Be visually appealing but readable; choose background colors and fonts wisely.
3. Be easily navigable.
4. Have correct use of Spanish vocabulary and grammatical structures.

Evaluation:

Refer to the multimedia presentation rubric to understand how your Web site will be evaluated.

- Samples of rubrics used to evaluate the tasks:

Rubric for Oral Performance

Name:	Excellent (5)	Good (4)	Fair (3)	Poor (2-1)
Language Usage/ Comprehension	Few or no errors; message highly comprehensible	Some errors but message is comprehensible	Several serious errors; at times message not comprehensible	Many serious errors; message not comprehensible
Fluency	Few or no pauses or false starts; thoughts expressed fluently	Some pauses or false starts but thoughts expressed completely	Frequent pauses but manages to complete thoughts	Many long pauses and false starts; incomplete thoughts; resorting to English
Pronunciation	Few or no errors; speech easily understood	Some errors but speech generally understood	Several serious errors; speech at times not understood.	Many serious errors; speech not understood
Vocabulary	Adequate and accurate use of vocabulary; several attempts at elaboration	Adequate and accurate use of vocabulary	At times inadequate or inaccurate use of vocabulary	Frequent inadequate or inaccurate use of vocabulary
Task completion	Superior completion of task; adds to required elements	Good completion of task; all required elements included	Partial completion of task; most required elements included	Minimal or no completion of task; few or none of required elements included

A = 21-25	B = 16-20	C = 11-15	D = 6-10	E = 5

Appendix

Rubric for Written Performance

Name:	Excellent (5)	Good (4)	Fair (3)	Poor (2-1)
Language Usage/ Comprehension	Few or no errors; message highly comprehensible	Some errors but message is comprehensible	Several serious errors; at times message not comprehensible	Many serious errors; message not comprehensible
Vocabulary	Adequate and accurate use of vocabulary; several attempts at elaboration	Adequate and accurate use of vocabulary	At times inadequate or inaccurate use of vocabulary	Frequent inadequate or inaccurate use of vocabulary
Task completion	Superior completion of task; adds to required elements	Good completion of task; all required elements included	Partial completion of task; most required elements included	Minimal or no completion of task; few or none of required elements included

A = 13-15	B = 10-12	C = 7-9	D = 4-6	E = 3

Rubric for Multimedia Presentations

Name:	Excellent (5)	Good (4)	Fair (3)	Poor (2-1)
Language Usage/ Vocabulary	Adequate and accurate use of vocabulary; few or no errors	Mostly adequate and accurate use of vocabulary; some errors	At times inadequate or inaccurate use of vocabulary; several serious errors	Frequent inadequate or inaccurate use of vocabulary; many serious errors
Task completion	Superior completion of task; adds to required elements	Good complction of task; all required elements included	Partial completion of task; most required elements included	Minimal completion of task; few or none of required elements included
Presentation	Well organized; effectively conveys message; shows creativity; very visually appealing	Adequately organized; conveys message; visually appealing	Needs some improvement in organization, appearance, and message communication	Poorly organized; presentation not visually appealing; does not convey message

A = 13-15	B = 10-12	C = 7-9	D = 4-6	E = 3

Works Cited

Grabe, Cindy and Mark. *Integrating the Internet for Meaningful Learning.* Boston, MA: Houghton Mifflin Company, 2000.

Jonassen, David H. *Computers in the Classroom.* Englewood Cliffs, NJ: Prentice-Hall, Inc., 1996.

About Maria Nuzzo

Born and raised in Naples, Italy, Maria Nuzzo has made Virginia Beach her home for the past 23 years. She has been a Spanish teacher in the Virginia Beach City Public Schools since 1995 and has taught at several of the city's middle schools. Also, she taught Spanish at Virginia Wesleyan College as an adjunct faculty member. Ms. Nuzzo received a Bachelor of Arts degree in Spanish from Virginia Wesleyan College and a Master of Science degree in Secondary Education from Old Dominion University. Currently, she teaches at Corporate Landing Middle School.

Section Four

Stiching Technology Into the Structure of Mathematics

Edward A. Obermeyer
Blue Mood

Description: My interest in this painting was to create a mood with the blue butterflies and blue computer chip pieces. The brush strokes on the butterflies are much looser than on the computer chips which point to the difference between technology and nature. Technology is so rigid and structured in contrast to nature, which is free flowing and wild.

Medium Used: Acrylic on Canvas, 48" X 72"

Educational Background: Edward Obermeyer received his Bachelor of Fine Arts from Virginia Commonwealth University and a Master of Interdisciplinary Studies from Virginia Commonwealth University.

Teaching Experience: Mr. Obermeyer has taught for twenty-five years in Virginia Beach. During this time, he has taught students at Kemps Landing Magnet School, a middle school for gifted students; Salem Middle School; and Larkspur Middle School. In addition, he taught beginning, intermediate, and advanced airbrush at the Old Donation Center, an elementary school for gifted children.

Awards: Mr. Obermeyer was recognized as Kemps Landing Teacher of the Year for 1987 and Salem Middle School's Teacher of the Year for 1989. His other awards include the "Artist Extraordinaire" in 1998, the Gold Brush Award in 2001, the winner of *Striped Bass Fisherman's Guide* cover contest (illustrated cover) in 1999, TVEA First Place in juried exhibition in 1999, and was published in *A Tapestry of Knowledge, Volume 1*, in 1998.

Stitching Technology Into the Structure of Mathematics

Eliminating math anxiety and finding qualified mathematics teachers are two problems that confront both teachers and administrators. Interestingly enough, both these problems can be solved by using technology. By utilizing the graphing calculator in algebra and geometry classrooms, Dean Howard, a mathematics teacher at Kellam High School, found that he could reduce students' fear of arithmetic and numbers while emphasizing important mathematical concepts that otherwise might be lost due to math anxiety. Howard explains how important it is to first familiarize the students with the calculator and all its functions. Then, when the students are comfortable with the calculator, he moves into applying the calculator to algebraic and geometrical analysis. His article describes in detail two tasks in which students use the graphing calculator in algebra and geometry with great success. Howard concludes that this technological tool shows great promise for helping students to overcome their anxieties, and with the elimination of this fear, they are able to concentrate on learning mathematical concepts.

Providing equitable educational opportunities in all schools for all students in a large school division is problematic when it comes to specialized courses in high school. With the advent of distance learning, it is entirely possible for one teacher to instruct students in locations across the city. In their article, "Ready, Set, Going the Distance with Mathematics," Monica Lang, Ann Zingraff-Newton, and Eva Roupas, describe how distance learning was designed and implemented in the Virginia Beach School Division. Starting in 1999 with one distance learning class with 20 students in two high schools to

Left to Right: Eva Roupas, Dean Howard, and Ann Zingraff-Newton

23 classes and 444 students in 2002, this program has allowed students to participate in courses that were not available to them in their own school for a variety of reasons: schedule conflicts, a shortage of qualified teachers, or lack of enrollment. The writers conclude that having a live teacher in the classroom with the students is still the best method for students to receive instruction. However, if a teacher is not available, distance learning provides a strong second.

Both these articles demonstrate not only how technology has become an integral part of the Virginia Beach School Division, but how it is being put to use in meaningful ways for students.

Using Graphing Calculators to Overcome Math Anxiety and Improve Test Scores

by Dean Howard

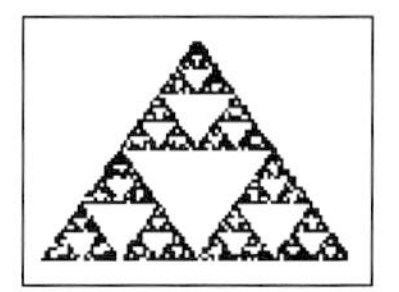

Ben is in mathematics class, and the teacher announces a pop quiz. Looking at the questions on the quiz, Ben realizes that he has forgotten some of the multiplication tables. His heart rate, which was at an all time high, has now shot up to astronomical heights; his mouth is dry, and he can't think of any way to solve the problems. He begins to rethink his future plans to include anything other than attending college. Anything to avoid math altogether! Ben is experiencing math anxiety!

> *With today's emphasis on standardized testing there is a tendency on the part of some students to freeze when confronted with a problem in mathematics.*

With today's emphasis on standardized testing, there is a tendency on the part of some students to freeze when confronted with a problem in mathematics. With each opportunity for an incorrect answer, many students shut down and refuse to try. Causes could be as simple as forgetting how to perform a mathematical operation, such as multiplying, or a lack of confidence in the ability to do the work. This fits the classic definition of math anxiety. When students forget a number fact and do not have the required knowledge to reconstruct that fact, they tend to get frustrated. This is apparent in the slower-paced math courses, such as the Introduction to Algebra/Algebra (X) or Introduction to Geometry/Geometry (X) curriculum, currently taught in Virginia Beach high schools. The curriculum in these courses covers four semesters of math in six semesters to allow students to earn three math credits for completing two math courses.

Is Technology the Answer?

We math teachers have the opportunity to use technological tools to improve learning and help students overcome the fear of incorrect answers. Even if there is not enough time to take each student into a computer lab, some extremely useful graphing calculators are available for use inside and outside the classroom. The TI-83 and TI-92 graphing calculators are examples of these tools. The TI-83 calculator is a multi-function, graphing calculator that is capable of graphing simple and complex functions. It may be used to simplify many algebraic concepts such as the line of best fit or solutions to higher order equations. It is capable of being programmed to perform repetitive calculations, thus allowing the student to concentrate on the concepts under investigation. The TI-92 Plus calculator is also a multi-function graphing calculator that has the added dimension of containing a fully functional keyboard. The TI-92 has more memory capacity than the TI-83 and is capable of storing course specific software applications. This capability makes the TI-92 Plus especially useful for geometry applications. Both calculators have link capabilities that allow data sharing between calculators and PCs. In fact, the graphics that accompany this article have been downloaded from the calculators to a PC. Both calculators have overhead viewscreens available for use with low heat overhead projectors. This enables the teacher's calculator to be seen by the entire class.

Mathematics teachers have several assumptions to overcome before they can make effective use of the calculator technology available

Mathematics teachers have several assumptions to overcome before they can make effective use of the calculator technology available. The first is that their students are technologically advanced. This is untrue. Teachers cannot assume this just because their students can program a VCR, and often, teachers cannot. They are just as leery of new technology as teachers are. The second assumption is that the technology is difficult to use. Nothing could be further from the truth. A step-by-step procedure does wonders to eliminate the "complexity" of graphing calculators.

By the time students are in high school they have encountered arithmetic every year of their school lives. Yes, there must be some emphasis on number sense and arithmetic, but it should not be at the expense of the concept teachers are trying to teach. If math teachers can use technology to reduce the fear of numbers while emphasizing important concepts that might otherwise be lost due to math anxiety, then they will have effectively prepared our students for the next step in their lives whether it is college or the work force.

TI-83 Graphing Calculator in the Algebra (X) Classroom

In order to overcome any fear of graphing technology in an Algebra (X) classroom, I tend to start each school year with a brief familiarization activity that covers the keystrokes required to perform specific functions. I cover the most common functions the students will encounter during the semester that they are in Algebra (X). For example:

TI-83 Familiarization Exercise

1. Turn calculator ON and adjust screen intensity as necessary.
2. Where can I go if I want to enter data in a list? Press [STAT] Select **1: EDIT**

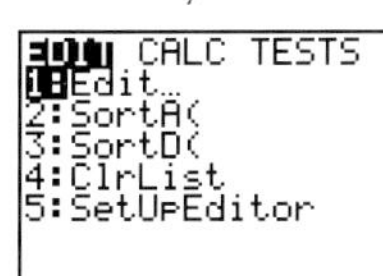

3. How many lists can be used? 6
4. How can I clear all data out of a list? **HIGHLIGHT LIST NAME; Press [CLEAR] [ENTER]**

5. What do I press to set up a statistical plot based on my data? [2nd] [Y =]

6. After a plot has been turned on and defined, how do I display my plot? [ZOOM] [9]
7. What screen is used to determine the line of best fit? [STAT] **Right arrow to (CALC)**

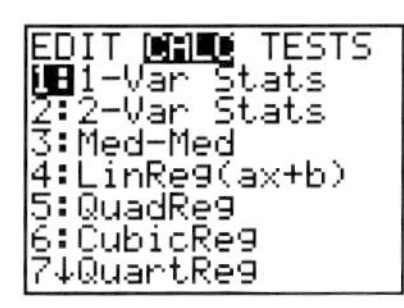

Now that students have become familiar with some of the functions of the calculator, we are ready to proceed with the next activity.

Algebra (X) Statistics Activity

Before the advent of graphing calculators, the procedure for performing an analysis on a list of data was to plot the individual data points on a sheet of graph paper. We asked the students to connect the dots to define a line. We told them to use a method, either something to provide a moveable straight line, such as a piece of uncooked spaghetti, or a formula to calculate a line-of-best-fit. (See Figure 1.) For some students this manual method provided another reason to avoid math. With a graphing calculator, this cumbersome process is reduced to some relatively simple steps, thus enabling the student to concentrate on the analysis instead of the method.

Figure 1

TI-83 Activity

Students are to pretend they began a business several years ago and want to be able to predict when their annual profits will exceed a certain amount. The following table displays their profits for the past seven years.

1	- 5000
2	- 3000
3	- 2000
4	0
5	500
6	1300
7	2100

1 Enter the data into L1 and L2:
Press [STAT] [1]
Enter each data item and press **[ENTER]** after each.

2 Display a scatter plot of the data:
Press [2ND] [Y=] [1] [ENTER] Highlight ON [ENTER]
Highlight appropriate plot type. Check that Xlist indicates the Listnumber in which you placed the x data; check that the indicated Ylist is appropriately selected. Press [ZOOM] [9] to display graph.

3 Determine line of best fit.
Press [STAT] arrow right to **CALC**
Press [4] [ENTER] to select a linear regression **RECORD RESULTS**

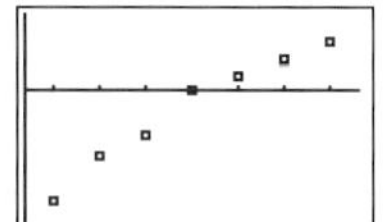

4 Enter the linear regression equation into **[Y=]** screen:
Press [Y =], then enter calculator values for "a"
Press [X,T,_, n] Then enter the value for "b".
Press [GRAPH].

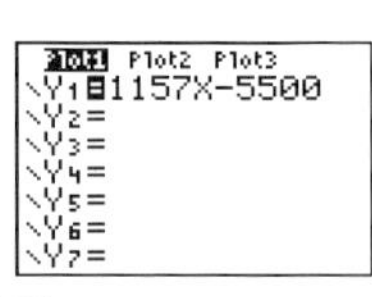

5 Do the two graphs closely match up?
YES

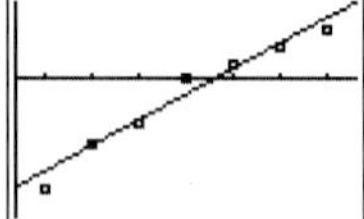

6 When will profits exceed $5000?
Press [2ND] [GRAPH](TABLE)
Scroll down until the Y1 value is greater than $ 5000.

Between 9 and 10 years.

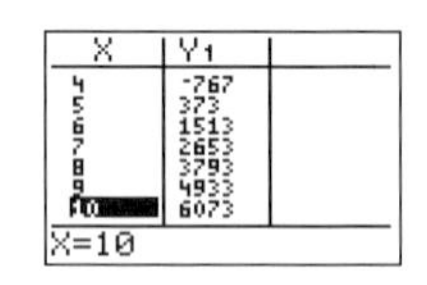

7 Can you predict when profits will be any value?
Yes. Scroll through the table until you find the appropriate value.

Figure 2

TI-92 Plus Familiarization Exercise

1 What keystrokes are used to enter the Geometry application?
Press [APPS] [8][ENTER]

2 Where do I find the "draw a point" tool?
Press [F2[[1]

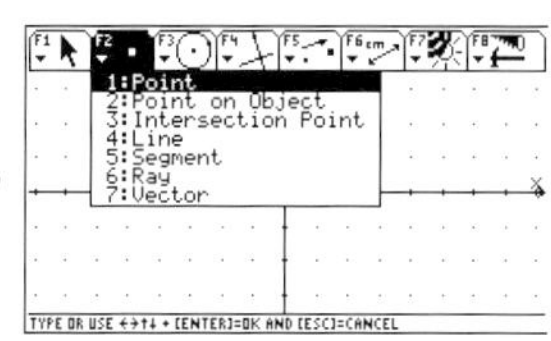

3 Where do I find the "draw a line segment"?
Press [F2] [5]

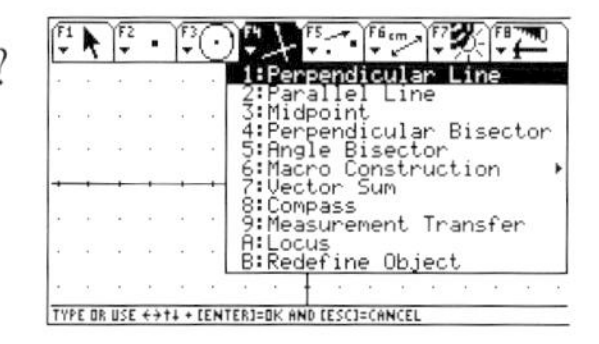

4 Where do I find the "draw a parallel line"?
Press [F4] [2]

5 Where do you go to define and label an intersection point?
Press [F2] [3]

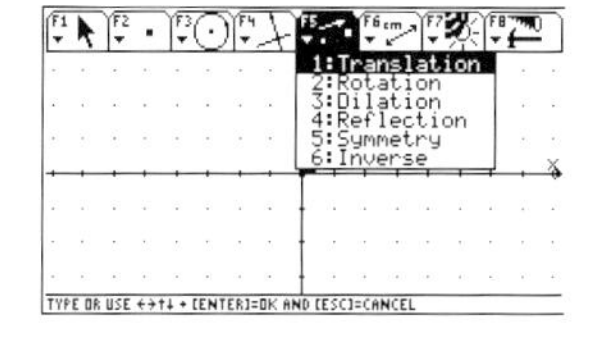

6 Where do you find the way to rotate an object?
Press [F5] [2]

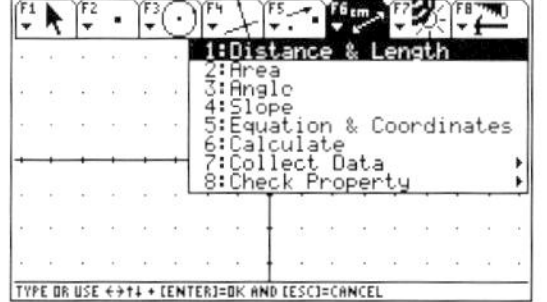

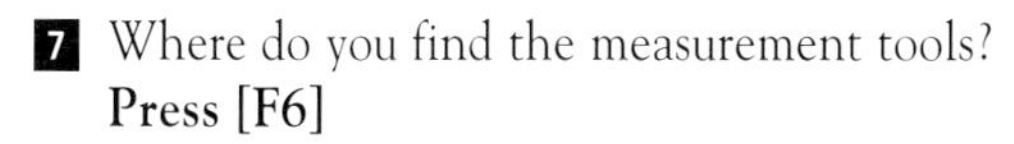

7 Where do you find the measurement tools?
Press [F6]

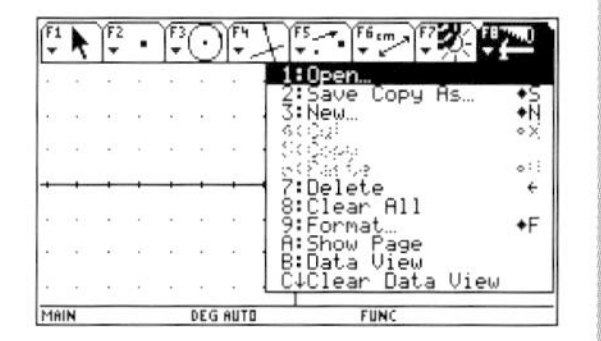

8 What keystrokes are required to clear your work and start over?
Press [F8] [8]

Figure 3

TI-92 Plus Transformation Exercise

1 Once in the Geometry application, ensure that the axes and grids are turned on.
Press [F8] [9] Set Coordinate Axes to

RECTANGULAR Grid to ON.

2 Draw a triangle in the first quadrant with one vertex at the origin.
Press [F3] [3] [ENTER]- Move cursor to any grid point.
Press [ENTER] move cursor to third grid point and press [ENTER].

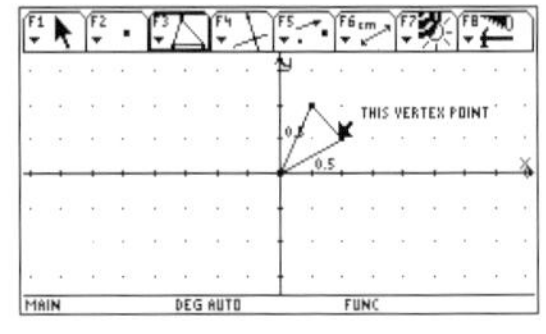

3 Enter degrees of rotation anywhere on the screen. **Press [F7] [6] Move cursor to a convenient location, [ENTER]**
Enter the number "90" Press [ENTER].

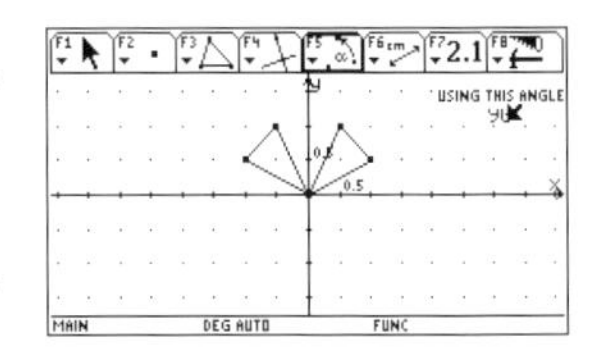

4 Rotate the triangle about the origin.
Press [F5] [2] Enter - Point to Triangle, until you see "Rotate this Triangle". Press [ENTER]. Point to origin until screen says "Around this Point." Press [ENTER]. Point to the label "90" until it says "Using this Angle." Press [ENTER].

5 Repeat step 4 until there are 4 triangles on the screen. **NOTE:** When you point to the "point of rotation," you may see "which object?" displayed. If so, press **[ENTER] [1].**

6 Draw the results on your graph paper.

7 Is there another way to accomplish this transformation, (i.e., reflection, transformation)?

8 How could you rotate the triangle in the opposite direction?
Enter "–90"instead of "90".

9 How many rotations of 90E will make a reflection?
2

10 Identify the symmetries that you see? **Rotational, Line**

TI-92 Plus Calculator in the Introduction to Geometry/ Geometry (X) classroom Most geometry concepts are of a visual nature; if the student can see what is going on, then there is a greater chance of understanding the concept. Using the graphing calculator is an excellent method to allow the student to explore geometric concepts that become apparent when conditions change, i.e., what happens to an object when several transformations are applied. This required multiple sheets of graph paper and was rather static before graphing calculators were available. Now the concept can be explored quickly and effectively without requiring students to perform multiple drawings.

The TI-92 Plus calculator can be rather intimidating at first glance as it looks like a small computer, which it is. Again using a step-by-step approach to familiarize students with its capabilities and features before launching them into the world of techno-geometry will alleviate much of the anxiety that is created when handling this calculator for the first time. (See Figure 2.)

Now that the students are familiar with some of the features of the calculator, they are ready to proceed with the next activity. (See Figure 3.)

Benefits of Technology in Algebra (X)/ Geometry (X) When I first began teaching in 1999, I did not know how to use technology to help my students. I tried to help the students overcome their math anxiety by using the methods with which I was familiar. Needless to say, I did not have a great deal of success with my Algebra (X) students and only slightly more with my Geometry (X) students. In Algebra (X) over two semesters in 1999/2000, I had one student out of 23 pass the Algebra I SOL test. This was a devastating result. The next school year (2000/2001) I committed to learning and using graphing calculator technology in all my classes, TI83 in Algebra (X) and TI-92 Plus in Intro to Geometry/Geometry (X). Combined with a team teaching concept, the use of calculators in the instructional process contributed to 10 students out of 26 passing the Algebra I SOL, a 38% improvement over the previous year. This improvement can be attributed to many factors, but I feel the primary reason is that the students are becoming more comfortable with mathematics because they are able to concentrate on concepts as opposed to being anxious about arithmetic.

> *There are resources available that will allow the student to explore more complex math concepts.*

Is There More? The sample activities in this article serve both as a familiarization to graphing calculator technology and as an introduction to what the technology can do to demonstrate some concepts in Algebra and Geometry. There are resources available that will allow the student to explore more complex math concepts. The algebra and geometry resource materials that come with the McDougal Littell textbooks have some excellent calculator activities that serve either to introduce a concept or to reinforce previously learned concepts. Texas Instruments has published a book of TI-92 Plus Geometry explorations that may be used as stand alone activities or may be used as building blocks of knowledge. There are resources available on the Internet that may be found with a simple search for calculator activities using any search engine. The Texas Instruments Web site has a wealth of activities that are tailored to specific grade levels.

Conclusion While graphing calculator technology may not be the final answer to solving the problem of math anxiety, it can go a long way toward relieving the stress that some students feel when faced with solving a problem that requires arithmetic skills. Calculator technology may even provide the confidence that some students need in order to do well on standardized tests.

About Dean E. Howard Dean E. Howard has been teaching for three years at Kellam High School. He began teaching as a second career after completing 20 years in the U.S. Navy and eight years as a government contractor.

Ready, Set, Going the Distance With Mathematics

by Monica Lang, Ann Zingraff-Newton, and Eva Roupas

Introduction

Lights! Camera! Action! (Eva Roupas, Distance Learning Coordinator)

The use of technology for technology's sake is not a choice that can be made in a field such as education, where budgets are tight and the stakes are high. One need only look to recent events in the news regarding technology, whether it be stocks, technology companies, IPOs, or the like, to realize how fluid and pervasive technology really is. That being said, it is also true that the effect technology has had in education can be compared to the effect the printing press had on the dissemination of knowledge in the Renaissance. This unprecedented access to knowledge and the potential for providing equity in education, as well as enhancement of curricula, has never been greater.

For Virginia Beach City Public Schools, technology—specifically, distance learning—has changed the way the division does business. Although the process has not been easy, the school division has progressed from offering one distance learning class to 20 students in two high schools to our present offering of 23 classes to 444 students spread across the division. Foreign language classes are the most pervasive, but mathematics courses served as the pioneers.

The technology has also liberated students from the confines of schedules, enabling students to participate in courses either not available when they need them or not available at all.

The distance learning initiative was launched in February of 1999 as a videoconferencing program. The program was initially designed to offer additional curricular choices to students and expanded training opportunities for staff. The program has grown exponentially from its beginning. The technology has also liberated students from the confines of schedules, enabling students to participate in courses either not available when they need them or not available at all.

Course Selection

Not only did Distance Learning highlight our master teachers, it also leveled the academic playing field. (Eva Roupas, Distance Learning Coordinator)

The majority of the experiences provided by distance learning for both our teachers and students have been successful. These experiences tended to provide motivation for those students who were previously unmotivated or unprepared and created additional academic opportunities for gifted and highly motivated students. In preparation for the creation of the first distance learning class, we knew we had two critical questions to consider: what courses would be taught and which teacher would teach it? Three schools were targeted to pilot the distance learning labs, and the mission was to have one school originate a class and the other two receive it by second semester of the 1998-1999 school year. The Discrete Mathematics course was selected as our premiere class. It had a collective enrollment of 20 students. This 18-week course, which is available to those students who have successfully completed Algebra II, focuses on modeling problems involving graphs, scheduling, optimization, and social decision-making. It premiered February 2, 1999, with Princess Anne High School's Discrete Mathematics course sent via distance learning to Bayside and Ocean Lakes High Schools. By the following school year, another high school shared AP Statistics via distance learning with two neighboring schools. In September 2001, enter Monica Lang, veteran, high school mathematics teacher who enthusiastically responded to the call to serve as a distance learning Pre-IB Algebra II/Trig teacher. The course originated from Monica's home school, Princess Anne High School, and was shared with Kemps Landing Magnet School—part of the division's gifted and talented program.

Teacher Selection

You are a special breed of teacher; one who believes 'No guts, no glory.'
(Eva Roupas, Distance Learning Coordinator)

As coordinator of the distance learning program, Eva Roupas made a conscious decision to be inclusive of all staff who were interested in providing distance learning instruction. This has proven to be a wise choice. The three mathematics classes offered have worked very well through the technology, largely due to the exceptional instruction of the teachers. In the three-year tenure of this program, excellent instruction by outstanding teachers has been the greatest key to its success. One of the major lessons

> *Whether they are excellent communicators and/or performers, unabashed risk-takers, or reticent traditionalists who have built a powerhouse of a program, distance learning teachers all begin at the same novice level.*

learned in this endeavor is that exceptional teachers make effective instruction happen, regardless of the facilities. Equally important is teacher buy-in, and, it is one of the determining factors in determining teacher selection. The selling points for some principals and teachers differed. For example, some were avoiding involuntary transfers due to low enrollment. Others were trying to save elective courses which had dangerously low enrollment and were close to being dropped from the master schedule. From the pool of good teachers, Eva had to search for those valiant few who were willing to place themselves into the new instructional mode of videoconferencing. Whether they are excellent communicators and/or performers, unabashed risk-takers, or reticent traditionalists who have built a powerhouse of a program, distance learning teachers all begin at the same novice level. Once the teachers are committed to using the distance learning venue, they must be convinced to stay the course.

Training

The technology magnifies and sensitizes ALL of your characteristics—the good, the bad, and the ugly. (Eva Roupas, Distance Learning Coordinator)

Because most teachers are not technologically savvy, validating the fear that accompanies the lack of experience is important. The 20-hour training program spotlights issues ranging from hardware manipulation, to interactive lesson planning, to on-camera performance requirements to troubleshooting equipment failure. During training, it is vital to put teachers in front of the cameras and microphones early and have them utilize the document camera and control keypad immediately. Any existing phobias will only persist and grow without an immediate and rich hands-on experience.

Equipment

One of my favorite lessons this year was in my distance learning class. . . the document camera transformed a fun lesson plan into a truly engaging one. (Monica Lang)

In Virginia Beach all distance learning rooms are similarly equipped and can be either origination or receiving sites. The equipment is permanently fixed and cannot be moved from room to room. At each site a primary camera (See Illustration A) is focused on the teacher who uses a touch pad to manipulate the camera (See Illustration B). The instructor also manipulates a document camera (See Illustration E) and the cameras at the remote sites, and can select the video sources seen by the students (See Illustration C). A monitor allows the teacher to preview each image before it is broadcast as well as make intermittent site checks. This also means that the students at any given site may not be aware that they are being seen. Each classroom has four television monitors, two at the front of the room, two farther back (See Illustration D). Each shows images of the teacher's choosing, such as his or her computer screen, document camera image, an instructional video, or the shot from another camera. At the receiving site, a student who wants to ask a question presses the button on a microphone on the table (See Illustration F). When the remote site camera zooms in on that student, the microphone allows the question to be heard by the teacher and students at the other sites. If a student wants to show the teacher his or her work (See Illustration G), she uses the document camera in his or her room. The initial experience can best be understood through Monica Lang's own account:

> After three full days of training and practice with the distance learning equipment, I still felt an overwhelming anxiety the night before the first day of school. I had stayed up late planning every button push, camera angle, and precisely at what times during the lesson I would view my distance learning students. I arrived to class well prepared and ready to sit in my "captain's chair" behind the "mother board" and navigate my way through my first distance learning Pre-IB Algebra II/Trig lesson. The lesson did go rather smoothly. To my surprise, I rarely had to glance at my notes. Over the next few weeks I would become more focused on my students and the lesson than on operating the equipment. Sometimes it would take a few seconds to remember a particular button sequence--but not for long--and fortunately my students were always patient. I soon became very comfortable guiding and pre-setting the primary camera to focus on different areas of the classroom. The students followed my lead—they also acclimated to the technology in the classroom, eagerly responding to a question or participating in discussion by "chiming" in to answer a question. I became able to respond instinctively by pushing the appropriate buttons, allowing them to speak into their personal microphones.

The merging of technology and instruction became almost seamless.

Undoubtedly, the most important asset to the distance learning classroom is the document camera. Little did I know that the (affectionately known as and brand-named) "Elmo" would become my best friend and the unifying instrument between the students and me at both sites. This apparatus alone is the best part about teaching in a distance learning classroom. It enabled me to invite a student to share his or her work directly from his/her paper or graphing calculator.

By the end of the first nine weeks, I was manipulating the keypad, operating the equipment, and facilitating instruction as though on automatic pilot. At first the distance learning classroom and all of its technology can be a bit frightful, but isn't that true with any new teaching assignment?

Beam me aboard, Scottie.

Special Considerations

The microphones are different because I'm used to raising my hand in class. . . I don't like to use them . . . I guess I'm timid. . . I like being on camera. . . be prepared for people to watch your every move. . . the monitors and cameras help me focus more because if I mess up, everyone will see or hear it—there's less distraction. (Student Survey Samples)

It must be noted, however, that instructing through the distance learning medium is neither for every teacher nor every student. While we determined that student need was a main factor in course and teacher selection, we recognized that there were several other crucial determiners as well. Essential qualities for potential distance learning teachers are superior organizational skills, the ability to be flexible, and a good sense of humor. However, to succeed as a videoconferencer is to relish the adrenalin rush that performing without a net provides. A broadcast presence, not to be confused with physical beauty, is essential. The ability to capture the viewers' attention and keep the "show" moving is the bottom line.

Distance learning students must possess unique features as well. Of primary importance, a hunger for the specific course must exist. No handholding—maturity, not necessarily age, and resilience are required

> *School is not "out" with downed equipment—students and staff must cope—the class must go on.*

by the student in order to learn without constant teacher presence. School is not "out" with downed equipment—students and staff must cope—the class must go on. Provisions were made at each site for equipment failure by installing a fax machine, cell phone, and computer with Internet access. In addition, teachers prepare extensive lesson plans that afford the teacher assistant the capability of continuing the class during down time. A final consideration of which the distance learning staff and students must be cognizant is that they will never know who is really watching the class in progress. Distance learning labs equipped with microphones, cameras, and monitors mean the classroom is no longer a private, intimate setting. This year Pre-Algebra II/Trig was open for, literally, the world to see.

Distance Learning and Teaching Standards

Regardless of the environment, profound learning requires actively engaged students communicating their understanding and experiencing the joy of learning—a math class should be the busiest, most energized classroom in the school. (Ann Zingraff-Newton, Mathematics Teacher Specialist)

The question of whether distance learning is an effective or an appropriate medium for the teaching and learning of mathematics is a critical one. Best practices espoused in the *Handbook of Research on Improving Student Achievement* and promoted by the Virginia Beach City Public School System are addressed by distance learning in many ways. For example, the "Opportunity to Learn" (Cawelti et al. 5-7) is provided to those students who might otherwise not have access to a particular mathematics course due to unavailability of staff or insufficient student enrollment. This was the case when Princess Anne High School mathematics instructor, Monica Lang, agreed to be the distance learning instructor for the previously mentioned Pre-IB Algebra II/Trig course. From another viewpoint, this "Opportunity to Learn" may be more of an equity issue. The National Council of Teachers of Mathematics in its *Principles and Standards for School Mathematics* paints a vision for school mathematics that demands "high-quality, engaging mathematics instruction" for all students. Its first principle, that of educational equity, "is a core element of this vision" (Martin et al.12). With the growing national shortage of qualified mathematics teachers, the concepts of equity and opportunity to learn will certainly become more critical issues, for which distance learning can provide an answer.

"Openness to Student Solution Methods and Student Interaction" (Cawelti et al.11) is uniquely enhanced through the use of the document camera. Students can share work directly from their notebooks with their distant peers. The possibility of this occurring can serve as motivation for more consistently organized work. Although a few students exhibit camera shyness, others frequently are eager to experience the new technology and often do so with an elevated air of professionalism. Understanding that powerful learning takes place when students have the opportunity to talk about mathematics, Ms. Lang regularly invited students to approach the document camera to share their solutions, to explain their thinking, and to demonstrate a solution strategy. Committed to this concept of communication of understanding, Ms. Lang went so far as to require that each student "ring in" for such an exposition a minimum of five times each nine-week grading period. She would pose a question and then say, "Ready, Set, Go!" Students eagerly pressed their microphone call button to "win" airtime at the document camera. This procedure eliminated the calling out of answers and gave the teacher the opportunity to select the shy student over those who may have rung in first. Distance learning teachers report that younger (middle school) students seem particularly willing to ring in to ask questions and contribute to class discussion. The opportunity for "Small Group Learning" (Cawelti 12-13) is not impeded but does require special consideration in terms of space and accessibility to microphones and camera. One of Ms. Lang's favorite, more active, cooperative learning activities was attempted with some apprehension. This activity involved student groups of four, carefully placing Hershey Kisses into a cup precariously hanging from strands of spaghetti. Students must experientially collect data, create a scatter plot, and determine a regression equation modeling how many kisses a given number of strands will hold. By focusing the cameras on the classroom sites, Ms. Lang was able to circulate around her room and still monitor progress at the receiving site.

Although a few students exhibit camera shyness, others frequently are eager to experience the new technology and often do so with an elevated air of professionalism.

Establishing Site-to-Site Rapport Classbuilding has a unique, yet critical, role in distance learning. It is very important to encourage bonds between sites. This was accomplished by carefully establishing pairs, groups, and teams across the distance. Students were often assigned to such cooperative formations with members at the remote site. "TV time" was incorporated into the class to enable cooperating members to discuss their solutions or to answer each other's questions. Games in a mathematics classroom have long been considered a viable instructional method. Distance learning requires a rethinking of how best to incorporate competition into the classroom. Being from different schools, already competing on academic as well as athletic teams, distance learning students arrive naturally competitive from Day One. "Whole class discussion" (Cawelti 14) as well takes on a different flavor. It is imperative that participants from each site contribute to the learning process, and herein lies the challenge. The necessity for the camera to focus on the speaker before other sites can hear him or her is, for some, a moment of fame while others experience an unfortunate rise in anxiety. An impatient few find the moment it takes for the camera to train on the speaker agonizingly slow. They want to voice their input immediately and spontaneously.

Distance learning requires a rethinking of how best to incorporate competition into the classroom.

Graphing Calculators and the Document Camera The intrinsic motivators of curiosity and ambiguity (Child 47) and the brain's innate drive to seek patterns and meaning (Caine & Caine 113) can be tapped through the use of concrete materials and calculators. Both tools can be employed in a visually pleasing and effective manner through the use of the document camera. One of the most important themes espoused by the *Principles and Standards for School Mathematics* (Martin et al.) is that of connections. Through the use of a graphing calculator and the employment of multiple representations, graphical, algebraic and numeric, connections not previously possible can be discovered. The document camera enables any calculator to be utilized and viewed easily by all students without extra cables or a specialized view screen. The student can display his or her own calculator while justifying individual thinking or posing a particular question. An example of this occurred while reviewing how to graph conic equations, one student asked, "How do I put these equations into my graphing calculator?" Knowing that graphing equations to produce a recognizable design is both fun and instructive, Ms. Lang quickly responded, "Let's make a smiley face!" After fifteen minutes of careful questioning, which enabled the students to lead the teacher through each required step, students had produced a simple smiley face. They were offered time in which to personalize their creations with additional features such as ears, lips, hair, eyebrows, etc. Ten minutes later, students had met the challenge. They had even incorporated linear, absolute value, and more advanced equations to create a unique face. As each student placed his or her calculator below the document camera for a quick and easy display of each creation, everyone was thoroughly entertained by the creativity shown. This would never have been possible with such ease in a traditionally equipped classroom. Clearly, this is an example of what is meant by how "technology enhances mathematics learning" (Martin et al.). Although distance learning requires attention to detail and careful planning, paradoxically, it can respond well to spontaneity.

Computers in Distance Learning Teachers need to "orchestrate the immersion of the learner in complex, interactive experiences that are both rich and real" (Caine & Caine 113). The distance learning lab enables an Internet-linked computer to be experienced by all participants at all sites simultaneously, providing real world, even real time, data and global access with ease. Multimedia presentations or video seem more powerful in a distance learning classroom.

Distance Learning and the Teaching Principle The mathematics teacher plays an important role in enabling students to construct understanding by providing a variety of rich experiences. Since the lens of the camera magnifies everything from flaw to forte, the distance learning teacher must embody NCTM's Teaching Principle. The teacher must not only possess profound content knowledge, but he or she must be well-versed in multiple representations of an idea, able to connect concepts, and possess an expertise in a wide array of pedagogical strategies.

Math-Friendly Environment Perhaps more importantly, the teacher must be capable of creating an environment that is supportive and conducive to students participating actively in their own learning process. The combination of technophobia and math anxiety could be a deadly combination. However, the use of games, simulations, and multimedia presentations through distance learning technology has proven to be effective in combating these two problem areas. A spirit of camaraderie can be developed through the encouragement of cooperation and competition, which are both valid motivators (Child 47). The ability to set an onscreen timer for such activities assists with time management, both from the teacher's perspective and that of the students'.

Feedback

If you have a bad hair day, it's broadcast all over the city. . . This is a great class; I like being on camera. . . this technology should be in every classroom.
(Student Survey Samples)

Through intermittent surveys taken since the inception of the distance learning program, we asked teachers and students how the distance learning technology affected instruction. Teachers were candid in their responses, looking for the positive, and suggesting methods that may improve a continually changing medium. Among the comments were the following:

- ✓ I would prefer different teaching options other than standing in one place.
- ✓ More training on hardware/troubleshooting tips is needed.
- ✓ More time is needed to prepare lessons.
- ✓ Having only one distant site, I was able to keep all the class sites on camera most of the time.
- ✓ The distance learning teacher assistant duties were much more enjoyable than previous possible teacher assistant assignments.
- ✓ Duties are different but not harder.
- ✓ Teachers need to come to the receiving sites more.
- ✓ I loved the moderators (distance learning teacher assistants).
- ✓ Support from school system and distance learning staff made instruction very doable.
- ✓ Interdepartmental mail proved unreliable.
- ✓ Students didn't take advantage of using email.
- ✓ I am more aware of the way I come across to my students.
- ✓ You must make an effort to contact your distance students.
- ✓ Be prepared for flexibility.
- ✓ Preparation beforehand is the key.

When asked, students provided refreshing, objective candor indicated in the following:

- ✓ It's cool to interact with different schools.
- ✓ I get to use the technology.
- ✓ Sometimes it can take forever for the teacher to "get" to you.
- ✓ Technical problems/Technology isn't clear/random tech problems.
- ✓ It was difficult to horse around too much since anyone could be watching.
- ✓ The experiments were neat because of the document camera.
- ✓ I don't get to talk to the teacher privately.
- ✓ Adding other schools is just like overcrowded classes.
- ✓ I didn't like that the teacher had the ability to zap you off the screen.
- ✓ I feel uncomfortable answering questions while people I don't know are watching.
- ✓ The camera zooming in on you to answer (a question) and you're not sure you have the right one (answer).
- ✓ Watch out for the microphone.
- ✓ Continue using it (distance learning technology)—it's very useful and effective.
- ✓ The best thing is you really do learn things from distance learning—you are kinda forced to pay attention.
- ✓ It was fun.
- ✓ I'd like to meet the other class in person.
- ✓ I'm used to raising my hand instead of pressing a button.
- ✓ The other class is really smart and I learn things from them.
- ✓ I respond more because I love being on camera!
- ✓ Some people intentionally hit the button but while there they fix their hair.
- ✓ I like it because it is sooo different! I've never seen something like this.
- ✓ You are on camera which I love! And you are expected to act more mature.
- ✓ You have a teacher, a pen, a pencil, paper, and a chalkboard. You learn, they teach and it's basically the same thing to me.
- ✓ Well, it's just odd.

Many of the suggestions offered by the first instructors were excellent building blocks for the program. A stipend for the distance learning teacher, a fax machine located in the classroom, a teacher assistant hired to not only support the receiving classes, but the sending classes as well—all are now regular fare in our distance learning program. Two previous mathematics teachers had more specific reflections regarding instruction using the distance learning venue. Both agreed that instruction changed dramatically as they utilized videoconferencing equipment. The tendency is for student participation to decrease unless 30-50% of instruction is interactive—regardless of the ability level of the students. There was a dire need for creative thinking on how to incorporate videoconferencing in a mathematics class in such a way as to actively engage students. For some students having to use the technology, coupled with a well-honed reticence to participate in a traditional class, made the challenge of getting a response like pulling proverbial teeth. However, on a lighter note, not all classes necessarily had a problem with the creative incorporation of videoconferencing equipment. The following reflection from one of our middle school distance learning teachers illustrates the adage, "the more things change, the more they stay the same."

There was a dire need for creative thinking on how to incorporate videoconferencing in a mathematics class in such a way as to actively engage students.

> During the fourth quarter in the 6th grade Creative Writing Class, two instances occurred that I shared with Eva. The first of which was when I was noticing errant spitwads on the right monitor. Try as I may, I could never catch the culprit in action. I contacted Eva to see if the technology still had the capability to record the class. She said yes. Upon notification that class would be taped thereafter, this, and problems of this nature, ceased. In the same class, a young man saw a window of opportunity to launch his paper airplane when my back was to him. I was facing the front of the room, which meant I could also see my class in the monitor. And there he was, a close-up of the youngster's first and last flight. And who says technology can't be used in the classroom? (Middle School Distance Learning teacher, 2002)

Teachers found the greatest gains from lesson-planning-for-TV included the following: increased instructional focus on interactivity; employment of state-of-the-art technology, especially the document camera; enhancement of instruction in non-distance learning classes, specifically, better organization, frequent use of PowerPoint®; and a brisk instructional pace. Overwhelmingly, the mathematics instructors found great value in enriching student academics by providing courses, especially at the upper level, that would not otherwise be available.

Probably the greatest interference to mathematics instruction was the teacher's inability to observe the students and their work as they attempted problems independently. In addition, because the interdepartmental mail between 85 schools takes days to deliver, teachers also found that lack of immediate feedback in grading homework and tests or quizzes hampered effectiveness in keeping students current and on task. Lastly, all teachers found the effectiveness of the teacher assistants at the receiving sites vital to student success.

Lessons Learned

When teaching via distance learning I found everything I see or do is two-dimensional. Some facial expressions or body language may look less friendly on TV than in person. Certain comments sound harsher. Lacking are personal relationships that I take for granted in a traditional classroom. Thus, it is critical to take the time to get to know all students on a personal as well as an academic level. (Monica Lang)

The one constant of our distance learning program throughout the three years of its existence has been the continual and successful marrying of mathematics courses with videoconferencing. However, the surveys made it clear that most students believe, and we concede the point, nothing will ever take the place of an excellent, live instructor. Distance learning, despite its advantages, will always remain a strong second.

The lessons we have learned are many. This medium is not for every teacher nor is it a venue for every student. The abstract nature of mathematics can create an unbreachable chasm for many. Distance learning can compound the psychological barrier experienced by some learners of mathematics. As in all educational situations, the teacher is the key and must bridge the divide. Because of the critical nature of the role of the teacher, it is not recommended that an inexperienced instructor should ever be directed to teach via distance learning.

In three years we have learned the many facets of a successful distance learning program. As we continue on our journey, we realize that as in Nature, the only constant we will find in this program is that of inconstancy.

Illustrations of VBCPS Distance Learning

(A)

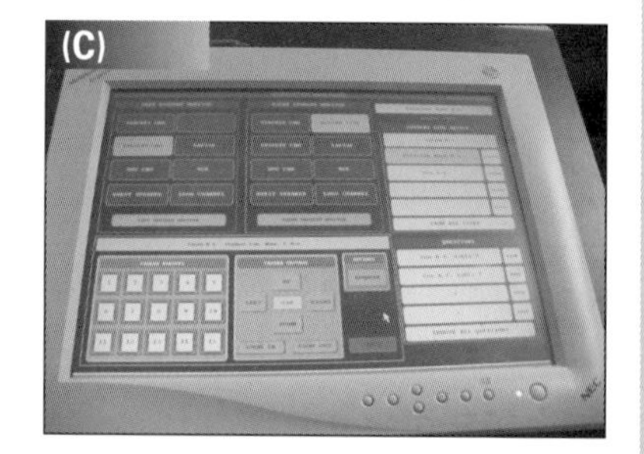
(C)

(B)

(D)

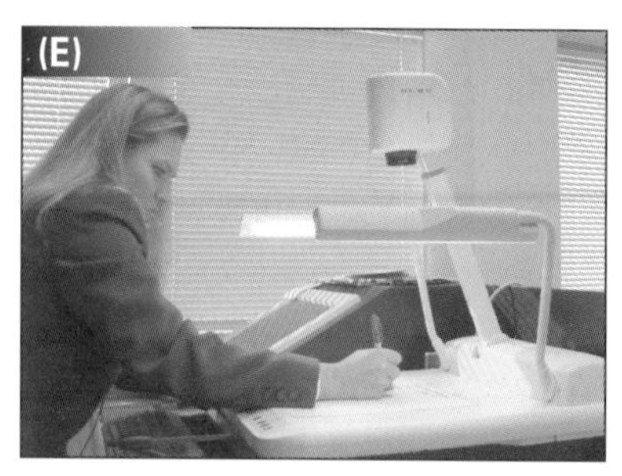
(E)

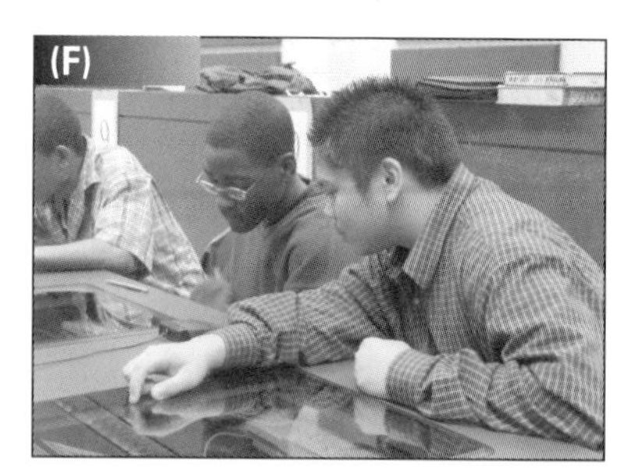
(F)

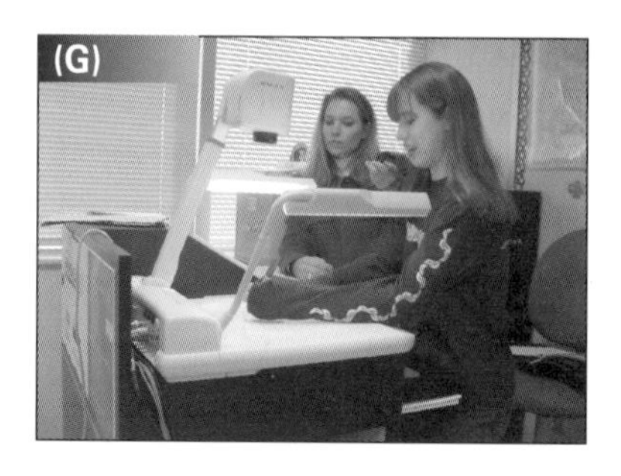
(G)

Works Cited

Caine, Renata, and Geoffrey Caine. *Making Connections: Teaching and the Human Brain*. Boston, MA: Addison Wesley, 1994.

Cawelti, Gordon, Douglas A. Grouws, and Kristin J. Cebulla. *Improving Student Achievement in Mathematics*. Arlington, VA: Educational Research Service, 1999.

Child, Dennis. *Psychology and the Teacher* (4th ed.). New York: Holt, Rinehart, & Wilson, 1986.

Lang, Monica. Personal Interview. 30 January 2002.

Martin, W.G., et al. *Principles and Standards for School Mathematics*. Reston, VA: The National Council of Teachers of Mathematics, Inc., 2000.

About Monica M. Lang

Mrs. Monica M. Lang has spent all ten years of her teaching experience at Princess Anne High School. During that time, she has taught Algebraic Foundations, Algebra I, Geometry, and Algebra II/Trig. In 1997 she completed a Master of Science degree in secondary mathematics education at Old Dominion University. Mrs. Lang was selected as Princess Anne High School's Teacher of the Year 2000. Also in that year, Mrs. Lang served on the citywide textbook adoption committee for Algebra II/Trig. and contributed to its current curriculum guide.

About Ann Zingraff-Newton

Mrs. Ann Zingraff-Newton, a Norfolk, Virginia native, has had twenty-one years of experience in secondary mathematics, fifteen of which have been with the Virginia Beach City Public School system. Her career has taken her to Hampton, Norfolk, Albemarle County, and finally to Virginia Beach where she taught at Old Donation Center for the Gifted and Talented, Kempsville Junior High School, Tallwood High School, and Ocean Lakes High School. She received a Master of Science degree from Old Dominion University in 1996. Mrs. Zingraff-Newton currently serves as the High School Mathematics Teacher Specialist in the Office of Instructional Services. Mrs. Zingraff-Newton was the recipient of the 1999 Presidential Award for Excellence in Mathematics and Science Teaching. She was selected as Ocean Lakes High School's Teacher of the Year in 2000. Mrs. Zingraff-Newton co-authored a related article with Ms. Eva Roupas and was invited to present at the International Conference on the Teaching of Mathematics in Crete, Greece, July 2002. The paper has been published in the official conference proceedings at htt://www.math.uoc.gr/~ictm2/Proceedings/ICTM2_Presentations_by_Author.html and released in compact disc form to conference participants.

About Eva Roupas Eva Roupas is a 24-year veteran teacher with ten of those years devoted to teaching theatre at Salem High School in Virginia Beach. Prior to coming to Virginia Beach City Public Schools, Ms. Roupas taught theatre, speech, and English at school divisions in Wisconsin and Illinois. From teaching she moved to the Department of Technology where she currently holds the administrative position of Distance Learning Coordinator for the school division. As part of her duties, Ms. Roupas designed and developed the distance learning program from its rudimentary beginnings of one class being broadcast to two schools to its present size of 36 classes, which are broadcast and received at eleven high schools and five middle schools across the city. Ms. Roupas is a former citywide Teacher of the Year (1998) and has won several awards for her distance learning program, among them the Governor's Silver Technology Award in 2001 and the National School Public Relations Association's Golden Achievement Award in 2002. In addition, she was published in the first volume of *Tapestry of Knowledge* and co-authored, with Ann Zingraff-Newton, an article for conference proceedings of the International Conference on the Teaching of Mathematics held in Crete in July 2002. In early summer 2003, she is anticipating publication of a special issue of *Computers in the Schools* which includes an article she has co-authored profiling the Virginia Beach City Public Schools' distance learning program. Ms. Roupas holds a Bachelor of Arts degree in Speech from the University of Wisconsin-Eau Claire and a Master of Education in Administration and Supervision from the University of Virginia.

Section Five

Creating Designs *to* Understand Science

Caroline Thietje

Growth

Description: This piece is about personal growth and the nurturing a parent gives a child.

Medium Used: Collage

Educational Background: Caroline Thietje received a Bachelor of Fine Arts from Virginia Commonwealth University.

Teaching Experience: Ms. Thietje taught for two years at Elizabeth City Middle School and has been teaching at Salem Elementary School for eleven years.

The Spade

Creating Designs to Understand Science

"No longer the sage on the stage, but the guide on the side" is a phrase coined by Chris Held, to describe how the role of the teacher must change to accommodate the massive amount of new knowledge made available by the technological age (McNear 4). Just as significant is the resulting change in the students' role. Students become more than passive recipients of information because the teacher is no longer just pouring information into the student's head but setting up different types of learning situations for them. As a result of this interactive learning environment, the students become all or several of the following: learners of facts, programmers, problem solvers, editors, designers, collaborators, adventurers, and/or sense makers (Yoder 7).

Karen Frederick, a fifth-grade math and science teacher at Providence Elementary, conveys in her article, "Oceans of Fear: Conquering Technological Anxiety," how frightened she was to use computers in her classroom. She describes in depth her feelings of inadequacy, and her article is an account of her psychological journey from fear of computers to computer literacy. During this journey, she found that she could take on the role of learner with her students as they were instructed by the Computer Resource Specialist. At other times, she discovered that she and the students could become problem solvers as she struggled to use technological tools such as the InFocus® machine in her classroom. Her journey makes clear that even though technological tools are sometimes frightening for adults, the students regard them as a natural part of their world and expect to use them in the classroom. Frederick's article illustrates that both the teacher and the student have multiple roles to play in the integration of technology into the classroom.

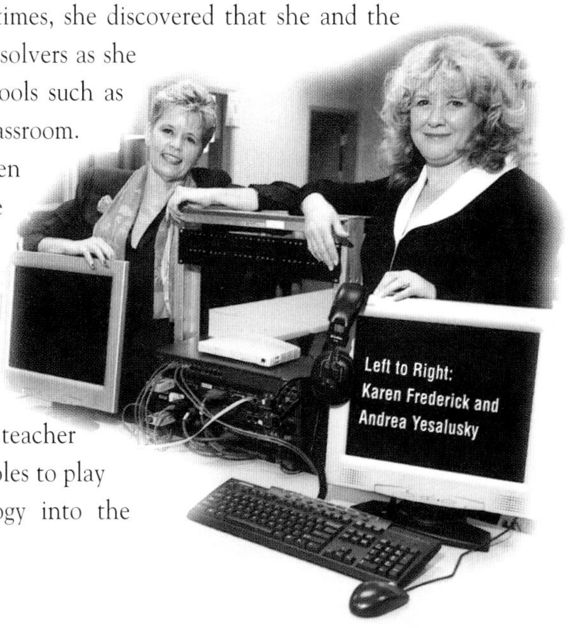

Left to Right: Karen Frederick and Andrea Yesalusky

Another example of how technology has changed both the role of the student and the teacher is examined in Andrea Yesalusky's article "Integrating Science and Technology into the Elementary Curriculum: Sit Down! You're Rocking My Boat!" In this article, Yesalusky describes how she has used activity-based software to design representations of the rock cycle and used graphics and colored boxes to differentiate between the parts of the food chain. In these activities her students play several roles: learners of facts, editors, designers, collaborators, and sensemakers. She concludes that technology has a major role to play in incorporating activity-based learning into the science classroom, and that this has placed the teacher in the role of a facilitator of learning. She applauds this change and describes the role of the science teacher as a "launch pad to spur thought and direction."

Both these articles illustrate how technology is a prominent force in changing the roles of teachers and students. The stories told in these articles demonstrate that working with students as facilitators, learners, leaders, and guides results in a far deeper and rewarding educational experience.

Work Cited

McNear, Anita. "The Changing Role of Students and Teachers." *Learning and Leading with Technology*. February 2003. 4-5

Yoder, Maureen Brown. "Oh, the Changes We've Seen." *Learning and Leading with Technology*. February 2003. 6-9, 16-17.

Oceans of Fear:
Conquering Technological Anxiety

by Karen Frederick

Fear: Getting my Feet Wet! The room was sparsely decorated, a few scattered pictures on the two bulletin boards, not a typical teacher's classroom. There were no student desks to be seen; instead there were wall-to-wall computers, one for every student. It was a computer lab. The air was filled with cries of, "It's frozen," Ms. Frederick. "What do I do next?" "How do I get out of this?" "How do I enlarge this picture?" These were only a few of the many cries for help. I felt inadequate, unable to reply to their troubleshooting questions. My usual answer was, "I don't know."

Attitude: Diving In! I thought a computer lab was great for the students, such a hands-on experience with educational fun, but it brought great fear and anxiety to me. Does this mean I have to teach computer skills to my class? I, who thought computers were complicated, confusing, and frustrating machines that just collected dust in the back of the room, secretly hoped they would go away. I realized that I needed an attitude adjustment. I reassured myself with the idea that there was a Computer Resource Specialist (CRS) to whom I hoped this responsibility would fall. How much would I have to know? How would I learn?

> *As a baby boomer teaching fifth-grade math and science, my adrenaline would pump and my heart would race at the thought of learning to use computers in the computer lab as well as in my classroom.*

As a baby boomer teaching fifth-grade math and science, my adrenaline would pump and my heart would race at the thought of learning to use computers in the computer lab as well as in my classroom. What motivated me was the desire to learn so that I was able to help my students when they were experiencing difficulty. After all, they looked to me for assurance. I wanted to help them and not feel helpless.

I am overcoming my fearful attitude of computers by slowly educating myself and learning to incorporate technology into instruction, taking it one step at a time.

Time and Patience: Taking the Plunge

I also took a class from Future Kids, a group hired by VBCPS, to help teachers in 1999 to prepare for and pass the Technology Standards for Instructional Personnel (TSIP) test.

Taking it one step at a time was my approach. "When the student is ready, the teacher will appear," according to Susan Jeffers of *Feel the Fear and Do it Anyway* (5). I felt I was ready to learn, to dive in, so I took several of the courses sponsored by the Virginia Beach City Public Schools (VBCPS) system. I also took a class from Future Kids, a group hired by VBCPS, to help teachers in 1999 to prepare for and pass the Technology Standards for Instructional Personnel (TSIP) test. This is a three-part test. All teachers are required by the VBCPS to pass this test, and one must take it on the computer! I told myself not to worry! 2004 was too far off for me to be concerned; maybe the school system would do away with the TSIP by then!

In the meantime I took my students to the computer lab once a week and began listening to the CRS instruct the students. I began participating with the students and learning with them. I really paid attention the following years because of the fifth-grade Standards of Learning computer test and my up-coming TSIP test. The feeling of inadequacy toward my students' trouble-shooting problems was lessening. I began to help my students in the computer lab which, in turn, gave me the certitude I needed.

More Fear and Anxiety!

In the summer of 2001, I took a science class sponsored by Hampton University at the Virginia Living Museum in Newport News, called Science in the Wild. I learned some very helpful and exciting fifth-grade science curriculum strategies. It was a hands-on course and I loved it. In order to receive full credit I had to complete a project produced with technology! More fear and anxiety! How was I ever going to do that? I had three months to teach a science unit and produce a written, documented, hard cover project. The students benefited as well because the science unit became a hands-on experience with several fieldtrips to collect live specimens of the five kingdoms in the school's pond.

I slowly tackled this project telling myself I could do it. I asked my CRS for Print Shop Ensemble II® to produce some graphics. I thought that would be enjoyable! I made awesome cover sheets of a jungle scene and page dividers, and I felt my first success. Next, I tackled Microsoft Word® and used word processing to write my thirty-page report on the classification system of the five kingdoms. In the computer lab, with the help of the CRS, my students used Inspiration Software® to produce a five-kingdom diagram. (See Figure 1.) They were able to relate to the kingdoms with first-hand knowledge, and were particularly excited when I incorporated their diagrams into my project. When I received an A, I felt that I had achieved both academic and technological success! My comfort with technology was increasing.

Figure 1

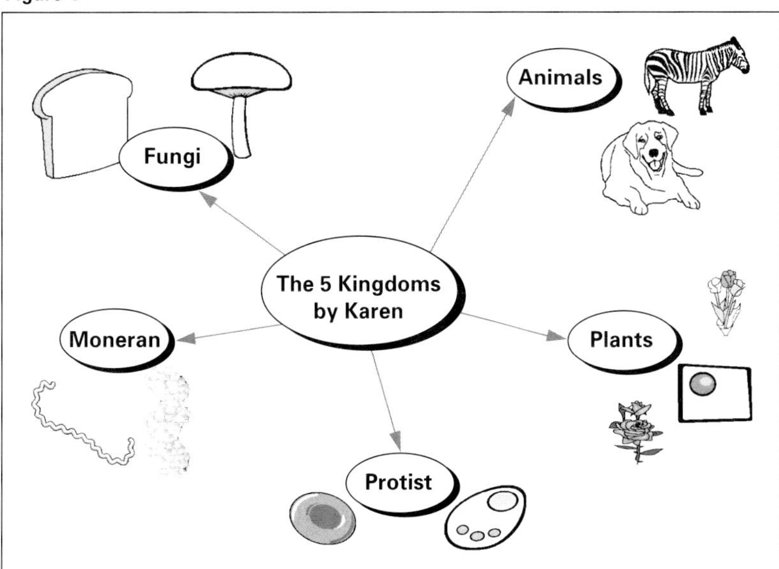

TSIP Trials

As the time drew near for the dreaded TSIP test, I studied the material from the Future Kids computer course. I knew a few terms and could identify the parts of a computer, and I remembered learning about spreadsheets and databases in the computer lab with my students. When I finished Part I of the test and pressed the "grade it" key, I was disappointed, as I failed by one question. I felt like giving up and leaving, but I didn't. I continued and successfully passed Parts II and III. Yeah, I felt great, even though I knew I would have to retake Part I again. Part I was on computer basics. So I dived into the booklet again and studied some more, feeling the anxiety build as the testing date grew near. Again when I pressed the dreaded "grade it" key, another major disappointment set in, and I cried on the way home as I had missed passing by one question again. I was very frustrated; I knew the correct answer. It was a matter of trusting myself and my knowledge of the computer. Now the fear and anxiety were at a maximum. Do I retake the test again or take a class offered by the school system specifically to help one pass the test? What if I fail it again? Will I lose my job? What will my coworkers, friends, and the CRS think of me? Will I ever be computer literate? I studied that booklet of terminology one more time and mustered enough courage to retake Part I. I felt confident this time; at the end of the test, I pushed the dreaded "grade it" button, and I hoped for the last time. Success! I passed this time with 90 percent. I had persevered and won!! The trust I built in myself with technology would slowly creep into the classroom, especially in the area of science.

Success! I passed this time with 90 percent.

Acceptance: Treading Water/Staying Afloat Today, each time I am challenged with technology and persevere, I feel more confident with the ever-changing world of computers. I do have one at home and practice with e-mail and Microsoft Word®. Just recently I was asked to write a letter of recommendation for my Volunteer in Education. My first reaction was negative, saying I didn't have time to sit down and write it on the computer, but I did. I now am able to produce science and math worksheets, quizzes, and tests on the computer. My attitude is changing to a more relaxed approach where I believe in myself although I still have a great deal to learn. The reward is that the fear has subsided, and I tackle technological opportunities with confidence, and I don't feel like a failure when I ask for help. I try to remember that I am interested in progress, not perfection.

Recently, one of my students brought me a Web site that he had looked up at home about Pangaea. (A hypothetical super continent that included all the land masses of the earth before the Triassic Period.) I immediately brought it up on the computer in the back of the room, and it was a slideshow on the Earth's continental drift occurring over the last 4.6 billion years. I was excited. Then, I arranged to use the InFocus® machine, a projector attached to the computer to display the slideshow to the whole class. I asked the CRS for the apparatus and rolled it into my room. In order to use the InFocus® machine, I had to unplug and plug in computers and connect to the Internet. It was a very complicated and frustrating experience. But, with the help of my students, I pulled up the Web site, only to receive a message that it needed a particular CD downloaded to produce the slideshow. I tried several times without success. As frustration set in, I reminded myself to be patient and to be flexible. So I unplugged, replugged, and reconnected, bringing the slideshow up on the computer in the back of the room. This success built faith in my ability to use technology in the classroom, and the slides now made a difficult concept much easier for the students to understand. They were able to see the world four billion years ago. Being able to watch the idea of Pangaea happen before their eyes rather than reading it from a book instilled a lasting impression on them.

Being able to watch the idea of Pangaea happen rather than reading it from a book instilled a lasting impression on the students.

A new way of incorporating technology is facing me now. I recently had the opportunity when first introducing the unit on matter to divide the science class into groups and place them at the three computers in my room. The students had to find information about atoms on the Internet. It was exciting for them as well as educational. Teaching information on matter and atoms is a difficult and abstract concept to visualize and understand for fifth-grade students. The computer Web site helped to enhance the lesson, making the concept clearer to the students.

My knowledge of science and my improvement in the use of computers to enhance instruction for my students have given me the confidence to take part in the *Tapestry* writing project. Moreover, I am the science lead teacher for my school, and I was asked to submit my lesson plans for the Earth Movement Unit for inclusion in the Science Curriculum. I am doing so with the help of the CRS at my school, and the lesson plans will be located on the Intranet for others to view.

Sink or Swim

Today I am more sure of myself when I am faced with a computer challenge. I am capable of helping my students in the classroom and in the computer lab. When I display more confidence, my students feel more confident and succeed. I no longer have to answer questions about the computer with, "I don't know."

Works Cited

Jeffers, Susan. *Feel the Fear and Do It Anyway*. New York: Ballentine Books, 1987.

About Karen Frederick

Karen Frederick was born and raised in New York State. She graduated from Daemen College (formerly Rosary Hill College) in Buffalo, New York, with a Bachelor of Science degree in Education. She has experienced different teaching assignments in various school systems across the United States including New York, Maryland, Florida, Hawaii, and California. She has been teaching for twenty years with sixteen years in the Virginia Beach City Public School System, with the majority of her experience in fifth grade.

Integrating Science and Technology Into the Elementary Curriculum: Sit Down! You're Rocking My Boat!

by Andrea Yesalusky

Before we begin, take a moment to think back to science lessons in elementary school. Are there fond memories filled with experiments, a great deal of exploration using the senses and outdoor discoveries, or was science class primarily focused on the textbook and lectures with limited connections to the world around us? I was fortunate to have experienced elementary science to its fullest. My memories are filled with lessons using experiments with changes in matter, the mixing of chemicals for surprising reactions, nature walks to collect and classify plants and animals, and the discovery of an amazing world through the view from a microscope.

Reflecting on those days, I wonder if it was because I am a visual learner and enjoy hands-on projects where I can see results, or if it was because my teachers were innovative educators

It is not surprising that I found science interesting. Reflecting on those days, I wonder if it was because I am a visual learner and enjoy hands-on projects where I can see results, or if it was because my teachers were innovative educators. I tend to believe it was a little of both. Regardless, learning was taking place, and my teachers heightened my interest and enthusiasm.

Being an educator, I now realize what a challenge it can be to present material over and over again with a new twist. Let's face it, an igneous rock is an igneous rock, no matter how you present it! Fortunately, education is constantly evolving, and opportunities for change are always on the horizon. New techniques and strategies continually become available to assist us with the various learning styles for successful student outcomes in the classroom. A demanding change has been the expectation of technology integration in all subjects. The public is expecting computers and technological resources to be utilized in our schools. They want to see science fair projects that Elroy Jetson, the son of the futuristic Jetson cartoon family, would create.

Tides of Change

The field of science is a great choice to begin to "test the waters of technology." Science and technology are a natural fit. Using all kinds of tools and gadgets has always been part of science instruction.

Science lessons are filled with scientific investigations and experiments. Plants are grown in empty milk cartons on windowsills in every school system, magnets are attracting paper clips, and the swamps are populated with frogs grown from jars and jars of tadpoles. All of these concepts and life processes will always be of extreme importance in the education of youth, but how can we use our advances in technology to expand our science curriculum? What can we do to put a new spin on our science lessons using technology?

As we brave the tides of technology integration, we need to ask the question, "Will these activities engage students in active and meaningful learning?"

Life Processes - Cast Off! Full Speed Ahead

Life processes and living systems in elementary education lend themselves well to visual examples and pictorial representations. A multitude of opportunities exist for students to create their own works to aid them in understanding animals, plants, life cycles, food chains, and our ecosystem.

> *A simple drawing of the parts of a plant, along with labeling these parts using a graphics program, is an excellent way to introduce a student to the capabilities of the mouse, text, and color within a program.*

Life processes focus on the various parts and cycles of living organisms. Computers, in most cases, have graphic applications programs that allow the student to create a picture using the mouse as a pencil. A simple drawing of the parts of a plant, along with labeling these parts using a graphics program, is an excellent way to introduce a student to the capabilities of the mouse, text, and color within a program. Dividing a computer screen into four quadrants by drawing lines with a mouse and creating the four life cycles of the butterfly is an example of a simplified use of technology.

Taking this a step further, first-grade students at our school were able to create a slide show presentation with these butterfly life cycle graphic designs. The students followed step-by-step directions to incorporate their art into slide presentations and added sound and transitions to the slides.

Our second-grade classes acquired butterfly eggs in the spring, and students were able to watch the life cycle transition actually happen in the classroom. Using a digital camera to record this process and incorporating pictures into presentation software and a timeline program deepened the learning process and strengthened understanding.

Life processes also address cycles that lend themselves well to webbing diagrams. Draw programs have the capability of creating webs, but there are applications such as Inspiration Software® that are designed for webbing diagrams as in Figure 1. By using these applications, students can focus on the connection between these life processes. These diagrams also can assist students with the organization and memorization of data.

The Five Kingdoms diagram in Figure 1 was created using the Inspiration Software® program. This webbing program allows students to click and create bubbles, then link the bubbles to their main idea. Students can also add graphics to clarify and expand their web. A simple click of a button can turn this diagram into an outline form for organization and writing activities.

Figure 1. Kingdoms created on Inspiration Software®

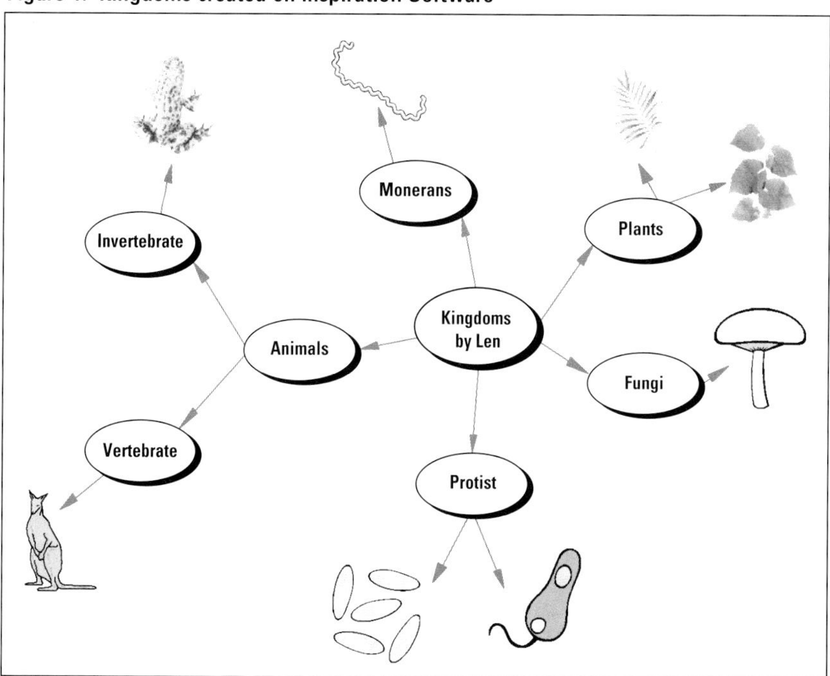

As educators, we all are well aware of the benefits of visual representations for learning subject matter. A new slant on an old concept can sometimes reach students with different learning styles. In Figure 2, a food chain with a different twist is created using Inspiration Software®. Using graphics and colored boxes to differentiate between the parts of the food chain, students can organize facts and determine the correct categories of plants and animals.

Figure 2. The Food Chain created using Inspiration Software®

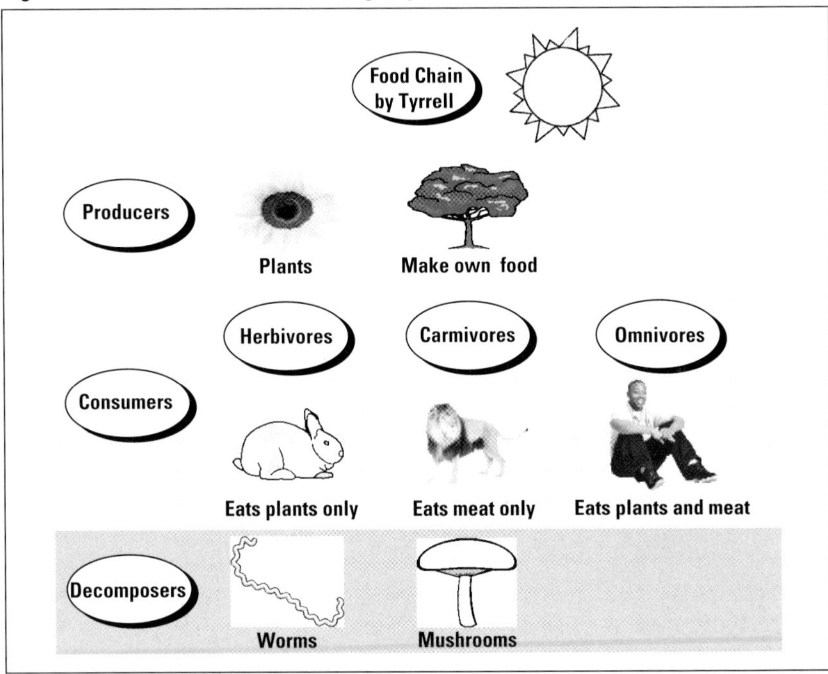

Living systems exist around us and live examples can be seen daily. Using digital cameras and video cameras, teachers can connect classroom lessons to the real world. Animal and plant changes, habitats, camouflage, herbivores, carnivores, omnivores, and the influence of humans on life are evident all around us. Using technology to capture these changes is particularly effective. Most schools have a digital camera, and training in its use is available for teachers. Pictures from these cameras can be inserted into word processing documents, timelines, and many types of multimedia applications. Also, these pictures may be copied, cropped, and altered to produce creative works for classroom activities. Applying this technology from our own backyard to visual representation is exciting and rewarding. Learning and understanding key concepts when connected to ourselves and the life that surrounds us bolsters learning opportunities for all levels of students. Life processes in the science curriculum can utilize technology with tremendous results.

The Earth and the Solar System - Sailing Beneath the Stars

The study of the planets is an interesting and exciting unit of study for students. Classroom lessons are filled with examples of the resources found on our planet. Incorporating technology may seem a challenge with this unit, but opportunities to utilize software and program applications are available and greatly beneficial.

Exploring the ever-changing Earth and creating graphic designs and models on the computer can assist students with understanding the key concepts of the Earth's structure. Using various drawing tools, students can create a visual cross section of mountain formations and geographic changes in plate tectonics. In Figure 3, students used the drawing tools in Kid Pix®

Exploring the ever-changing Earth and creating graphic designs and models on the computer can assist students with understanding the key concepts of the Earth's structure.

Figure 3. Mountain Formations created on Kid Pix® software

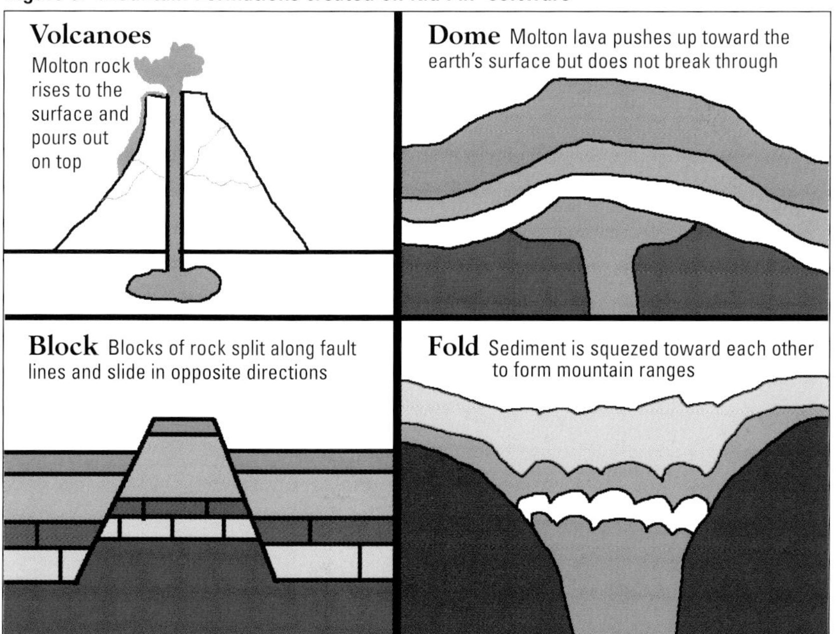

Volcanoes
Molton rock rises to the surface and pours out on top
Dome Molton lava pushes up toward the earth's surface but does not break through
Block Blocks of rock split along fault lines and slide in opposite directions
Fold Sediment is squezed toward each other to form mountain ranges

software to draw mountain formations. Using the mouse as a pencil, the different layers of the earth are drawn by the students. By using the paint feature, color can be added to accentuate the features. By adding text and printing the document, students have a clear and concise representation of mountains and how they are formed.

The rock cycle, shown in Figure 4, is another example of a visual representation that students can create using Inspiration Software®. With the use of bubbles, graphics, and links, the rock cycle and its properties become more understandable and relationships between the various steps in the cycle more logical.

Figure 4. The Rock Cycle created on Inspiration Software®

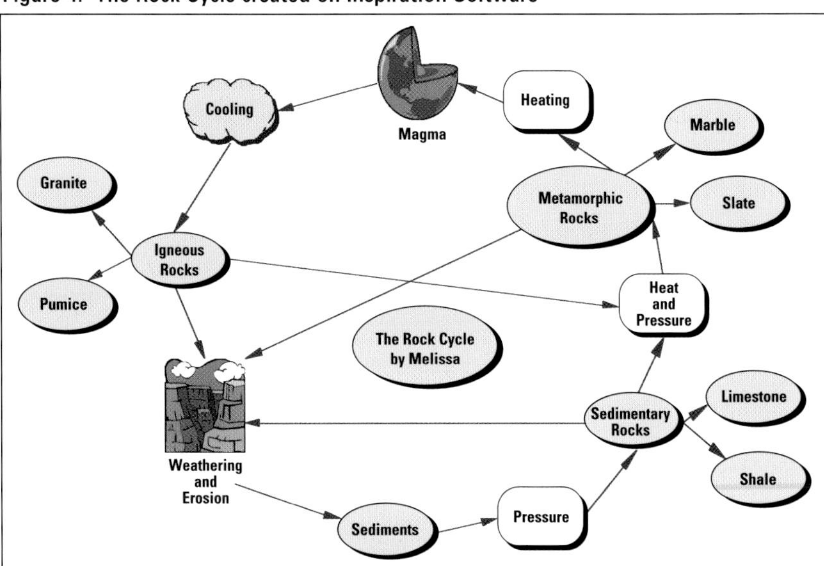

Computer applications such as spreadsheets and databases can be incorporated into the science curriculum. Being creative with data collections and combining them with software can reap multiple benefits. Not only are students becoming familiar with different computer applications, they are reinforcing their knowledge of the subject. An example of this concept would be creating a database of facts about the planets of the solar system. Entries could include the size of the planet, planet composition, the distance from the sun, number of moons, daily rotation, and length of orbit around the sun. Students not only can research and gather data from various resources, but also can enter and sort the individual facts. The characteristics of each planet are determined with a quick click of the mouse.

Spreadsheet and database applications found in programs such as AppleWorks®, Microsoft Excel®, and Microsoft Access® are wonderful tools to use for collected scientific data. Daily weather observations locally and in other locations around the world can be charted and graphed. Weights and measurements on Earth and other planets can be an interesting and insightful project for students. Documenting plant growth or the circumference of various trees along with their location, environment, and conditions could produce more analysis and in-depth thoughts and conclusions regarding the life that surrounds us. Science and data collection go hand-in-hand. Technology can be used to document and organize scientific findings. This data may then be presented to encourage discussion among students. Multiple Standards of Learning and educational objectives can be met with the benefit of technology.

Forces, Motion, Energy, and Matter - Anchors Away!

Magnets, machines, and matter have always found their roots in a lab setting. Physical properties and changes within different materials are well explained and justified by experiments with student participation. Sometimes for safety reasons, teachers are unable to demonstrate these changes. Electrical investigations are one example of changes that occur from the mixture of chemicals. Software programs can demonstrate and allow interaction of subject matter without the safety issues. The *I Love Science*™ and *Thinking Science*™ software have wonderful features that allow the student to manipulate items to achieve the desired results. These programs include experiments with magnets, light, sound, machines, and many other science related topics. I have found that students thoroughly enjoy this software for the presentation of the information, for the freedom to try different scenarios, and for the opportunity to see results.

> *Software programs can demonstrate and allow interaction of subject matter without the safety issues.*

The study of the different states of matter also allows great opportunities for hands-on activities with students. Along with classroom experiments, technology can be used to document their findings and expand their choices. An example of this is in Figure 5. The use of Inspiration Software® to illustrate the various states of matter initiates discussion and reinforces the students' knowledge and understanding of this topic.

Figure 5. States of Matter created on Inspiration Software®

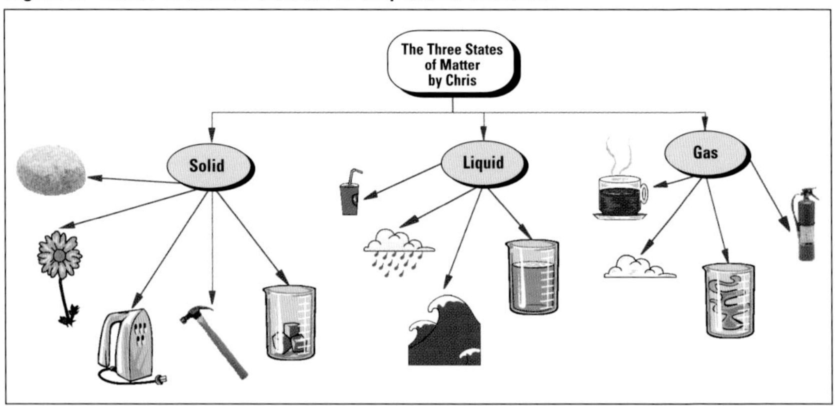

Other technology can also be used along with this unit of study. Microscopes that allow display from a computer screen or a projection device are now available for computers. Physical properties of objects can be magnified and displayed for the entire class to view. These microscopes are fairly inexpensive and provide new opportunities for learning in a classroom or in a computer lab.

Conclusions - "Don't Give Up The Ship!"

Activity-based learning has reformed science education, and the teacher has become more of a facilitator of learning. The educator's role as a launch pad to spur thought and direction has achieved positive results, demonstrated better understanding of concepts, and become an effective model for education.

Technology can play a major role in activity-based learning in education. Computer applications are designed to increase productivity and allow students to see results from their efforts. Whether the computer functions as a tool that allows the student to utilize drawing applications to design a representation of the rock cycle or as a tutor that interacts with the student as in the *I Love Science*™ activity-based software, computers are being used to facilitate learning. Even when the computer acts as a tutee that allows the student to teach the computer to perform an operation, such as creating graphs and charts from data, students are active learners, acquiring knowledge and developing skills in varied and unique ways.

It's time to weigh anchor and continue the journey into new frontiers of education and as James Lawrence said, "Don't Give Up The Ship!"

Works Cited

Broderbund LLC. Electronic Sources: Kid Pix® Software: http://www.broderbund.com [May 10, 2002].

Inspiration Software®, Inc.: http://www.inspiration.com [May 10, 2002].

Kindersley, Dorling (2002). Electronic Sources: *I Love Science Software*: http://www.dk.com [May 8, 2002].

Riverdeep Interactive Learning Limited. Electronic Sources: *Thinking Science*: http://www.riverdeep.net/edmark [May 7, 2002].

About Andrea Yesalusky

Andrea Yesalusky is a product of a Tidewater area public school system. She graduated from Old Dominion University with a Bachelor of Science in Business Administration and is pursuing a Master of Science degree in Technology Education. She taught technology and curriculum integration in adult education for ten years and became an elementary Computer Resource Teacher in 1997. Mrs. Yesalusky is presently teaching at Providence Elementary School in Virginia Beach. Mrs. Yesalusky has also served as a Parent Teacher Association (PTA) President and received a lifetime membership for her service and dedication to children. She has presented numerous training sessions for classroom teachers and administrators to expand their knowledge of technology and to introduce techniques which integrate curriculum and technology into the classroom.

Section Six

Envisioning Real-World Experiences Through *the* Web

Sue Loudon Frost

Old World Journey of the Elusion

Description: The work is a commemorative 50th birthday present for Kirt Schuldt in honor of his forthcoming sailing trip (when he retires from teaching computer classes at the new Virginia Beach City Public Schools' Advanced Technology Center). It is one of a body of work based on Journeys that I completed in 2002.

Medium Used: Mixed Media

Educational Background: Sue Loudon Frost received a Bachelor of Fine Arts in Education from the University of North Carolina, a Master of Science in Guidance and Counseling from Old Dominion University, and a Master of Arts in Art Education from Virginia Commonwealth University.

Teaching Experience: Ms. Frost has been teaching art at various Virginia Beach City Public Schools for thirty-three years.

Awards: Ms. Frost was recognized as the American Automobile Association Teacher of the Year for 1993, 1994, 1996, and 1999. She was the Teacher of the Year at Thalia Elementary School in 1972. Also, she has been recognized as an Outstanding Educator of America for several years and as an Outstanding Young Women of America in 1986.

AMERICA
MAR
DEL
NORT
SEPTENTRIO
Keith
ELLISON

Envisioning Real-World Experiences Through the Web

Each election year, newspaper headlines assail the public with the lackluster performance of the American voter. It seems that fewer and fewer Americans take advantage of their right to vote. Political pundits fill the airways with explanations for the apathy of the American voter. Many feel the reason for this apathy is the public's insufficient knowledge of how the political process works. Marion Broglie, an eighth-grade civics teacher at Lynnhaven Middle School, has used a Youth Leadership Initiative program (YLI) to make sure that his students will understand the political process and will not fall in this apathetic category.

Broglie found the YLI Web site as he was writing a research paper for a graduate course in which he was enrolled one summer. Through this Web site, his students were able to participate in an online mock election. By using the lesson plans found on the Web site, Broglie's students were able to learn about the major political parties and research the candidates for Governor of Virginia and their positions on major issues. He concludes that this program enabled him to add excitement and hands-on experiences to his classes. In addition, the students were able to use the most up-to-date technology which, in turn, gave them access to some of the country's greatest political minds.

Left to Right: Marion Broglie and Sheryl Nussbaum-Beach

Entering the Web of Politics Through Technology

by Marion F. Broglie

Three days in a row, eighth-grader Billy Dunbar approached me outside my classroom and asked if I had heard whether his group's bill had passed or not. Why? Was his the only name on the bill, I teased, even though his group included four other conscientious, hard-working students who had proposed an increase in the minimum wage? His interest in the fate of his bill was a pleasant reminder of why I made the switch from high school to middle school.

After eighteen years of teaching primarily World History at the high school level, I found myself in front of an eighth-grade classroom teaching civics at Lynnhaven Middle School. The e-Congress, for which Billy Dunbar's group had written the bill, is part of the Youth Leadership Initiative (YLI) program, which was a lifesaver for me in my first year at the middle school.

As I struggled at the end of the summer to put together a comprehensive course plan, I recalled the YLI Web site that I had found while writing a research paper for the Introduction to the Gifted and Talented course I had taken earlier that summer.

As I struggled at the end of the summer to put together a comprehensive course plan, I recalled the YLI Web site that I had found while writing a research paper for the Introduction to the Gifted and Talented course I had taken earlier that summer. I had chosen leadership as my topic for the paper, and the site provided numerous resources for the teaching of citizenship skills.

Youth Leadership Initiative

YLI is a program created by renowned political scientist Larry Sabato through the University of Virginia's Center for Governmental Studies. Dr. Sabato is perhaps the leading political scientist in the country and, according to the University of Virginia's president, John T. Casteen III, "the most quoted college professor in the land" (Scott and Theodoridis 29). For example, "On the day the Clinton-Lewinsky scandal broke in 1998, Sabato received 963 media inquiries in a 24-hour period" (Scott and Theodoridis 28).

YLI's purpose is to encourage middle and high school students to take an active part in their role as citizens and to inspire them to become tomorrow's leaders. It allows students, with the thousands of others across the country, to take part in a mock election and mock Congress. Also, it includes a variety of excellent lesson plans to teach both basic and complex concepts of the political process, and it conducts the largest online mock election in the nation.

Mock Election

The year 2001 began with a gubernatorial election campaign in Virginia between Democrat Mark Warner and Republican Mark Earley. YLI conducted an online mock election for middle and high school students across the Commonwealth of Virginia. They also conducted a similar program for students in New Jersey for their gubernatorial election.

The Web site provides options which make it useful in any classroom. As a new civics teacher, I attempted to incorporate as much of the program as I could into my teaching. I was not disappointed; the experience that I gained this year will enable me to make better use of the program in the future. YLI has previously run a mock presidential election in 2000 and 2002 and should continue with mock Senatorial campaigns in 2003.

> *YLI has previously run a mock presidential election in 2000 and 2002 and should continue with mock Senatorial campaigns in 2003.*

Registration

The basic requirements to participate in the mock election are very simple. Teachers need to log onto the Web site, www.youthleadership.net, and register their classes. With only a few simple items to complete (e.g., school name, teacher name), this takes less than five minutes.

After registering the classes, individual students are required to register online during a specified period. A list of all students who have registered, along with their passwords, is accessed by the teacher and approved before the students are able to vote. A second period of several days is set up for online voting. The students use their passwords to access the "voting booth," and, in this case, get the chance to vote for governor, lieutenant governor, and attorney general of Virginia. These very basic steps can be completed with access to a single computer. With access to a computer lab, registration and voting for an entire class can be completed in less than ten minutes.

Extended Activities for the Mock Election However, much more can be accomplished with the resources that YLI offers. I started with the *Formation of an Ideological Spectrum* lesson plan that allowed the students to create and understand the political spectrum. My students then took the *Political Ideology Survey* to see where they best fit on the political spectrum. We also discussed the basic political beliefs of the two major political parties, Democrats and Republicans, and where they would fall on the political spectrum.

My classes next used the Internet (via my implementation of a lesson plan [*Mark My Words…*] that YLI created) to research the two candidates for governor and their positions on the major issues. My students became well informed about the candidates. One student, Roberta Sheradan, said, "It was nice to be able to inform my family about the two candidates' stances on the issues. My parents had not had time to do the research themselves."

We adapted the Campaign Survey that outlined the basic positions of the two gubernatorial candidates and allowed the students to match their views with the candidates. After discussing the candidates and their merits, my classes were divided into two groups, those supporting Mark Warner and those supporting Mark Earley.

We adapted the Campaign Survey that outlined the basic positions of the two gubernatorial candidates and allowed the students to match their views with the candidates.

Since the other eighth-grade civics teachers at Lynnhaven Middle School were not using the YLI program, I volunteered my students to help instruct the other students about the mock election and to register the other classes, giving them the opportunity to vote. Three eighth-grade teachers graciously gave me time from their classes to complete the necessary tasks to engage my students in the election process.

First, my students were required to register the other civics classes for the mock election. Small groups of the students went to each of the other classes, escorted students to the computer lab, and walked them through the registration process. They explained how to access the YLI Web site and took them through the directions for registration, helping individual students who had difficulty in following the directions.

In addition, the student groups created campaign posters for their candidates. Each group went through the process of deciding what aspects of their candidate's positions would most appeal to the audience of eighth-grade civics students at Lynnhaven Middle School. These posters were then displayed in each of the other civics teachers' classrooms in the days leading up to the election.

The most difficult task was for the students to create campaign "speeches" or presentations to the other classes to persuade them to vote for the candidates that they supported

The most difficult task was for the students to create campaign "speeches" or presentations to the other classes to persuade them to vote for the candidates that they supported. Warner supporters and Earley supporters had fifteen minutes each to convince the students for whom they should vote. Some students used the medium of television and created videotapes to show the classes. Others took a more traditional approach and made campaign speeches. "It takes time to think about a well-written speech to the voters," wrote Susan Elliott.

Finally, after having the opportunity to vote in the mock election themselves, the students took the other classes to the computer lab to vote. Again, they were given full control over the process with the caveat that, as in real life, campaigning could not take place near the polling place.

Additional Lesson Plans for the Mock Election YLI also provided lesson plans that allowed my students to investigate campaign expenditures, analyze television campaign ads, and evaluate bellwethers or indicators of future trends. All of my students are now aware that Fairfax City and Fairfax County have picked the winning candidate in every gubernatorial election for the past thirty years. I extended this lesson by having my students investigate which states were bellwethers in presidential elections. I gave them presidential election maps for the past nine elections, and they had to determine which states had selected the winner most often.

Gubernatorial Debate YLI hosted one of the gubernatorial debates between Mark Warner and Mark Earley and gave the students participating in the mock election the chance to submit questions. Two of the student questions were chosen, and the students who submitted the chosen questions had a

It also gave me an opportunity to discuss the differences among national, state, and local government responsibilities as the class discussed which questions would be appropriate to ask the candidates for the state's top political officer.

chance to videotape their question for the candidates to answer. While no Lynnhaven Middle School student's question was chosen this year, it generated ample excitement and anticipation as my students struggled to come up with a unique question that would be worthy of being selected. It also gave me an opportunity to discuss the differences among national, state, and local government responsibilities as the class discussed which questions would be appropriate to ask the candidates for the state's top political officer. For instance, many students were upset about local ordinances and issues (skateboarding restrictions, the school calendar, the school dress code) or national concerns (September 11th , the war on terrorism) that would have to be rephrased to be applicable to the future governor or, in some cases, could not be made appropriate and had to be discarded.

Evaluation of the Mock Election The greatest problem that I encountered was the evaluation of the campaign speeches/presentations, since I was unable to be in all of the classes at the same time and see the entire presentations. My solution to this was to create a very short rubric for the classroom teacher to fill out while watching the presentation. One could also schedule the presentations at different times, but that would be more difficult if one is not on the block schedule, as Lynnhaven Middle School is.

A possible extension of this program in the future would be to include the entire eighth grade and have them register, campaign, and encourage the rest of the school (sixth- and seventh-graders) to vote. This could also be done at the high school level; an election day could be created.

All in all, the mock election went very well and my students gained both knowledge and experience from it. In a survey to evaluate the program, Ann Monroe wrote, "There really isn't anything I didn't like. I learned a lot about how elections worked. There was nothing wrong with the project; it was the perfect simulation."

e-Congress YLI also gives students an opportunity to participate in the lawmaking process through its e-Congress in February. Again, it provides the resources necessary to execute this program in a simple or complex manner. While I was impressed with this program as well, I will begin the drafting of legislation earlier next year (in January) in order to have enough time for the students to proofread and to evaluate their legislation.

Students, working in groups or on their own, write a bill on an issue that concerns them. Again, this provided an excellent opportunity to decide what issues members of Congress would consider. Bills that dealt with state or local concerns had to be re-worked or reconsidered. Eighth-grader Lisa South wrote that the one thing that she learned from the e-Congress was "not to make a Virginia bill for the U.S. Congress." Working with middle school students, I did have to consider what topics would be appropriate for this level and limit the range of bills that my students could create.

After the deadline for bills to be submitted, YLI then assigned a number of bills to each of my classes. The bills assigned to us were written by students from across the country and none of the bills assigned to our classes were ones that they had crafted. They acted as a committee to consider each of these bills and their merits. They then had the option to *pass*, *fail*, or *table* each of the bills. In order to save time, I divided my classes into subcommittees and gave each of them three or four bills. Only those bills that made it out of our subcommittees were considered by the class as a whole. Acting as members of Congress and discussing possible laws is a much better way of teaching lawmaking procedures than reading about it in a book. This hands-on experience for the students is invaluable, as it remains in their minds that this is the way our Congress works.

Acting as members of Congress and discussing possible laws is a much better way of teaching lawmaking procedures than reading about it in a book.

The bills that made it out of committee were then put on the floor of the House. My students were taken to the computer lab and given the opportunity to vote on each of the bills as an individual member of Congress. Again, due to limited time and the many bills that made it to the floor, I directed them to the bills that they had to consider first (bills we had passed out of committee and the bills we had written) and with their remaining time, the students could consider other bills that were of most interest to them.

Lesson Plans on Other Topics

YLI also includes lesson plans which I have previewed on other civics topics, and of which I have made ample use over the course of the year. For instance, there are lessons on Thomas Hobbes, John Locke, Baron de Montesquieu, Jean-Jacques Rousseau, and William Blackstone and their ideas that are the foundation of our form of government. There are also lesson plans on the Bill of Rights and amending the Constitution. Just recently, I used a YLI lesson plan (*How Do Campaigns Channel their Information?*) on propaganda, and we analyzed the election advertisements of the candidates for our 2002 city council races. There is a veritable wealth of information on government and the political process that is accessible to teachers and students.

Conclusion

On the fourth day, Billy Dunbar and his four other group members discovered the fate of their bill that raised the minimum wage. H.R. 1311 was one of only eleven that passed on the House floor. In fact, it had passed with over fifty-eight percent of the votes cast, the second highest percentage of any of the laws passed. Their excitement about getting their law passed was genuine and a very satisfying experience for me. It also gave the class the chance to discuss how difficult it is to get a bill passed into law and the reasons why most of their bills failed.

> *The students were able to use the most up-to-date technology to access information on how the political process works.*

The mock election and the e-Congress were invaluable experiences for my students, and YLI provided me the wherewithal to add excitement and hands-on experiences to my classes. The students were able to use the most up-to-date technology to access information on how the political process works. I was able to develop lessons using these plans that made it possible for me as a first-year civics teacher to tap the knowledge base of some of the country's greatest political minds. The Youth Leadership Initiative's prepackaged lesson plans are the best that I have come across in nineteen years of teaching. I would have been lost this year without the use of this program. I look forward to the future, when I have gained the experience to utilize fully the resources being made available to me. I believe that the possibilities are limitless, and the potential for the growth of my students through this program is endless.

Note: All student names are pseudonyms and all student work has been used with permission.

Works Cited

Scott, Joshua J. and Theodoridis, Alex. "Talking Head." *UVA Alumni News*, Spring 2002, pp. 24 – 29.

"Youth Leadership Initiative." [Online] Available: www.youthleadership.net. April 20, 2002.

About Marion F. Broglie Marion F. Broglie has been a social studies teacher for nineteen years. For the past fourteen years, he was a World History and Advanced Placement European History teacher at Green Run High School in Virginia Beach, Virginia. At the beginning of the 2001-2002 school year, he moved to Lynnhaven Middle School in the same school district.

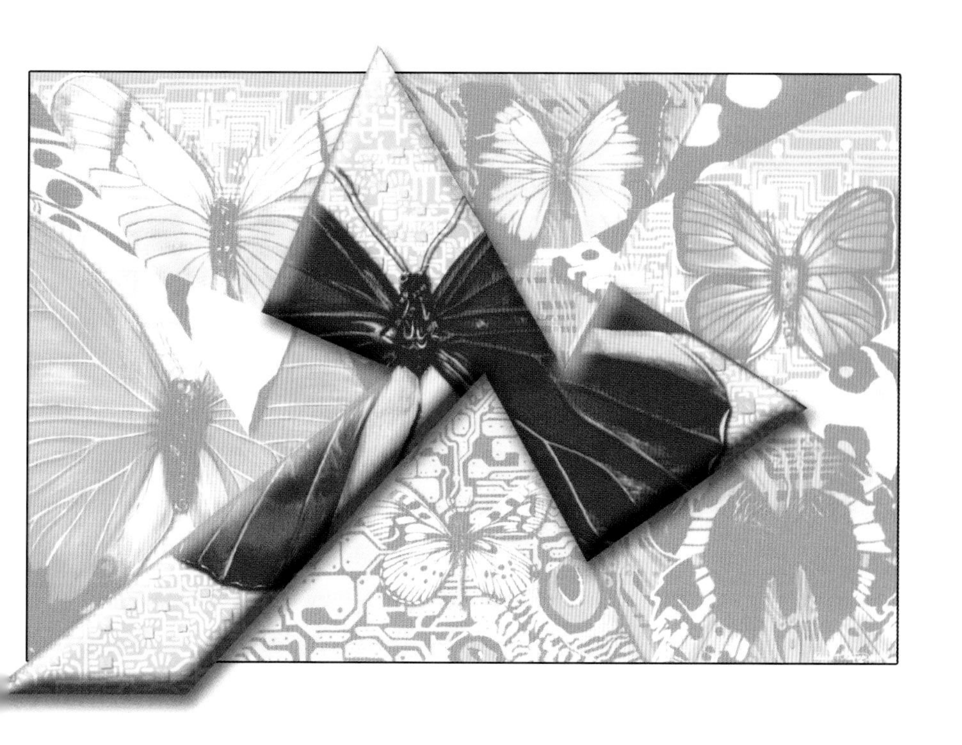

Section Seven

Interlacing Technology *With* Instruction in Support Services

Nan Leach

The Connection

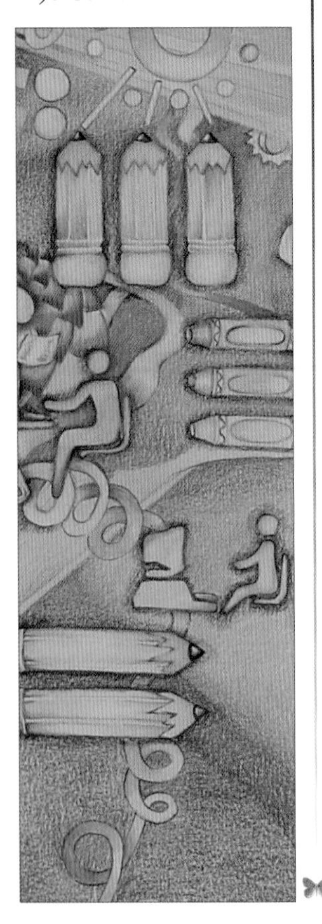

Description: Students in today's classrooms are lucky to have technology as a part of their education. In art class, we are always using computers to help us create artwork. This design reflects the ways education and technology are one and the same.

Medium Used: Prisma color pencils

Educational Background: Nan Leach received a Bachelor of Science in Art Education from Daemen College, Buffalo, New York.

Teaching Experience: Ms. Leach taught art in New York State for three years and has been teaching in Virginia Beach for twelve years. Also, she has taught at the Contemporary Art Center in Virginia Beach.

Awards: Ms. Leach is a commercial artist and does illustrations and designs for several companies and magazines such as *Crafts Magazine*, *Stitchers World*, and *Dollfus, Mieg & Cie* (DMC) Corporation, an embroidery floss company.

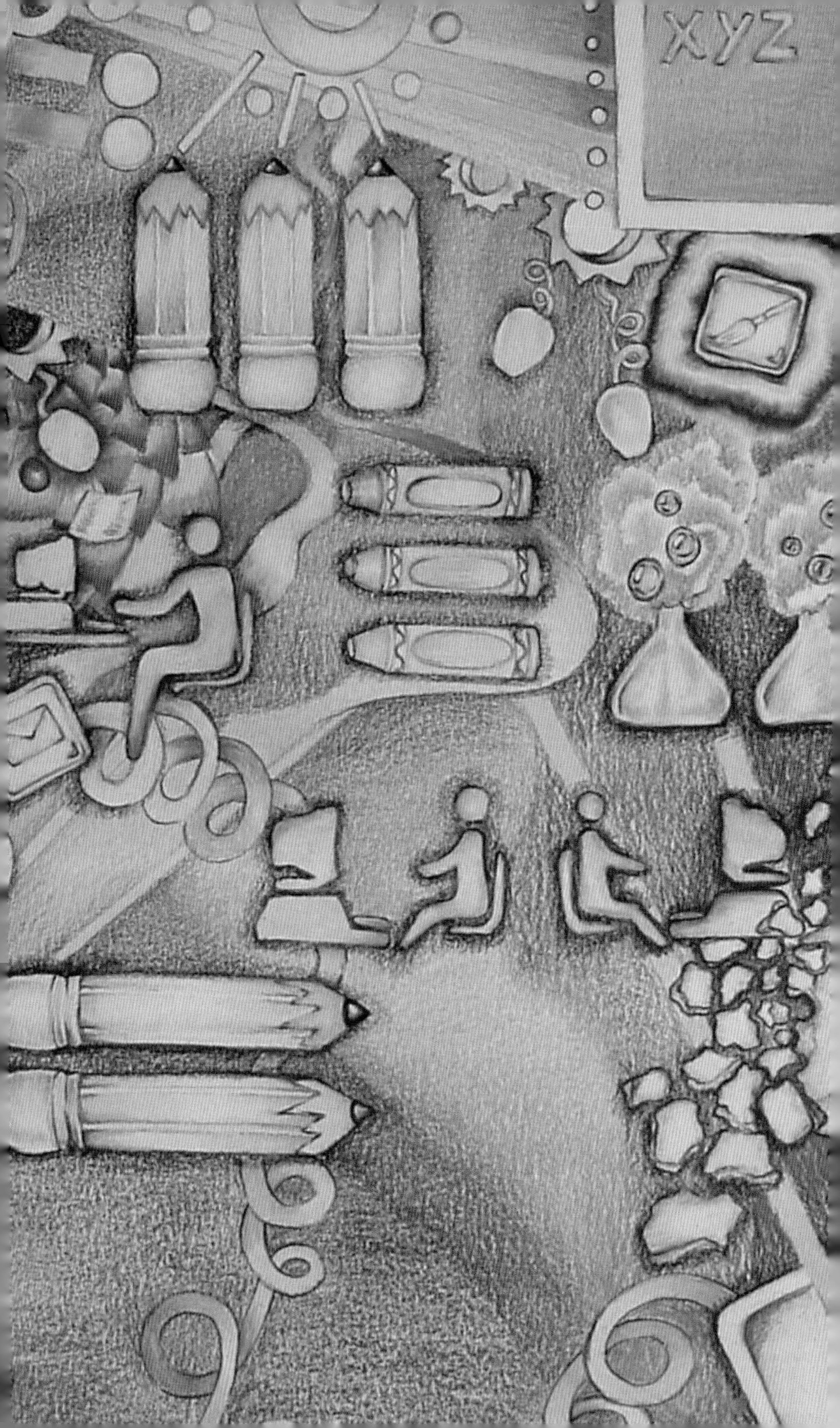
XYZ

Interlacing Technology With Instruction in Support Services

Villages, teams, school-wide themes, all are different words and phrases to describe how specialists are working with classroom teachers to integrate technology into the curriculum so students receive exciting and diversified experiences in their academic classrooms. All the articles in this section confirm that the isolated teacher struggling to teach all things to a roomful of students is more and more a thing of the past. In Virginia Beach Schools, Library Media Specialists, Computer Resource Specialists, and Speech Pathologists, among others, are trained and available to assist teachers as they integrate technology into the curriculum to meet instructional goals.

In "Walking in Miranda's Shoes: Believing 'We Can'," an Ocean Lakes Elementary School team consisting of Carol Koceja, a kindergarten inclusion teacher, Kelly O'Brien, a speech pathologist teacher, and Carl Peake, a Computer Resource Specialist, describe how they worked together to help a disabled student. This student arrived in Koceja's classroom able to do little more than respond to limited instruction by using a paddle switch. The article describes how the team interacted with each other to adapt technological tools to ensure that the student had access to the curriculum.

Dona Leigh Caldwell uses the image of the village to symbolize the team of teachers who worked together at the Old Donation Center to create two units that combined information from language arts, science, research, and technology into integrated units of study. The resulting instruction not only met many curriculum goals, but assured the students of a deeper understanding of the connections of both academic subjects and their relationship to the outside world.

While reading Dr. Christopher Moersch's article in Learning and Leading with Technology, which includes his framework describing the eight different levels of technology

Front Row Left to Right: Dorothy Kidwell, Carl Peake, Carol Koceja
Back Row Left to Right: Kelly O'Brien, Patricia Norfleet, Dona Caldwell

integration, Dorothy Kidwell, a Computer Resource Specialist at Rosemont Forest Elementary School, realized that some of the teachers at her school could fit into each of the eight levels. This led her to plan a diversified program of staff development sessions for the teachers at Rosemont Forest. To achieve this, Kidwell spent many hours planning instructional activities that helped teachers use curriculum objectives to determine the best use of technology. At the end of the article, Kidwell describes with pride how the resulting lessons and projects created by the teachers caused students to be involved in problem-solving activities that encouraged divergent thinking.

Dreams do come true; however, Patricia Norfleet, a Computer Resource Specialist at Centerville Elementary School, found that the teachers at Centerville did not share her dream; at least, at first. Her dream was to have a class set of AlphaSmart® keyboards; and, in her dream, she saw herself helping students and teachers incorporate them into daily instruction. After she persuaded her principal to buy these keyboards, she found that teachers were not enthusiastic about using them. Her article recounts how she devised a plan to make these technology tools a necessary and popular element of classroom instruction at Centerville Elementary School.

Providing staff development opportunities for teachers to become technologically proficient was the task that Sheryl Nussbaum-Beach took on when she arrived at W.T. Cooke Elementary School as the Computer Resource Specialist several years ago. Her goal was to help the teachers move along a continuum from being non-users of technology to becoming creative appliers and integrators of technology. To accomplish this, she created staff development sessions that were teacher-centered and diversified. In the ensuing years, the school's standardized test scores improved, and the faculty was the second school in the division to have 100 percent of its teachers pass a required division technology assessment test. In her article, Ms. Nussbaum-Beach describes in detail how she worked with the teachers and administrators to accomplish their dreams of student success.

In her article, Dorothy Kidwell refers to a statement made by Norman Vincent Peale, "Change your thoughts and you change your world." All the articles in this section illustrate how resource teachers and specialists working with classroom teachers have changed the educational environment for many students.

Walking in Miranda's Shoes: Believing "We Can!"

by Carol Koceja, Kelly O'Brien, and Carl Peake

Where Do We Begin?

Miranda could not speak; she could not walk without the use of an assistive device. She could grasp items and hold them but had great difficulty with writing because her elbows and wrists did not move in a way to allow her to place her hands flat on a table or grasp items. She is a child with an undiagnosed neurological disorder resulting in a variety of issues that make it difficult for her to access curriculum in the routine manner. Miranda could be characterized as a "miracle baby."

"Miracle babies" are born every day to families waiting with loving, open arms to embrace the "perfect child." Medical technology has made it possible for babies to be born as early as during the fifth- or sixth-month of gestation, and these premature babies characteristically experience developmental delays and physical disabilities that range from mild, to severe, or profound. These babies are taken to Infant Stimulation programs as early as possible and subsequently are referred to Early Childhood Special Education programs. The two- to five-year-old children in these programs are often eager to learn but have had little social experience beyond the home or medical environment. How does our team, consisting of a classroom teacher, a speech therapist, and a computer resource teacher begin to work with students like Miranda with disabilities ranging from mild to severe?

How does our team, consisting of a classroom teacher, a speech therapist, and a computer resource teacher begin to work with students like Miranda with disabilities ranging from mild to severe?

In these situations our team must ask some very basic questions. In Miranda's case, such questions would be "Where do we begin?" "How do we know what Miranda understands?" "How do we know what she is thinking?" "Where are the opportunities for her to express her ideas, questions, and creativity?"

It was obvious that Miranda had many needs. The team approached Miranda as we would any student with disabilities, one issue at a time. Our hope in writing this article is to encourage colleagues who work on a daily basis with these students to consider using technology as a pivotal part of the curriculum.

Why Even Consider the Use of Technology? Why use technology in our curriculum? It has been our experience that when integrating technology into curriculum, students who otherwise could not be reached make progress toward educational goals. In classrooms that serve students with disabilities, technology provides access to the curriculum. Access to the curriculum is the focus, and technology is the means to that end. When viewed this way, the use of technological devices is not simply a frill that entices students like Miranda into participation; it is a basic need.

> *After the first few activities have been created on a specific piece of software, the time invested on future activities will diminish.*

Creating activities that use technology may appear daunting at first. After the first few activities have been created on a specific piece of software, the time invested on future activities will diminish. The success of the activities will serve to inspire teachers to create more and more activities that invite full participation from students. Spending hours making costumes and manipulatives, home made access devices, and other such instructional materials to motivate students may not evoke the joy in teachers that computer generated activities command, but, by spending the same amount of time moving methodically through available software and customizing a wide variety of language-based and math-based activities, the desired educational outcomes will be attained. Access to the curriculum made possible by these technological tools provides opportunities for students with disabilities to successfully complete SOL objectives. Our successful experiences with using technology with disabled students persuades us that it is essential that teachers consider its use whenever possible.

I'm Hooked! Where Do I Go From Here? Perhaps teachers might think that incorporating technological devices into the daily routine and curriculum could be overwhelming. However, once a teacher is "hooked" by the ease with which lesson plans can be developed using technology, it becomes a joy. The use of the computer is rarely problematic, nor are most of the augmentative devices available on the market today. It is more often the software that causes problems and questions.

Over the years, we have learned one piece of software after another (i.e. Speaking Dynamically Pro®, Boardmaker®, Intellipics®, and Intellitalk II®).

Figure 1

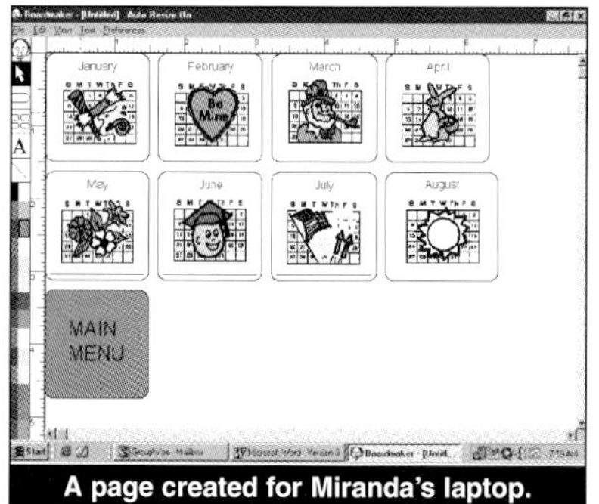

A page created for Miranda's laptop.

If someone had told us five years ago that we would be using a variety of software on a daily basis, we would have laughed. In actuality, our learning curve started out slowly. The speed with which our team can now create programs has increased tremendously to the point that "boards," brief-sequencing activities and functional picture clues, are sometimes developed on a laptop computer "on the spot" as they are needed. (See Figure 1.) We prefer to create these accommodations as lesson plans are created; however, there are those moments when we realize that if we had that one simple board or activity, we could reach this student immediately. The software not only serves the purpose of increasing communication options, but it develops language skills as well.

The Use of Technology Simply Overwhelms Me!

Reviewing Miranda's needs could have been overwhelming, but we started with Miranda exactly where we begin with every child who is new to the learning environment. Our efforts included learning about what made her happy, what made her sad, and what appeared to best motivate her in a variety of learning environments. In Miranda's case, weaving technology into the curriculum took place naturally as her specific needs became evident.

Miranda came to us using a "clock scanning" device, which is also called an "All-Turn-It Spinner" from Ablenet™. (See Figure 2.) Miranda used a paddle switch to move an arm around the dial to the preferred response, then she released the paddle. That served her well as long as the options and numbers were limited. The question was, what will happen when her vocabulary expands and her sentence structures move beyond two word utterances? As time progressed, we saw signs that Miranda's language skills were developing and her desire to communicate was evident despite her limited physical abilities and lack of speech.

Figure 2

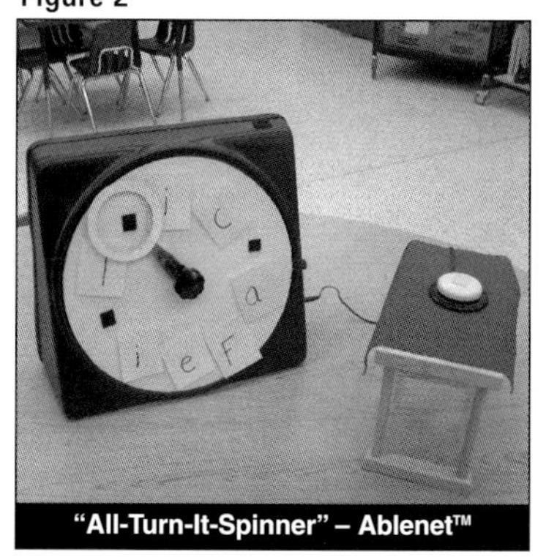

"All-Turn-It-Spinner" – Ablenet™

The concern was transitioning Miranda from using the "All-Turn-It-Spinner" to the device that required her to hold down the switch until the correct response was highlighted on a computer. This functional switch in accessing responses is a monumental transition for many students. Miranda made the transition and began using a laptop computer to scan options until the desired item appeared. The laptop computer was slightly modified to include the use of a paddle switch instead of the mouse so that Miranda could select answers as they were scanned on the screen. (See Figure 3.) At this point we were able to get a better picture of what Miranda's comprehension skills were and what information she was receiving and retaining.

Figure 3

Laptop computer with paddle

Miranda came to us knowing how to use a device called "Step-By-Step," that records simple phrases for the student. As an example, during music class, simple refrains to songs were placed on the device so that Miranda could "sing" the repetitive verses with the rest of the students. Short responses such as "yes," "no," and "help please" were placed on the device and made available to her at all times so that she could have basic wants and needs met immediately without someone bringing up a page on her laptop. (See Figure 4.)

Figure 4

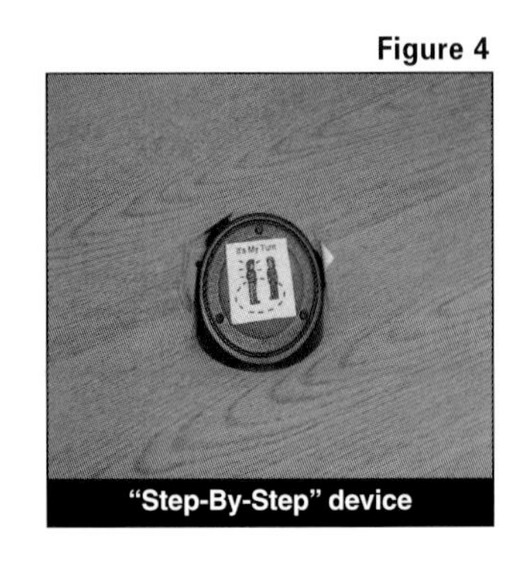

"Step-By-Step" device

During guided reading lessons, each page of the book was placed in sequence on the Step-by-Step device. Miranda's book was placed on a slant board and "page fluffers" were used to thicken the corner of each page so that Miranda could turn each page and tap the device to read in sequence. It is interesting to note that at the end of the book, she not only closed the book to the back cover, but she also pushed the device aside indicating that she was finished. These are simple yet powerful tools of communication.

I Don't Have Any Special Software! What Now? Although a wealth of outstanding software is available, not all of the software we use with special-needs students is special-needs-specific. Often we use standard software in non-standard ways to achieve our goals. Common software, like Microsoft Office® can be used to reach special-needs students once teachers begin to think "outside the box." In one instance we wanted the students to scan the computer keyboard and match letters to pictures that appeared on the monitor. We used Microsoft Excel®, placed outlined cells under the graphics, and locked the worksheet. (See Figure 5.) By locking the worksheet, students were restricted from altering the cells other than those we specified. Each student was then able to come to the computer, type a matching response in the appropriate cell, tab to the next open cell, and continue until all cells were complete. When students were ready, we altered the document to include lower-case captions. Since Miranda did not possess the dexterity to select individual letters on the computer keyboard, the activity was modified for her so that she could scan potential letters and use a paddle to select appropriate responses when the teacher assistant placed the mouse over them. This proved to be a particularly successful lesson for us. (See Figure 6.)

Figure 5

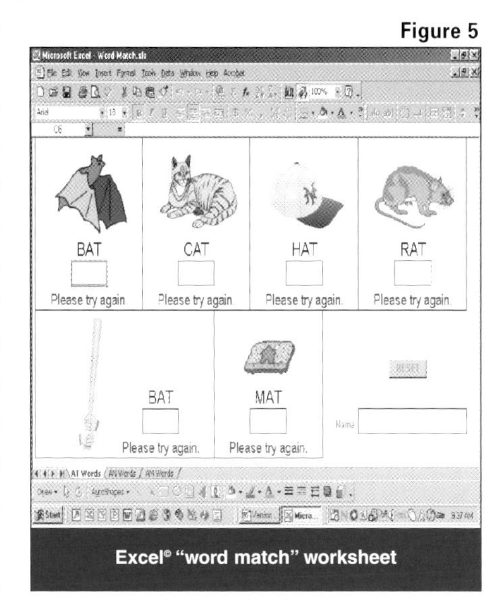

Excel© "word match" worksheet

Figure 6

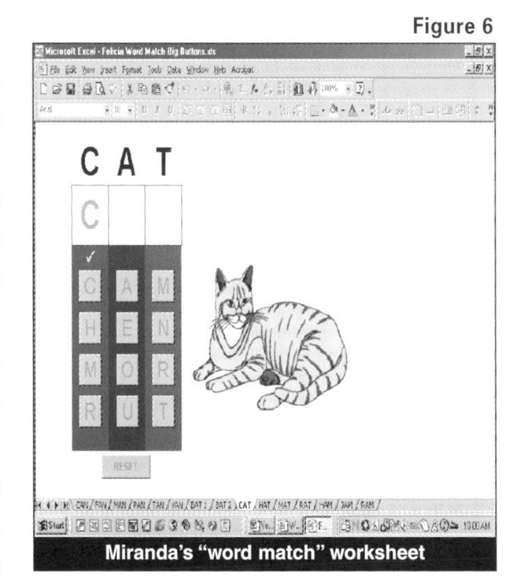

Miranda's "word match" worksheet

Figure 7

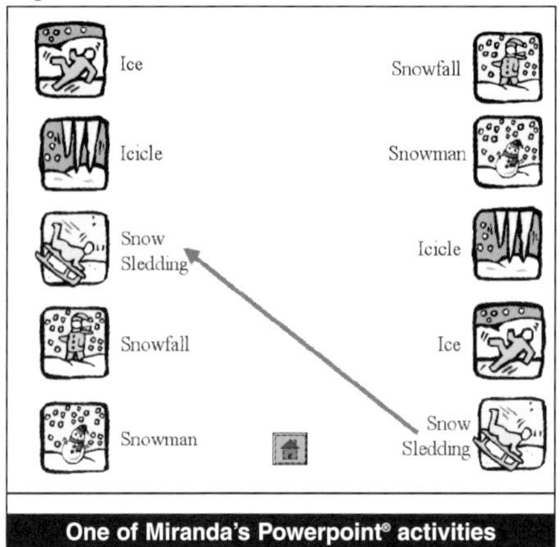

One of Miranda's Powerpoint® activities

Miranda required assistance in using the mouse, so we created several interactive Microsoft PowerPoint® documents in which the teacher assistant opened the file and asked her to click a paddle when the pointer was over a particular item on the screen. (See Figure 7.) By linking each slide to an appropriate response slide and/or sound file, we were able to encourage Miranda to scan the monitor and click to identify a number of different items, including pictures/names of classmates and seasonal pictures. The occupational therapist was particularly helpful with this project. She was able to make suggestions such as changing from a dark background to a lighter one to ensure that Miranda could see the page more clearly. This helped other students as well.

Figure 8

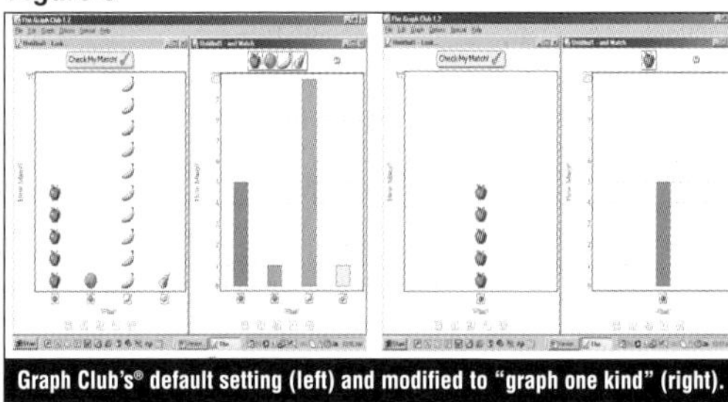

Graph Club's® default setting (left) and modified to "graph one kind" (right).

Sometimes, software intended for mainstream students can be customized easily for use with special-needs students. One example of this is the way in which we easily adapted a lesson using The Graph Club©. The mainstream kindergarten classes were doing an activity in which students matched items in a pictograph by creating a matching bar graph. By changing one setting in the program, we were able to teach the same lesson but with only one item to match instead of the default value of four. (See Figure 8.) Standard or mainstream software can be adapted to meet students' needs. Once the initial files are created, it is not a time-consuming task to update and further adapt them for a variety of new activities. It is no different from updating and adapting existing lesson plans to accommodate new situations. By keeping in mind the students' needs and the curriculum goals, the lessons we can create are limitless.

How Do We Integrate Technology Into the Daily Routine?

Critical to the success of weaving technology into the curriculum is the fact that ideas are implemented one at a time, one day at a time, and one unit at a time. Our initial interest in using technology started when we realized that we were serving several students who were pre-verbal or who had such poor articulation that speech was unintelligible. These students needed a simple way to communicate that would lessen frustration and encourage participation. Augmentative communication devices were introduced during the functional times of day first, such as snack time, restroom time, and other daily living skill moments of the day.

The first device of this kind used with Miranda only presented two options. It is commonly referred to as a "Cheap Talk" device. (See Figure 9.) She basically touched a picture, and the device would verbalize the request. It was a great cause/effect activity that eventually had functional meaning to her.

Figure 9

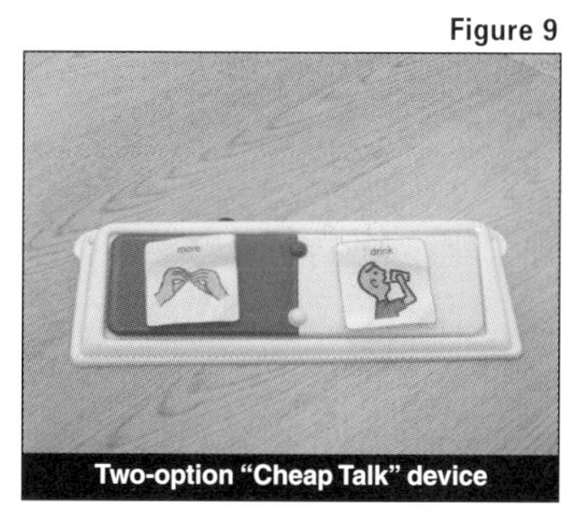

Two-option "Cheap Talk" device

Students who can speak are encouraged to repeat the verbal model and couple that verbal expression with sign language. We encourage them to communicate simple requests like "more drink please," "toilet please," etc. We couple the device with sign language. For many children who have the potential for speech, requiring the use of the device connected to the sign with a verbal approximation of the request results in total communication. Over time this proved to be highly successful in developing functional language for the child. From the start, the child is required to verbalize two word requests. The device never replaces verbal utterances; it is only there to enhance and provide an opportunity for basic needs to be met without frustration. In this case, the device serves multiple purposes. It eases the communication process and reinforces discrimination of correct sound and word production. This is a particularly vital skill for students who are experiencing significant speech disorders.

> *For many students who have the potential for speech, requiring the use of the device connected to the sign with a verbal approximation of the request results in total communication.*

Figure 10

Blackhawk® keypad

When the student relates with ease to a two-option device, we move the student to four-options, and then eight. There are devices that provide many options such as a "Blackhawk©." (See Figure10.) As the student becomes familiar with touching a pad or a paddle switch, we move him or her to scanning responses on laptop computers and larger computers with paddle switch activation in the classroom.

How Do I Move Beyond Functional Skills Using Technology?

It is never enough to rest on the success of seeing a student learn functional skills. There is always that moment when a teacher realizes that this is just the window opening to a host of educational opportunities.

In dealing with all the students in Miranda's class, the team found that we were faced with a "melting pot" of varying disorders (Downs Syndrome, Cerebral Palsy, Autism, Language and Communication Disorder, and children born prematurely). The speech therapist realized that we needed to provide more opportunities for our students and composed a number of nonsense rhymes that were placed on a software program called Intellitalk II® to meet the needs of this varied population. (See Figure 11.) This program provides picture clues, which are coupled with simple written language and auditory reinforcement. Once again, with the special expertise of one of our team, we addressed a vital pre-reading skill required for understanding where print is associated with verbal output. In addition, we reinforced sound play through rhyming, another necessary skill for successful reading skill development.

Figure 11

Intellipics® keyboard connected to computer

Given a sound basis in a variety of pre-reading skills, a student like Miranda is ready to attempt a kindergarten level curriculum. The kindergarten curriculum includes excellent literature as the basis of all unit work. Students are required to begin sight reading of high frequency words and to sequence stories; they must be able to tell a story with a beginning, middle, and end. With many of the topic books, we created at least one sequencing activity using a software program called Intellipics©. When that sequencing activity was used in the classroom, we found that "on task" behavior was at 100 percent for each and every student in the learning environment. They were "glued" to the computer screen! The students were absolutely mesmerized by the activity and had up to 80 percent retention of the sequencing following participation in the activity. Miranda was able to access Intellitalk II© programs using a paddle switch connected to the main computer. She could select the item she thought should come first, second, third, and so on when it was highlighted and verbalized on the screen. This provided her with success oriented feedback and provided the teacher with the information necessary to assess her sequencing abilities. In addition, it provided Miranda an equal opportunity to retell a story.

> *This provided her with success oriented feedback and provided the teacher with the information necessary to assess her sequencing abilities. In addition, it provided Miranda an equal opportunity to retell a story.*

Story sequencing activities often provide the threshold for opportunities to incorporate technological activities into the curriculum. Realizing this, we moved from sequencing activities related to the language arts curriculum to a large variety of activities introducing nouns and action verbs. We were able to use the computer activities to extend the curriculum and to encourage clarity in articulation. Functional movement activities were connected to verbs and prepositions, and a multitude of fine motor and cognitive objectives were connected to entire story lines. This provided the opportunity for students to tell stories with a beginning, a middle, and an end with ease.

At the same time that we were working on story sequencing, we needed to incorporate phonemic awareness. We decided to leave a blank for some of the rhyming words in the nursery rhymes. Then, many of the nursery rhymes were placed on the Intellitalk II© and Intellipics© software programs. This provided wonderful animation to familiar rhymes and encouraged verbal participation on the part of the students. They loved singing and saying the rhymes with the program. The speech therapist has subsequently taken some of what she initiated in the preschool classroom and provided the kindergarten classroom with lessons on the laptop computer that reinforce literacy skills at that level. These skills include beginning sound development, association of printed letter with an individual sound, and songs and stories connected to "the letter of the week."

How Do Related Services Personnel Work With Technology?

When Miranda came into our lives, we could have panicked, resulting in grasping for just about anything that would help us through the day, but we did not. Teaching is not a solitary endeavor. We asked mentors, teachers, teammates, volunteers, and related services personnel to collaborate with our efforts in serving the needs of this student. We looked for input at every turn. We worked cohesively as a teaching team.

Sometimes this input comes to us from sources we hardly expect. "Nurse Bobbie" accompanies Miranda to school every day to ensure that health issues are addressed minute-to-minute. She is an outstanding professional resource in the classroom because in addition to being a skilled nurse, she is a natural teacher. She has developed any number of accommodations for Miranda to provide access to activities and to extend learning opportunities of presented materials. Many students love to play *Concentration*, and for Miranda, any card game is of high interest. Nurse Bobbie created the idea of using small color cards to place on the back of the *Concentration* cards. Miranda could then decide which card she wanted to choose by scanning her choice using her laptop computer and a paddle switch. Once the two options were chosen, Miranda was asked whether or not her choices were the same or different. If they were the same, she could keep the cards. If the choices were different, they were turned over and the game proceeded to the next student. This simple accommodation made the difference between independent access to the game or reliance on others to continue to make decisions "for" Miranda. Miranda loved the freedom and challenge of this *Concentration* game.

Certain activation ideas and creative access tools would not have been available without the expertise of our occupational therapist. Switch activation is easy to attach to the computer, but how does the classroom teacher make the switch accessible to the student? That is where the occupational therapist comes in. In one case, the occupational therapist made a small "stool-like" stand for one switch so that Miranda could access the switch from a sitting position on the floor. (Miranda was working on sitting independently as one of her physical therapy goals. We blended that goal into circle time academic goals and provided access to her switch.)

We were able to integrate seven objectives from her Individual Educational Plan into a fifteen-minute block of time. Without the creative practicality of the occupational therapist, this access may not have been possible.

Outstanding volunteers in the local community provide faithful service to classrooms. Cynthia, a high school student volunteer, is an incredibly talented natural teacher who shares her compassion and joy with all students. Cynthia loved to create enjoyable activities for the students that highlighted the alphabet letter for the week. When we studied the letter "Q," Cynthia took it as a personal challenge to find an activity that the students would enjoy and participate in fully. We played with "Q" words, and the word "Quest" seemed to catch the students' interest. Then, Cynthia used the knowledge that earlier in the year the students enjoyed reading a book called *Treasure Chest*, connected it to the fact that we were studying positional words such as "on," "off," "under," "over," "around," "through," etc., and created an activity using Microsoft PowerPoint® to combine all of these experiences into one.

> *Cynthia loved to create enjoyable activities for the students that highlighted the alphabet letter for the week.*

First, she caught the student's interest by inviting them to participate in her computer-generated lesson. Then, she created cards that led them on a quest to find a treasure. Each card read, "look under table," "look on desk," etc. The students would read the card and, based on their participation in the PowerPoint® activity, they were able to find the next clue card. Finally, when they actually found the treasure chest, it was filled with books that Cynthia had purchased from a dollar store for them to keep. The students were enthusiastic, and they loved the wonderful books they took home.

Conclusion

Every day of every school year, students with disabilities like Miranda may be unintentionally denied access to the curriculum. Teachers diligently work to facilitate life skill development but are frustrated when a student is unable to reach instructional goals. As a consequence, these students become observers of the curriculum with little opportunity to participate in it. It is a mistake to think that they cannot learn the same information as their less disabled peers because they are poor communicators. Students with disabilities are entitled to every opportunity teachers can create to learn academics.

Many students, such as Miranda, can function and thrive in inclusion settings with technological assistance. More and more, professionals are consolidating efforts, collaborating, and creating dynamic teaching situations. By using technology effectively, the teacher is able to provide education for a broader spectrum of students with disabilities and reach greater numbers of students in need. The use of technology with students with disabilities is no longer a creative gesture but an imperative response to their educational development.

About Carol Koceja Carol Koceja presently teaches a kindergarten inclusion all-day program at Ocean Lakes Elementary School. She has been teaching for 32 years at all levels of education from infant intervention through graduate school education. She is a strong advocate for servicing the needs of students with disabilities and enjoys serving as a consultant to peer professionals in her field. Mrs. Koceja graduated from the University of Wisconsin, Whitewater.

About Kelly O'Brien Kelly O'Brien has been a speech/language pathologist for nine years. She has worked in a variety of settings, including home health care and public school. Currently, she is the speech pathologist at Ocean Lakes Elementary School and is working on a project integrating technology in therapeutic strategies. Ms. O'Brien has a Bachelor of Science in Speech pathology from James Madison University and a Master of Science from Old Dominion University.

About Carl Peake Carl Peake is currently the Computer Resource Specialist at Ocean Lakes Elementary School. He has 16 years of teaching experience in the City of Virginia Beach at both the middle and elementary school levels. His approach to computers in education emphasizes the use of the computer as a tool for learning and not as an end in itself. Mr. Peake earned his Bachelor of Science in Secondary Education from Old Dominion University.

Technology Instruction in the Elementary School: A Team Approach

by Dona Leigh Caldwell

"It takes a whole village to raise a child" is an African proverb that has meaning in today's classroom. With the changes in information technology during the last hundred years, it takes a team effort to prepare students for the information age. Classroom teachers need the expertise of a library media specialist and a computer resource specialist to assist them in implementing a technology rich curriculum.

Changes in Classroom Technology

In 1923 my grandmother completed six weeks of teacher training sponsored by East Carolina State Teachers College. She entered her first classroom in rural eastern North Carolina in the fall of that same year. As a first year teacher, my grandmother used the available technology to ensure that her students would enter the world with the skills to be successful. This technology was basically pencil and paper. For the most part, it was a pencil and paper world in 1923. Society dispersed information through printed materials, such as books, magazines, and newspapers. Students needed the skills to interpret and find meaning in the information provided in those resources. Most of the students my grandmother taught would complete their education at the eighth-grade level and then become farmers and housewives. At that time the manual typewriter was the technology encountered by the few students who would go into the business world.

At that time the manual typewriter was the technology encountered by the few students who would go into the business world.

Forty years later it was the beginning of the space age. President John F. Kennedy challenged the people of the United States to reach the moon by the end of the decade. Classrooms across the nation raced to teach students the skills they would need to meet this challenge. Even though technology was beginning to emerge in businesses and the military, in the classroom most information was obtained and dispersed through printed materials, such as books, magazines, and newspapers. When my mother began her teaching career in 1963, she taught her sixth grade students with the technology of the time, which was primarily pencil and paper. Most classrooms were not equipped with television sets and when the Mercury and Apollo rockets were launched, my mother brought her own television set to her classroom so that her students could see the events occurring around them. Teachers used overhead projectors, filmstrips, films, and books to motivate and instruct their students throughout the 1960s.

Technology was just beginning to become an instructional tool when I entered the teaching field in the 1970s. Like my mother, I received the traditional teacher certification in a four-year college program. The only technology training occurred in a semester course in which I was taught how to prepare lessons that used record players; overhead projectors; filmstrip, movie, and opaque projectors. My college professor had us practice operating and trouble-shooting these pieces of equipment. In order to pass the course, I had to correctly thread and operate a movie projector. Because my access to technology was limited both in school and at home, I remember how nervous I was as I approached and threaded the projector for the big test.

During my first few years of teaching, I relied on overhead projectors, filmstrips, films, and books in the planning of my instruction. But beginning in the early 1980s computers were in the schools, first in the library media center, then in the classroom, and finally in computer labs with trained computer resource specialists with the expertise to guide both teachers and students in acquiring and in using information retrieval skills. At first, computers were used to reinforce or remediate basic skills. The school system provided after school training sessions in which teachers were taught computer basics. They practiced using various software programs to enhance their instruction. With the advent of the Internet and the electronic encyclopedia, teachers worked to include the use of computers as information sources and as a method of sharing knowledge in the curriculum.

At first, computers were used to reinforce or remediate basic skills

Today students receive information in a variety of formats. These formats range all the way from simple picture books to complex multimedia packages. Information comes to them from television, radio, the Internet, computer software programs, and printed sources. Students must be taught to access, interpret, analyze, evaluate, and disseminate the masses of information they encounter through these resources. Many students do not understand that much of the information on a Web site can be advertisements for products or that the facts may be the opinions of the individual or group sponsoring the site. Occasionally, students will want to search the Internet looking for basic information about a subject, rather than obtaining the information from a printed resource. Using a printed resource, such as a nonfiction book or encyclopedia, can be much easier and quicker than searching through numerous Web sites using various search engines. Students need to understand that the kind of information they are looking for can determine the type of resource they use.

The Technology Team

Classroom teachers use technology as instructional tools and as information resources to enhance their teaching. Computer software programs, videotapes, laser disks, digital cameras, and camcorders can enable teachers to impart curricular objectives to their students in a stimulating fashion, one that more closely mirrors what students encounter in their everyday lives. Teachers incorporate student use of the electronic encyclopedia and the Internet as informational resources when designing their instruction. Word processing is used to develop and reinforce language arts skills, particularly writing.

In my teaching experience the teacher alone cannot effectively implement this technological approach to instruction. It requires a team effort. Three people—the classroom teacher, the library media specialist, and the computer resource specialist—have an active role in incorporating technology into the curriculum. Each member of this instructional team contributes singular expertise, skills, and knowledge to the successful technology-based curriculum.

Classroom teachers communicate to the other team members the objectives, learning standards, expected outcomes, and overall design of the curriculum. They use their knowledge of the learning styles and strengths of their students and of curriculum requirements to design effective lessons that incorporate technology. Students are taught appropriate classroom and personal behaviors that will enable them successfully to use technology. Classroom teachers maintain records of the progress made by their students. They report this progress to parents and to other team members.

Library media specialists identify print, nonprint, and electronic resources available in the library media center and the school division's central media center to the members of the technology team. They develop and maintain a collection of materials that supports the goals and objectives of the curriculum. Their instructional role is to teach students methods of information retrieval from both electronic and print materials. They work with the classroom teacher to ensure that information skills are not taught in isolation, but as an essential part of the curriculum. The library media specialists provide opportunities for individual, small group, and whole class instruction on the location, evaluation, and use of information resources.

The role of computer resource specialists is that of technology instructor. Not only do they have the expertise to address mechanical problems encountered when using technology, but more importantly they assist in reinforcing the skills teachers and students need to operate equipment and retrieve information. They have knowledge of the various software programs students can use to summarize findings. The computer resource specialists work with teachers on integrating technology skills within the curriculum. They also provide opportunities for teachers to receive training in order to strengthen the classroom teacher's technology skills and to become familiar with current trends in technology.

> *The role of computer resource specialists is that of technology instructor.*

Rationale for a Technology Team

Including technology in the curriculum might appear at first to be simple with the expertise of three professionals working toward the same goal. But there are other concerns facing each member of the technology team.

In most elementary schools, classroom teachers must plan and implement instruction in the major subject areas of language arts, mathematics, social studies, and science. Planning for this instruction, conducting parent conferences, and evaluating student work and progress often consume the teachers' time after school, in the evenings, and on weekends. Classroom teachers also provide guidance to their students in good work habits, citizenship, and discipline to ensure that they become independent, self-reliant learners. With all these demands on teachers, it can be a challenge for them to spend time surfing the Internet for appropriate sites to use in their classroom instruction and to be completely knowledgeable about current and effective software to use with their students.

Classroom teachers can rely on computer resource specialists to provide assistance in identifying technology systems, resources, and services to meet curriculum objectives and student learning styles. However, these are not the only concerns of computer resource specialists. They must work with teachers at each grade level to ensure that suitable technology skills are included in the classroom curriculum. The computer resource specialists demonstrate appropriate strategies through direct instruction with students. They plan and implement inservices for teachers on the current developments in the utilization of technology. The maintenance, installation, and upgrade of both software and hardware are other important tasks for computer resource specialists.

Like computer resource specialists, the library media specialists' duties pull them in many directions. Not only do they maintain a collection of materials to meet curriculum needs of all students at every grade level in their assigned school, but they also work collaboratively with classroom teachers to plan and implement instruction in information retrieval skills. Library media specialists are advocates for reading literacy, making sure that students develop into competent and self-motivated readers who appreciate literature. The management of the library media center and its staff is another major responsibility of library media specialists.

The Technology Team in Action

My most recent classroom teaching experience was as a second-grade teacher at the Old Donation Center which is a school for academically gifted students. The integration of technology into the curriculum was a high priority among the staff. Teachers at each grade level worked with the library media specialist and the computer resource specialist to ensure that technology was an integral part of the curriculum.

The curriculum developed there by the second-grade teachers was divided into four major integrated units of study, with the final unit designed to enable students to become involved in a community problem-solving project. Each unit required collaboration among the second-grade teachers, the library media specialist, and the computer resource specialist. In the first

The curriculum developed there by the second-grade teachers was divided into four major integrated units of study, with the final unit designed to enable students to become involved in a community problem-solving project.

three units, each member of the technology team worked to include skills and objectives that would enable students to become independent users of technology. The fourth unit of the year required students to take increasing responsibility for their own learning. They learned to use technology as independently and as meaningfully as possible.

The direction of the fourth unit encompassed some aspect of nature. Each year the "trigger" for this unit came from an article or event highlighted in the local newspaper. During my first year at the Old Donation Center, the local newspaper reported on the decline in the local frog population. Using these reports, we studied the life cycle and behavior of frogs, the importance of frogs to the environment, and the effect that changes in the environment had on frogs. The library media specialist and computer resource specialist met several times with the members of the grade-level team to map out and plan ways their services best could be utilized in this unit.

Roles and Responsibilities

The beginning of any unit requires the most energy and cooperation from each of the team members. It is imperative that they understand and are comfortable with their roles and responsibilities in order to effectively integrate technology into the instruction. Once these roles and responsibilities have been established, they can be slightly modified during the unit as the students' skills and abilities progress. Listed below are the objectives the team members created for themselves for the first week of our unit on frogs.

The classroom teacher will

- develop language arts and science lessons using frogs as a focal point,
- introduce students to the objectives of the unit,
- assist students in identifying and analyzing important information from newspaper articles about frogs, and
- work with students to develop a list of what they need to know about frogs.

The library media specialist will

- supply the classrooms with print materials about frogs from the school's media center,
- locate and obtain print resources from the public library,
- identify and program appropriate laser disk selections to be used in classroom science lessons, and
- instruct students on how to use the Dewey Decimal system to locate nonfiction books on frogs.

The computer resource specialist will

- identify a variety of Web sites about frogs for students to use on the computers in the classroom,
- supply the teacher with electronic encyclopedia programs such as *Compton's Interactive Encyclopedia* and the *Children's Ultimate Encyclopedia*,
- assist the classroom teacher in instructing the students on how to use the electronic encyclopedia *Ultimate Children's Encyclopedia* to answer questions they had developed about frogs, and
- conduct an inservice for teachers on strategies for using Internet resources.

Changing Roles and Responsibilities

During the second week of the unit, the classroom teachers used literature selections about frogs in language arts instruction. These selections were suggestions made by the library media specialist. At the beginning of the week, the library media specialist used the nonfiction series *Nature's Children* to instruct students on how to take notes from a printed source. The computer resource teacher came to the classroom during the second week of the unit to instruct the students on how to use the digital camera, which they used throughout the unit to record the progress of tadpoles being raised in the classroom. Some of the pictures were used in the students' creative writing assignments and projects.

Station	Activity
One	Using the *Ultimate Children's Encyclopedia*, students worked at three computers in the classroom to record facts about the life cycle, habitat, and food requirements of frogs.
Two	Students received language arts instruction from the classroom teacher using the literature selection, *Frog and Toad All Year* by Arnold Lobel.
Three	Students wrote and illustrated creative stories about what it would be like to be a frog.
Four	Students went to the media center to work with the library media specialist. She used *The World Book Student Discovery Encyclopedia* with students to reinforce the note-taking skills she had taught in the first week in the unit. Students recorded facts about the differences between frogs and toads.
Five	Students worked independently on grammar skills by correcting sentences about frogs.
Six	Students silently read both fiction and nonfiction books about frogs.

Students were introduced to six learning stations during the second week of the unit. These stations would be held twice a week throughout the duration of the unit. During each of the two-hour time periods, the students worked in three of the six stations.

The objectives of the stations changed focus as the unit progressed. In the third week, the computer resource teacher taught students how to use Web sites to learn about frogs. The students used these sites while working in stations. By the fourth and fifth weeks, students were using their time in stations to summarize their research on frogs. Students continued to visit the media center where the library media specialist worked with them on accessing and analyzing information from other electronic resources such as *Compton's Interactive Encyclopedia.*

The computer resource teacher also helped students to plan, organize, and implement a slide show based on their research. At the end of the unit, students wrote letters to city council members highlighting the need to preserve and maintain wetlands and gave multimedia presentations to other classes summarizing their research findings.

Other Opportunities for Teamwork

Once we established this method of planning and working as a team, we were able to implement technology into a variety of subjects. In my second year at the Old Donation Center, students participated in a project called "Journey North." In the early fall of the year, the computer resource specialist introduced students to the Internet when they visited a Web site that tracked the flight of monarch butterflies from the United States to Mexico. Students wrote letters to Mexican school children asking them to watch out for the monarch butterflies and to help protect the forests where the butterflies hibernate during the winter.

Students wrote letters to Mexican school children asking them to watch out for the monarch butterflies and to help protect the forests where the butterflies hibernate during the winter.

Later in the year, we received letters from students in Mexico stating that the butterflies would soon be headed back our way. Once again, the Internet was used to chart the progress of the migration. The students became extremely interested in the plight of butterflies. The classroom teachers worked to ensure their lessons on butterflies met the Virginia State and local school division's Standards of Learning. The library media specialist reinforced student research and note-taking skills when using print and electronic resources. As in the previous year, the computer resource specialist assisted students in locating appropriate Internet sites for research. She also instructed students in methods to find, retrieve, save, and print clip art for their individual reports on butterflies. At the end of the unit, students planted a butterfly garden on the school grounds after investigating the life cycle and environmental needs of butterflies.

During my last year at the Old Donation Center, students studied sea turtles after reading several newspaper articles about dead and stranded sea turtles on the beaches of Virginia and North Carolina. Once again the roles and responsibilities of the members of the technology team remained basically the same as in the previous two years. The classroom teachers ensured that the Virginia Standards of Learning were included in their instruction. Using literature recommended by the library media specialist, students received language arts instruction using books about sea turtles. She also assisted students in research methods using both print and electronic resources. As a culminating activity to the unit, the computer resource specialist worked with students to create a slide show on sea turtles that could be used as an instructional resource by teachers and other students in the school.

Each year this final unit was the most challenging to plan and to implement, but it was the unit in which I took the most pride...the pride coming from the ownership my students took in their own learning; the mastery of curriculum objectives; and the collaboration of the library media specialist, the computer resource specialist, and me, the classroom teacher. We exemplified the proverb, "It takes a whole village to raise a child." In our case we provided an environment that stimulated and motivated our students to learn. Our students helped to direct some of their learning and were given opportunities to use technology. Through the use of both nonprint and print sources, our students became experts in the subject we were studying, whether it was butterflies, turtles, or frogs.

Conclusion

My students live in a world vastly different from the one encountered by the students of my grandmother and of my mother. The world has been changed by the availability of information in a variety of formats, and this amount of information is constantly growing. There has been an explosion in the methods of obtaining, storing, and dispersing information. Teachers need to integrate technology in their instruction in order to prepare their students for the future. Students need skills they can use as they progress through school and as they enter the work force. These skills include the ability to effectively use information tools and the ability to analyze, evaluate, and synthesize the information held within a variety of nonprint and print sources. This is a monumental task for a teacher to face alone. Effective teaching can no longer be achieved by a single individual. It is the result of a team effort, an effort managed best by the planning and collaboration of classroom teachers, library media specialists, and computer resource specialists.

Works Cited

Compton's Interactive Encyclopedia. CD-ROM. The Learning Company, 1997.

Doyle, Dan. *Nature's Children.* Danbury, CT: Grolier Educational, 1997.

"Journey North: A Global Study of Wildlife Migration." Annenberg/CPB. April 2002: On-line. Internet. 11 May 2002 Available: http://www.learner.org/jnorth

Lobel, Arnold. *Frog and Toad All Year.* New York: HarperCollins Publisher, 1976.

----------*Frog and Toad are Friends.* New York: HarperCollins Publishers, 1970.

---------- *Frog and Toad Together.* New York: HarperCollins Publishers, 1971.

Ultimate Children's Encyclopedia. CD-ROM. The Learning Company, 1996.

The World Book Student Discovery Encyclopedia. Chicago: World Book, Inc., 2000.

About Dona Leigh Caldwell

Dona Leigh Caldwell has taught in the Virginia Beach City Public Schools for twenty-six years. She received a Bachelor of Science degree in Education from Radford University and a Master of Science degree in Education from Old Dominion University. She holds endorsements in Early Childhood Education, Gifted Education, and Library Media Science. Ms. Caldwell taught grades kindergarten through three at Aragona and Windsor Oaks Elementary schools. For three years, she was a resource teacher in the gifted program. After working as a second-grade teacher for seven years at the Old Donation Center for the Gifted and Talented, she is currently the library media specialist at Plaza Elementary School. .

Close All Windows

by Dorothy K. Kidwell

Our Goal—Integration

The room was filled with fifteen bodies showing various signs of fatigue. They had worked hard, and I was pleased with their progress. There was a collective sigh of relief when I said, "Close all windows and return to your desktops." One of the fifteen rose, walked across the room, lifted the shade that had been drawn against the angled rays of the afternoon sun, and shut the window. Beaming, she returned to her seat. Could I hide my frustration? The last two hours had been spent using precise computer terminology, and now it seemed to have been wasted. I might as well have been speaking a foreign language.

Slowly smiles spread on the faces of others in the room. They chuckled and then laughed out loud. "Oh," she said, "you meant in computer terms," and quickly carried out my direction properly. Now I smiled along with the class and knew that soon those computer terms would be second-nature to them.

> *Our goal was true integration, not merely using the computer during a lesson.*

This class needed to learn much more than terms, however, for their task was to integrate technology with curriculum. Our goal was true integration, not merely using the computer during a lesson. This classroom was filled not with children but with professional educators. And yet, I worried that these "students" did not know enough about the computer's capabilities to imagine all its applications. The challenge was to design staff development activities that would meet the needs of the teachers in the school.

"Tomorrow is as yesterday unless we learn the lessons of today." - Anonymous

In the evolution of staff development for teachers in the area of technology, some disturbing trends can be noted. Dr. Christopher Moersch, president of Learning Quest, characterizes it as often insufficient, misdirected, and unrelated to instructional themes. Additionally, it is offered under two assumptions:

1. teachers can easily make connections between available technology and curriculum, and
2. teachers are ready to make changes in their delivery of instruction. (40)

Unfortunately, one or both of these assumptions may be inaccurate. In the *Journal of Computer-Based Instruction*, Olivier and Shapiro wrote on the theory of self-efficacy (81-85). They found that individuals who rated themselves low in the area of achieving results were less likely to accept change and innovation than those who rated themselves high in self-efficacy.

Another factor to consider when designing technology staff development was documented by McLaughlin, writing with Berman and again with Marsh, when he cited the significance of a principal's interest in the successful implementation of effective program change (71).

Therefore, it seemed logical to conclude that effective technology staff development must not only expand teachers' skills but also bolster their computer literacy confidence and have the endorsement of the building administrators.

...it is the learners who inherit the future. The learned usually find themselves equipped to live in a world that no longer exists." - Eric Hoffer

Why should we be concerned about staff development in the area of technology? The mission statement recited in my school every morning by students and faculty alike expresses one fundamental reason: "Our mission is to educate each child for success by providing the knowledge and skills required by a changing world." Obviously, technology-infused lab lessons and classroom experiences are essential to the achievement of this mission.

Moving beyond this very obvious reason, there is evidence that effective computer use positively affects standardized test scores. In 1998, both Middleton (19) and Wenglinsky (32), working separately, found that students scored higher in classrooms where teachers used technology applications associated with higher-order thinking skills with their students, and that students performed better when their teachers had participated in staff development for computers.

> *Did using technology foster teaching methods conducive to higher test scores, or did the presence of those teaching methods lead to the use of technology?*

It was easy to see this dynamic reflected among the teachers at my school. Did using technology foster teaching methods conducive to higher test scores, or did the presence of those teaching methods lead to the use of technology? Fortunately, I did not have to answer that question to plan staff development for the teachers in the building. I did, however, have to assess each teacher's level of computer proficiency and prepare challenging activities for everyone.

It would be necessary to employ flex-grouping in the planning to give both low-level and high-level users appropriate projects. Basic computer applications could be presented as teacher productivity tools to spark interest. Using spreadsheets for grades, databases for student information, or mail merges for parent letters could be effective lessons. I wanted teachers to make connections to the technology curriculum just as the teachers want the students to make connections to the core curriculum. Only then would they understand each concept well enough to envision its useful application in their students' activities.

Basic troubleshooting skills would need to be presented. Each teacher should be able to successfully direct a class working on the computers to open files, to save, or to print to produce a final product. Teachers could even load paper in the network printers and clean lint from each mouse to foster feelings of control and reduce technophobia. Partnering high-level with low-level users in mentoring relationships could also prove useful in the technology staff development plan.

Another component of the plan had to address the fact that while most of the learners would be classroom teachers, specialists and administrators had specific technology needs that must also be met through the staff development.

"Change is giving up what we are, to become what we could be." - Author unknown

Dr. Christopher Moersch has developed a framework defining the levels of technology integration. It has become known as LOTI and is summarized in the table below (42). (See Figure 1.) Upon review, it is an ambitious undertaking that the Virginia Beach City Public Schools has proposed when directing that technology be integrated with curriculum.

Figure 1

Category	Description
Non-use	Existing "technology" is predominately text-based as with ditto sheets and an overhead projector.
Awareness	Use of computers is generally removed from the classroom teacher and applications have little or no relevance to the teacher's instructional program.
Exploration	Technology tools supplement the existing instructional program as extension or enrichment activities.
Infusion	Technology tools including database, spreadsheet, graphing, multimedia, desktop publishing, and telecommunications programs support isolated instructional events.
Integration	Technology tools are used to identify and solve problems pertinent to student understanding of instructional themes and concepts.
Expansion	Technology access is extended beyond the classroom to business, government, research, and university partners in student activities related to major themes.
Refinement	Technology is perceived as a process, product, and tool for students with ready access to and complete understanding of an array of applications.

All too often in the busy school day, technology use rises only to the level of Awareness. This level is technology-centered, meaning the technology determines the instruction. A person other than the regular classroom teacher delivers the instruction. It has little or no relevance to student mastery of appropriate content. Student work is produced to develop or practice technology skills rather than having the content drive technology use. Technology use occurs only at scheduled times and is offered as a reward activity or allowed when "real work" is completed.

It is tempting to boast of including Exploration level activities in the classroom. Exploration involves teacher-centered, teacher-directed instruction in which student assignments are low-level cognitive tasks (content drill and games for skill practice) requiring little analysis or creativity and resulting in "cookie cutter" products. The primary purpose for using technology is to sustain student interest in content or to increase student time on task and is optional or unnecessary to achieve the learning goals.

Activities on the Infusion level occur most often in the school where I teach. Infusion implies teacher-centered, teacher-directed instruction where technology use for mastering content is adapted to fit with traditional goals and tasks. Isolated lessons are adapted to include the use of technology, and technology skills are learned within the academic curriculum. Although incorporated as an integral part of the learning activity and used with little or no management problems, technology is an alternative component in the lesson and is not essential for achieving the lesson goals.

> *Infusion implies teacher-centered, teacher-directed instruction where technology use for mastering content is adapted to fit with traditional goals and tasks.*

Integration level activities indicate student-centered instruction wherein technologies are used for collaborative project-based instruction. Students engage in high-level cognitive tasks to solve problems related to the topics of study. Technology tools are fully and appropriately integrated throughout the learning activity. In fact, some activities would not be possible if the technology were not present. Students work within a rubric to make some of the decisions regarding the use of technology in planning, completing, and evaluating their work.

Technology integration is, indeed, a lofty goal. The school system already requires all employees holding teaching certificates to pass the test of Technology Standards for Instructional Personnel by 2004. However, this test requires no submission of projects or portfolios. It can be passed by memorizing terms and definitions. Many teachers could "talk the talk." Now they needed to "walk the walk." How could staff development bring them to the level of computer literacy that would allow them to integrate technology within their curriculum? Only then would they reach the potential envisioned by the Computer Resource Program.

"We must become the change we want to see." - Mahatma Gandhi

Strategies for flex-grouping are a necessary component of effective staff development. It is very important to keep in mind that the teachers in any given school will always be at varying levels of proficiency and will need different resources. The gifted user should not be neglected while addressing the needs of the less able user, even in the technology curriculum. And, all the while as the instructor, I will walk a fine line between the roles of colleague and instructor.

Where was the incentive for the teacher to learn new strategies? I encountered what the classroom teacher faces everyday but without the cooperation of a concerned parent or the leverage of detention. There were no grades. Often there was no concept of usefulness on the part of the teacher/administrator. "Why must we learn this?" they moaned like fifth-graders studying factors and exponents. "I'll retire first!"

Teachers of elementary students are used to knowing and providing answers. The area of technology is one where the answers change from day to day. Nobody has all the answers. As teachers, we would have to fall in love with the *process* of learning rather than with the *product*. What better way to exhibit independent, life-long learning to our students than by modeling it as we learned new technology strategies? Could I create an atmosphere where the teachers accept change and innovation and even reinvent their approach to the curriculum?

So we put grades on spreadsheets and entered student data in databases. We took digital camera pictures of science fair projects and newly hatched chicks. In years past, the camera and disks had been returned to me for the development of finished products. Now teachers opened Microsoft Word® and inserted pictures; they edited wrap points, cropped and resized, added

Figure 2

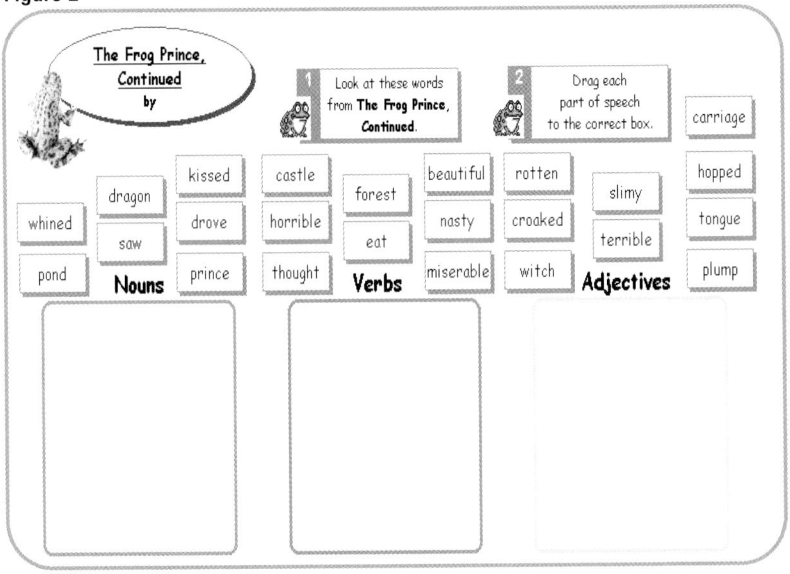

borders, and formatted the text. They were so proficient! They contributed ideas for the creation of lessons like the one in Figure 2 which uses Inspiration Software®.

They pulled files like the one in Figure 3, created in Microsoft Word®, from the server to their classroom computers.

Figure 3

Holiday French Toast

Ingredients

12 slices cinnamon raisin bread, dry and firm
2 cups prepared eggnog
$^{1}/_{2}$ cup butter or margarine
confectioners' sugar

Instructions

- ☺ Cut the bread into 1" strips.
- ☺ Pour the eggnog into a shallow bowl and dip each strip of bread into the eggnog.
- ☺ Melt butter in a skillet over medium heat.
- ☺ Cook the bread strips on all sides until golden brown.
- ☺ Dust with confectioners' sugar.

Makes 12 servings

Math Questions

- ❶ If a loaf of cinnamon raisin bread has 20 slices in it, how many slices would be left after you make this recipe?

- ❶ How many slices of cinnamon raisin bread would you need to make 6 servings of French toast?

- ❶ If you buy 1 quart of eggnog, can you make this recipe?

- ❶ How many cups of eggnog would you need to make 24 servings of French toast?

- ❶ How much butter would you need to make 24 servings of French toast?

- ❶ If Santa, his 8 tiny reindeer, and Rudolph came for breakfast, would you have enough French toast?

They found wonderful Web sites and bookmarked them for regular use. They started to teach in the computer lab and, as their students called their names instead of mine when asking questions, their confidence grew. In a very unscientific study, I observed the teachers who implemented what they learned in staff development sessions and noted the differences in their classes. Changes were apparent in the computer lab as well as in the regular classroom.

"Judge a man by his questions rather than his answers." - Voltaire

The more they learned, the more they questioned. They saw possibilities everywhere. "Can we use spreadsheets to practice formulas for area and perimeter?"

"Will Inspiration Software® work for a book report lesson?"

"Can I divide my class into groups for cooperative learning in the computer lab?"

"Do you think the children can use PowerPoint® for multimedia presentations rather than Kid Pix®?"

"Can we make a slide show in the classroom about each child's favorite activity and show it during Open House?"

"Yes" became my favorite word.

As teacher confidence grew, so did student curiosity. They were eager to try more difficult lessons employing technology. I enjoyed every minute spent creating extension activities for these classes. Those students, with their eyes bright, never failed to beg, "We're finished! Now what can we do?"

Conclusion

Norman Vincent Peale said, "Change your thoughts and you change your world." Teachers who embraced technology changed the environment in which their students learned. Lessons conducted in the computer lab were completed more quickly. There was abundant evidence of student initiative and problem solving. Answers showed divergent thinking. Smiling faces entered and left the lab.

Will scores improve? That remains to be seen. Has student performance improved? Yes. Has teacher proficiency improved? Oh, my, yes! "Learning is infinitely joyous. A nimble mind constantly replenishes itself. With it, the world is ever new..."

Works Cited

Berman, Paul, and Wilbrey Wallin McLaughlin. *Federal Programs Supporting Educational Change. Vol. VIII: Implementing and Sustaining Innovations.* Santa Monica, CA: The Rand Corporation, 1978.

Inspiration Software®, version 6. Inspiration Software, Inc. Jan. 2003 <http://www.inspiration.com>.

McLaughlin, Milbrey Wallin, and David D. Marsh. "Staff Development and School Change." *Teachers College Record* 80.1, (1978: 69-63).

Microsoft Office. Microsoft Corporation. Jan. 2003 <http://www.microsoft.com>

Middleton, B. "The Impact of Instructional Technology on Student Academic Achievement in Reading and Mathematics." DISS. South Carolina State University, 1998.

Moersch, Christopher. "Assessing Current Technology Use in the Classroom: A Key to Efficient Staff Development and Technology Planning." *Learning & Leading With Technology* 26.8, 1999: 40-43, 49.

Moersch, Christopher. "Levels of Technology Implementation (LOTI): A Framework for Measuring Classroom Technology Use." *Learning and Leading with Technology* 23.3, 1995: 40-42.

Olivier, Terry A. and Faye Shapiro. "Self-efficacy and Computers." *Journal of Computer-Based Instruction* 20.3 1993: 81-85.

Wenglinsky, Hugh. "Does It Compute? The Relationship Between Educational Technology and Student Achievement in Mathematics." *ETS Policy Information Center*, 1998 Educational Testing Center. 8 May, 2002. <http://www.starcenter.org>.

About Dorothy K. Kidwell Currently, Dorothy K. Kidwell is a Computer Resource Specialist at Rosemont Forest Elementary School. After graduating from Kempsville High School in Virginia Beach, she attended James Madison University in Harrisonburg, Virginia. There she earned a Bachelor of Science in Elementary Education with a dual endorsement in Nursery/Kindergarten as well as endorsements in third, fourth, and seventh grades. She and her husband have four sons who also received an education from the Virginia Beach City Public Schools and Virginia universities.

AlphaSmart®: One Solution for Eliminating Grumbling From the Writing Process

by Patricia Norfleet

Dreaming "Wouldn't it be great if I had a word processor or computer sitting on the desk of every student in my classroom?" I remember thinking this when I was struggling to get my fourth-grade students to write paragraphs of any description or length. I knew that if I had writing assignments to complete, I would be writing on my word processor at home.

When the Grumbling Starts... My students would begin each writing assignment with a great deal of enthusiasm, and their ideas would come easily when we were brainstorming. They would get out their paper and pencils and develop their plan for writing by using Webs, lists, Venn diagrams, or sentences. When I walked around the classroom and spoke with students as they were working, I could see that they had many things to say and were excited about their ideas for writing.

After an initial writing session, we would move on to sharing and revising. Often the students would work with a partner to revise and then make changes to their paragraphs. Each student would have a conference with me during this stage of writing, and we would make suggestions to revise, add, or move sentences. It was at this point in the writing process that I started to hear grumbling from the students. Some of the complaints included: "I forgot to skip lines when writing the first draft. Do I have to copy it over?" "My hand is tired," and "I don't have any mistakes," or "I'm finished prewriting, and this is my published copy." I knew then that the students did not enjoy writing, not because they did not have the ideas, but because they were tired from the physical aspect of writing the words on paper and then rewriting the paragraphs to revise or present a published copy of their work.

It was at this point in the writing process that I started to hear grumbling from the students.

Teacher's Writing At this time, I was working toward a Master of Science in Education, and I had quite a few writing assignments myself. The focus of my research was the writing process, which included prewriting, writing, revising, editing, and publishing. I remember bringing a piece of my own writing to school to show students how many times I had written a paper, having marked all over it making numerous changes and corrections, and then reprinted the revised copy. The students noticed that I did not have to write my work in cursive. I only had to print revisions because I was using a word processor. I analyzed my own approach to writing and concluded that if I had to revise, edit, and proof everything I was working on without the aid of a word processor, I would not be a happy writer either. If my professor had suggestions for improvement or put editing and revising marks on my paper, I knew I would be frustrated if I had to handwrite it all again to make those corrections.

Budget Realities I knew that providing a piece of equipment for word processing to every student in a classroom would be extremely expensive. I tried to put the thoughts out of my mind and to encourage my students to write in the traditional way with paper and pencil. The best I could do for them during our writing sessions was to try to think of exciting topics and to let them take turns at the one computer in our classroom. As the years went by, the thought of every student having his or her own word processor would often pop back into my thoughts. I would push the thought away, thinking that public schools would never be able to afford this idea.

Then one year our school set up a computer lab with fourteen computers and four printers. It was not long before it occurred to me that we had half the number of those word processors that I wanted for every child in my class. I arranged for a parent volunteer to work with half of my students in the computer lab one half-hour each week. Together we used computer lab time as part of our writing workshops. The parent volunteer would help the students in the computer lab while I helped students with writing and revising in the classroom. It was an uphill battle, but it did help when the students became a little more efficient with word processing skills and when they were able to add graphics to their writing. I tried to find time in the computer lab schedule for extra computer lab visits.

Progress I started to see that the students did not mind the revision process quite as much when they could just make the changes using the word processor and then print a published copy. They were writing more, and they seemed to enjoy putting their ideas on paper. They were proud of their work, as was I, and pleased that they seemed to enjoy writing more than before we started using the computers. Their writing portfolios included a wide range of writing samples. It was easy to see that the students wrote more when they could use the word processor.

Changes Eventually, I had the opportunity to leave my classroom teacher role and begin a new role as a Computer Resource Specialist. I was both excited and apprehensive. That first year I learned much about integrating technology into the curriculum. I took classes, taught myself about using computers, and attended a technology conference in the spring. One of the many vendors at the conference displayed small keyboards called AlphaSmart® keyboards. These keyboards are smaller than most laptop computers, but they still have a full-sized keyboard and a small screen capable of showing five lines of text. AlphaSmart® keyboards can be used for word processing and spell checking. The keyboards have eight separate files to store writing. Each file is capable of storing eight typewritten pages of text. The keyboards are small and very portable. The vendor described them as "kid friendly" because they are very durable. They operate on batteries or by using a rechargeable plug-in station. They also have an infrared port that can "beam" writing to a printer or to a computer.

> *I took classes, taught myself about using computers and attended a technology conference in the spring.*

Dreaming Again, Budget Again Needless to say, I was dreaming about having a set of the keyboards for my school. Excitement quickly died, however, when I learned that each keyboard would cost slightly more than $220 and we would also need a printer with an infrared port. Again, I just knew that the possibility of obtaining a classroom set of keyboards was very small. Still excited about these portable keyboards, I told my principal about them. She thought they were a wonderful idea, but reality compelled her to tell me that there was little money left in our budget and it would need to be spent on other instructional items. I was not surprised, but I was still disappointed.

The next year we had a new principal assigned to our school and, of course, I shared my enthusiasm for these keyboards. Our new principal liked the idea but warned me that our budget did not have room for many large purchases of this nature. She did, however, tell me to remind her later in the year and maybe we could purchase a few of these keyboards with any money we might have "left over."

Reality A few months later our principal asked me if I had suggestions for spending some equipment money from the school budget. It was no surprise when I suggested that we purchase as many AlphaSmart® keyboards as possible. I never dreamed that we would be able to purchase a full classroom set. We completed the paperwork and, finally, my dream of having a classroom set of word processing keyboards was a reality. I was disappointed only in the fact that I was no longer a classroom teacher where I could use the new keyboards with my own students. I could envision my students using these keyboards in the course of a school day just like they use paper, pencils, and books. Any teacher would welcome this opportunity. My dream of having a word processor for every student in a classroom was a reality.

Developing Enthusiasm Knowing that my colleagues would eagerly welcome the AlphaSmart® keyboards into the school, I created a plan for checking out the set of keyboards. The teachers only needed to decide what time of day they wanted the keyboards in their classrooms. To my dismay, after a week the students had still not even seen the keyboards. Possibly, the teachers were too busy to take time to investigate using the new technology. Using a hands-on approach, I took ten AlphaSmart® keyboards to a faculty meeting so that the teachers could touch them, try them, ask questions, and see for themselves how wonderful this resource was. I even had the printer set up so they could see how easy it would be to print with the built-in infrared port. I described the checkout procedures and waited to see the results, when the students and teachers would use the keyboards on a daily basis.

> *To my dismay, after a week the students had still not even seen the keyboards.*

Disappointment and Regrouping After waiting another week for teachers to run with this idea, I was quite disappointed that no one had used the keyboards, but I would not give up. I had convinced our principal to spend thousands of dollars on this equipment and I did not want it to go unused. I asked myself how I could get teachers to use this expensive investment.

I knew that showing this technology to the students would ensure their excitement about the keyboards. Maybe the students could convince their teachers to give the keyboards a try. I also decided that I had to show teachers how to operate the keyboards, but I needed to show them in a way that would not require them to come to an extra meeting or require them to use their valuable planning time. My plan for accomplishing this task was to teach the teachers and the students how to use the keyboards myself and to teach both groups at the same time. I e-mailed all of the teachers in my building with an offer to come to their class and to teach a demonstration lesson on using the AlphaSmart® keyboards.

To convince teachers to use a new piece of equipment, I felt I needed to show them that it would be simple to use and would take very little extra effort. The planning that a teacher does for writing with paper and pencil would be the same planning they would use to plan for writing using the AlphaSmart® keyboards.

Successful lesson planning requires time and effort. I needed to show that planning for using the AlphaSmart® keyboards would fit into the constraints of allotted planning time, that the AlphaSmart® keyboards enhance instruction, and that they could be used with any writing lesson even if it is just a spelling test or a daily oral language activity. By demonstrating a lesson, I hoped that teachers would see that the keyboards could be used for the most routine writing assignments as well as more involved writing projects. I believed that after teachers saw that it would add very little time to planning writing lessons that the teachers would accept these keyboards and, in fact, make them an item to use daily in the classroom.

By demonstrating a lesson, I hoped that teachers would see that the keyboards could be used for the most routine writing assignments as well as more involved writing projects.

A few teachers accepted my offer for a demonstration lesson in their classrooms. After several lessons, the keyboards were becoming more popular. The students in the school started asking me when I was coming to their class with "those little computers." I would respond that I would come to their class as soon as their teacher could schedule a time for me. This plan worked, and soon I had demonstrated lessons in every lower grade classroom and almost all of the upper grade classes.

Opinions Students in my school who use the keyboards say that they are wonderful. In fact, in classrooms where the keyboards are used daily, the students are very disappointed when they do not get to use the keyboards. Some children say that they think using the AlphaSmart® keyboard also improves their typing skills because they use the keyboards regularly.

One teacher said, "My students beg to use the keyboards for assignments other than just writers' workshop. Sometimes we look for an empty file that we can just use temporarily for a short assignment." Another teacher said, "Sometimes my students have two or three pieces of writing going on at the same time in the same file. They just skip a few lines and start another piece of writing while they are waiting to conference with me."

Success There are many teachers at my school using the keyboards now. In fact, juggling the schedule can sometimes be difficult. Some teachers just use five of the keyboards for writing activities during daily flex group sessions. Other teachers use the keyboards just for special writing projects. A few teachers in my school use writers' workshop as a daily form of writing instruction. These are the teachers that seem to use the keyboards most often. The students in those classrooms pick up the keyboard just like they used to pick up a piece of paper and pencil. When I am in one of those classrooms and I see students working on the various stages of the writing process, some using the keyboards, some editing and revising with pencil, some conferencing with the teacher using a printed copy of their writing, and some "beaming" their work to the printer for publishing, I am truly jealous that I am not still a classroom teacher teaching writing with my own group of students.

The students in those classrooms pick up the keyboard just like they used to pick up a piece of paper and pencil.

Conclusion When I think back to the days when I was dreaming of having a computer or word processor for every student in my classroom, I really did not think it would ever be possible. Even so, the thought never really left my mind. Even when I saw an opportunity with the AlphaSmart® keyboards, I still did not think it would be possible because of financial issues. Once our school was able to obtain a set of keyboards, I just knew we had a wonderful resource, but I also knew that as the Computer Resource Specialist I was the person in our school who could make the use of the keyboards a success or a failure. Failure did loom in front of me at first, and I decided that I could not give up. I had to think of another way to present the keyboards so that teachers and students would begin to use them daily. Success did not come as quickly as I had expected, but it did come. Now many students and teachers use the keyboards regularly. I still have work to do because I would like to see the keyboards used even more. My next dream... how about five keyboards for every classroom, or maybe a set of keyboards for every grade level? Then again maybe I should dream about a keyboard or even a computer for every student. After all, dreams can come true.

About Patricia Norfleet Patricia Norfleet has taught for twenty-eight years in Virginia Beach. She is currently a Computer Resource Specialist. She taught fourth grade for twenty-four years. She is recognized as the 2003 Teacher of the Year at Centerville Elementary. Mrs. Norfleet earned a Bachelor of Science in Education degree from East Carolina University and a Master of Science in Education Curriculum and Instruction from Old Dominion University.

The Last Generation

by Sheryl Nussbaum-Beach

Blending Learning and Technology

We are the last generation that has the prerogative of deciding whether or not to master technology. Many of us have chosen not to acquire proficient skills and still have experienced success in our professions. However, the children we teach today do not have that choice. Students must acquire a high degree of technical skill to be marketable in the 21st century. As educators, we do our students a great service if we allow them to gain these skills within the safety net of our classrooms.

Administrators and teachers alike must focus on the blending of learning and technology to help shape students' technological effectiveness, especially within schools serving at-risk populations. Time must be found during the school day or year for teachers to become comfortable and knowledgeable about the technology tools that support the objectives of their curriculum so they can collaborate with other teachers in order to design and implement technology supported projects.

Professional Development

Therefore, the most important task ahead for leaders in education today is to provide the time and opportunity for teachers to become technologically proficient. Teachers need professional development not just about learning how to use new technologies, but also about which software programs or devices will lead to improved instruction and learning in their classrooms. These thoughts were uppermost in my mind when I arrived at W.T. Cooke Elementary School. My goal was to help teachers to move along a continuum from being non-users of technology to becoming creative appliers and integrators.

Cooke has a very diversified student body with one of the highest transient populations in the Virginia Beach City Public School (VBCPS) division and a high percentage of at-risk and homeless children. Technology can open doors for <u>all</u> children, regardless of race, socioeconomic background, or exceptionalities, and for that reason I spent each day looking for new ways to instill in these children a proactive vision of who they were and what they could do.

Part of the success at Cooke was a result of creating staff development sessions that were teacher-centered and full of energy; many times these sessions were "standing room" only. To help the teachers move along developmentally, they had to become reflective learners and researchers in their own classrooms, so they kept journals in which they could describe how their students were using technology to master the given objectives. They noted the successes and disappointments, and what conclusions they could draw from them. I also offered additional teacher training before school, during planning time, and after school. The training was integration specific; skills of the actual technologies and applications were taught within the context of the curriculum. Over time, the various developmental levels of the teachers began to emerge, and I was better able to address even more specific areas of need.

As the more advanced level teachers began to use technology seamlessly in their classrooms, they were identified as trainers. Each trainer was then assigned a smaller group of teachers to mentor. This "train the trainer" approach exponentially sped up the technology development. It was like cloning myself! Our state standardized test scores improved to the point where Cooke became a fully accredited school. Diagnostic test scores also began to improve. It was obvious we were all growing from the collaboration, and the school's at-risk population seemed to be benefiting the most!

Cooke's teachers worked hard to master the skills they needed to usher their students into the 21st century. Proof is in the fact that our school was the second in the district to have 100 percent of its teachers pass the Teaching Standards for Instructional Personnel (TSIP) test, a division assessment for teachers and an employment requirement. Teachers who earlier were too intimidated to turn on a computer and lacked the most basic mousing techniques were now teaching their own computer integrated lessons with ease.

Producers of Knowledge

Strategies and methods to empower at-risk students and reluctant teachers are highly replicable. As the Computer Resource Specialist at W.T. Cooke, I had the opportunity to design and implement many technology driven initiatives that impacted the most challenged students in a positive way. We developed the idea of teaching students to be Tech Assistants. A Tech Assistant is a technology support person in a pint-sized package. These third-fourth-and fifth-grade special and regular education students were trained to help peers, teachers, and others to use technology more effectively, to act as troubleshooters, and to maintain technology equipment in the school. The teams enabled us to keep all the equipment running and up-to-date. And, as a result of the self-esteem acquired from holding the title of Tech Assistant, many of these students experienced academic success in the classroom for the very first time.

Because a large number of the school's highly transient children needed extra help in preparing for the Virginia mandated Standards of Learning (SOL) tests, the whole faculty was encouraged to find creative learning strategies.

Because a large number of the school's highly transient children needed extra help in preparing for the Virginia mandated Standards of Learning (SOL) tests, the whole faculty was encouraged to find creative learning strategies. Armed with the knowledge that technology levels the playing field for academically challenged students, we instituted Cooke TV, a student-run television station where students would direct, anchor, film, script, and digitally edit copy for each morning's broadcast. The scripting team was comprised of at-risk learners who used laptops to create copy in PowerPoint© prompter format for the anchors to use in the morning broadcasts. A student director set up equipment and signaled anchors and special guests and then switched between video and live shots. The motivation for students in such a program is obvious. The students mastered technologies most adults had never used. Moreover, they developed oral presentations, improved writing ability, fostered leadership skills, and took ownership for their own learning.

The educational community has believed for years that students learn more if they are producers of knowledge rather than consumers. Believing that the use of technology to deliver standards-based curriculum in a project-based format will result in increased retention in the classroom, we initiated a unique school-wide twist to SOL tutoring using a "dream school" approach. We developed Utopia University, a technology based, thematic curriculum structured around ancient civilizations. Students reviewed state-mandated objectives by creating projects and worked in virtual environments. Toward the end of the program, one child said, "Hey! You tricked me!" When asked how he was tricked, he responded, "All along I thought we were having fun, but this is really school, isn't it?"

Finally, students of varying abilities shared information and worked together in teams to make decisions and solve problems that brought W.T. Cooke regional and national attention. By putting together a ThinkQuest® competition team, we were able to design activities that allowed every student to offer something towards the project. Students who previously had experienced little success in traditional classroom activities felt very successful in a technology-rich classroom that emphasized meaningful, authentic tasks. Together students created a *Growing Up in Afghanistan* Web site. http://library.thinkquest.org/CR0212462/ that was recognized nationally by ThinkQuest®. With many at-risk students participating, Cooke also took first place in several district and state level technology competitions. These at-risk students always emerged from the events filled with pride in their accomplishments! The positive feelings spilled over into their performances in core subjects as well.

Technology and Educational Reform

Recent federal legislation has mandated high standards and challenging learning activities for all children, but especially for those at risk of educational failure. For true learning to occur, students must have experiences that allow them to attach new ideas and concepts to what they already know. This allows them to "construct" their own understanding of the world. Technology that is integrated with the curriculum provides the perfect medium for offering children this chance to build on their own experiences, construct their own meanings, create products, and solve problems successfully.

An emerging body of research suggests that this thoughtful integration of technology into classroom instruction can be especially advantageous for at-risk children. Unfortunately in the past, when schools have used computers with their most at-risk populations, teachers and administrators have concentrated on the drill and practice programs that emphasize basic skills rather than using the technological tools to enable students to be producers of knowledge. In an ideal learning environment, the teacher can arrange the classroom activities so that students can work together on a project and use technology to solve problems and construct meaning in ways that make sense to them. In this way, teachers serve as guides as well as sources of knowledge, allowing for exploration, inquiry, curiosity, and active engagement to propel the learning. Technologies can be used in the classroom to produce real world applications that support research, design, analysis, composition, and communication.

Socrates once said, "Let the questions be the curriculum." By asking students to participate in lesson planning by asking them questions such as, "What do you know about this topic?" "How do you know what you know?" and "What do you want to know?" provides for engaged, collaborative partnerships in the learning process. It is essential for teachers to involve learners in active discussions and then step to the side to guide students in their quest for information and knowledge. Dynamic teachers use strategies such as arranging video conferencing with experts, demonstrating the latest "must have" electronic gadget, or allowing students to use a virtual interface to collaborate with E-pals (electronic pen pals) on a standards-based project. These strategies result in students taking ownership of their own learning.

Outstanding educators teach not only what they know, but also what they want to learn. In doing so they become co-learners with the students in the process. When students are drawn into planning their learning, they often become enthralled because they are given choices about what they can learn. Working with themes of study that correlate to the mandated curriculum, students and teachers can develop a course of study that provides both individualized and whole group activities. Based on the information from the students about their interests, the teacher can divide the class into small "interest" groups. These smaller groups of students become experts in one area of the theme. As the students research and complete creative tasks related to their topic, they design a method for sharing what they have learned with the class through the use of technology. Teacher facilitation of the groups ensures the students' success with such items as scanners, digital cameras, presentation software, or other forms of electronic communication that they may use to share their ideas.

Children today grow up in an environment where they control the flow of information and the graphic format in which they receive it. Think about it. Children use remote controls, push button phones, and have instant access to information in entertaining formats. Almost everywhere they go, they find a stream of multimedia. They are moving toward the future at full speed. The schools they attend, however, may often be locked into the past with out-of-date technology delivery. As a result, school seems rigid, uninteresting, and unyielding to many students.

Children today grow up in an environment where they control the flow of information and the graphic format in which they receive it.

It is essential for education to be restructured to reflect the technological advancements that are available. Technology must be more than an add-on, more than just another requirement the overburdened teacher must fit into the school day. Technology must become the collaboration and communication tool through which content area curricula are delivered.

Technology Teaching Strategies

Whenever I learn a song, it seems that I learn both the music and the words at the same time. I don't learn one then the other. This is also true of technology and content knowledge. Educators must think in terms of content objectives and then decide which technology would best facilitate teaching that objective. Students learn to use the technology while creating products that provide mastery of the content-based outcomes. A question each teacher should consider in planning for instruction is, "Which technology tool could I use to best deliver the curriculum content?"

For example, a typical Internet lesson-planning strategy would first involve determining the educational outcomes. What should students learn? Which standards will be covered? The next step is drafting the project by identifying the content/topic area, student roles, and audience. Next, instructional tasks for students must be designed. Asking questions such as, "Where will students gather information?" "What thinking skills and processes will be emphasized?" and "What student products and/or performances will communicate evidence of understanding or proficiency?" All these questions and their answers provide direction for the project's activities. And finally, the teacher must determine the evaluative criteria used to evaluate the student products and performances.

Technology is a delivery tool for organizing curriculum in an innovative, engaging fashion. The technology itself should be invisible. Video games and other virtual play experiences have prepared even the most at-risk child to use technology. Futuristic strategies such as video conferencing with authors and other subject matter experts seem natural to them. Our goal as educators is to teach students how to harvest the vast amounts of information out there, analyze it, and synthesize it into meaningful outcomes.

Conclusion

We are just beginning to truly understand the many possibilities that technology offers. Some of us are further along the continuum than others in turning these possibilities into reality in the classroom. After my experience at Cooke, I have confidence that more and more teachers will become believers and users of technology as they see the tremendous impact it has on student learning. Witnessing this transformation and watching students benefit reminds me of why I became a teacher in the first place.

Work Cited

Nussbaum-Beach, Sheryl. "Traveling the Techno Trail: Training Teachers to Use Technology." *Education World*. 29 January, 2003 <http://educationworld.com/a_tech/tech157.shtml>.

About Sheryl Nussbaum-Beach

Sheryl Nussbaum-Beach has seventeen years experience integrating and managing technology in a variety of educational environments. She has taught in public, private, and home schools, at the elementary, secondary, and postgraduate levels. She has also taught industry certification courses as a Microsoft® Certified Trainer.

Ms. Nussbaum-Beach received her Bachelor of Science and Master of Science in Education degrees from Valdosta State University, Valdosta, Georgia, in early childhood education where she also served on the faculty of the Early Childhood and Reading Education Department.

Currently, she serves as an electronic communications specialist for the Virginia Beach City Public School system, and is a faculty member of Connected University, an online professional development community. Ms. Nussbaum-Beach is a former citywide Teacher of the Year (2002) and has won several awards for her teaching expertise, including a National Albert Einstein Distinguished Educator Fellow Finalist in 2002; the Distinguished Service Award, Virginia, Parent Teacher Association 2002; and inclusion in *Who's Who in American Education* 1996. In addition, she has had several articles published in online journals, been featured on local television and radio shows, and is a regular presenter at local, state, and national conferences, speaking on topics of technology integration and implementation.

Ms. Nussbaum-Beach joined the Virginia Beach Schools in 1997 as a Computer Resource Specialist at W.T. Cooke Elementary School and is currently a Teacher Specialist for Electronic Communication. Her favorite pastime is spending every spare moment possible keeping up with her four active teenagers.

Section Eight

Building a Technology Framework *for the* Future

Sharon L. Clohessy

Puzzle Pieces

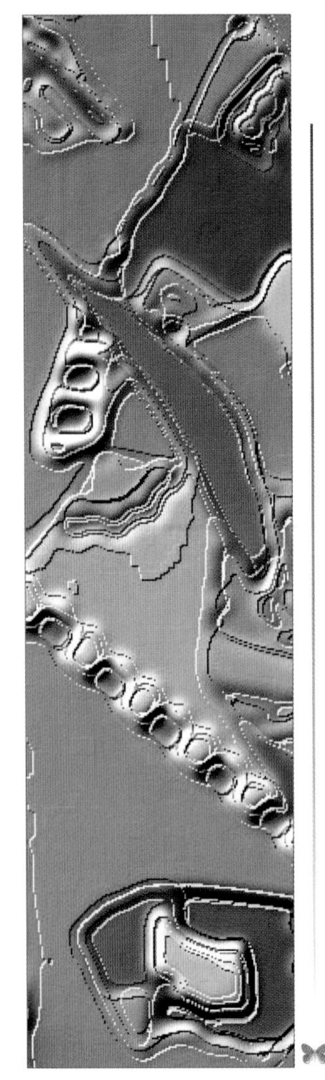

Description: In my work, I enjoy experimenting with the relationship of colors and making the painting come alive on the canvas. That is why I was fascinated the first time I used the computer to transform my artwork with the touch of a button and not a brush stroke.

Medium Used: Acrylic Paint on Canvas

Educational Background: Ms. Clohessy received a Bachelor of Arts in Art Education from Virginia Wesleyan College and a Master of Arts in Education from Virginia Commonwealth University.

Teaching Experience: Ms. Clohessy has been an art teacher at the Contemporary Art Center of Virginia, an adjunct professor for three years at Old Dominion University, and has been employed with Virginia Beach City Public Schools for eight years. She is currently an Art Teacher Specialist in the Office of Instructional Services.

Awards: Ms. Clohessy has exhibited at the Boardwalk Art Show in Virginia Beach, the Commonwealth Collects at the Contemporary Art Center, and the Tidewater Artist Association Art Show. Her artwork, Trevi, was included in *A Tapestry of Knowledge, Volume I* in 1998.

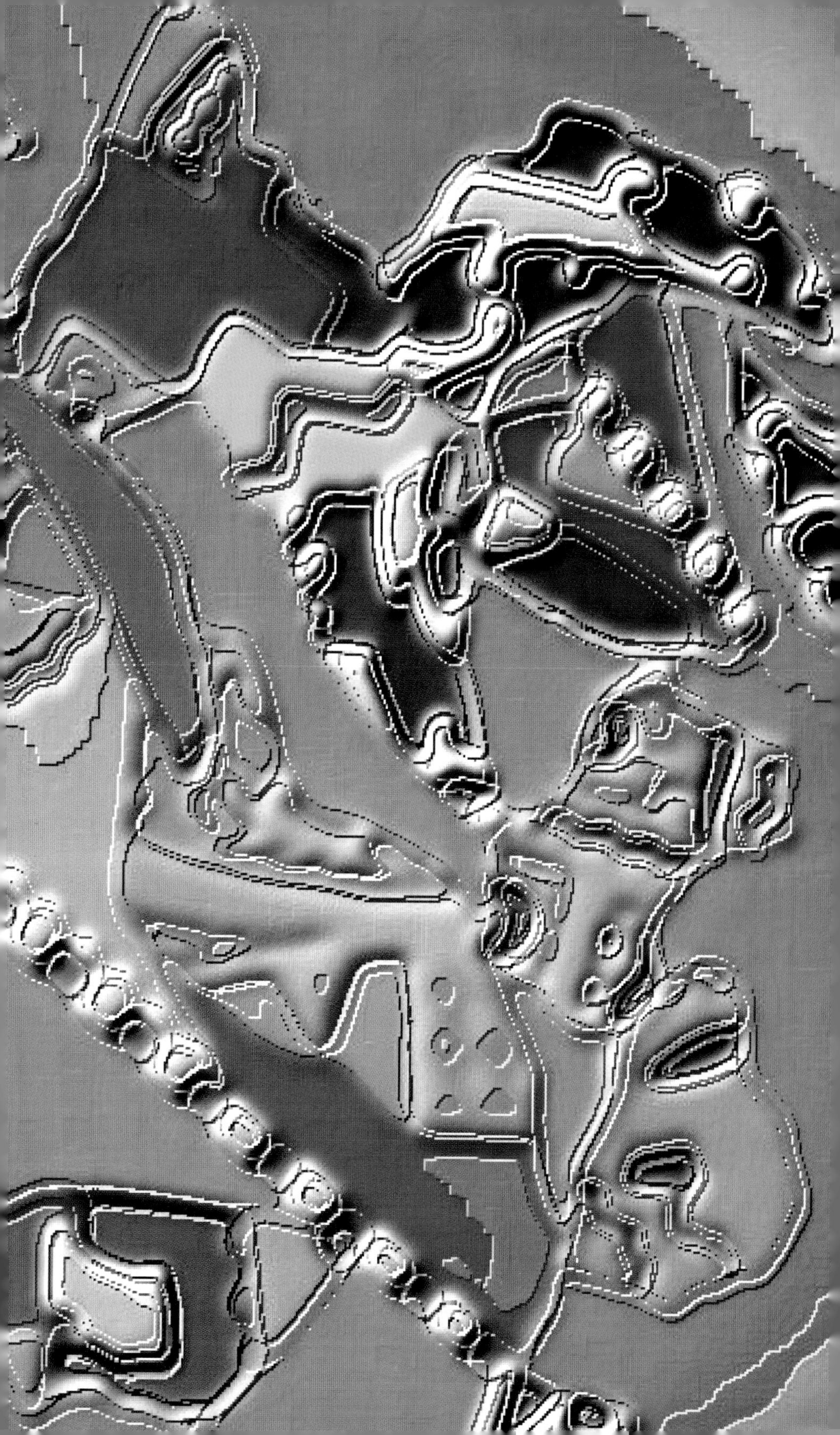

Building a Technology Framework for the Future

What will students need in the future? Computer technology changes daily, and in ten years the cutting edge technology tools of today will be obsolete. This means that future technicians will always need opportunities for lifelong learning and the infrastructure to support that training.

The authors of the two articles in this section discuss the current status of training possibilities, the provisions for the future, and the scope of the Advanced Technology Center which was dedicated this year, but is designed to meet the needs of the future.

Linda Lavender, a Computer Network Administrator, describes how the computer networking field has unfolded in the Virginia Beach Schools. Her article gives a brief history of the program at the Technical and Career Education Center, but looks forward to the move to the Advanced Technology Center which will provide partnerships with Tidewater Community College and the City of Virginia Beach's Economic Development department.

How do you get a mayor, a city manager, a school board, and city council all moving in the same direction? By building a facility that can be used by the school division and the local community college. The school division began to plan for an expansion of the Technical and Career Education Center in the late 1980s, but the vision for the grander collaborative venture was not realized until 1999 when an architectural firm completed an initial schematic design.

In his article, Dr. Patrick Konopnicki, the Director of Technical and Career Education for the Virginia Beach City Public Schools, relates how the plan moved forward, partnerships were formed, and grants were written to make this building a reality.

Both these articles illustrate how Virginia Beach as a school community is preparing for the future and is "Ahead of the Curve."

Patrick Konopnicki and Linda Lavendar

Building Information Technology Skills, Byte by Byte

by Linda Lavender

Steps Toward Becoming a Computer Technician Mark bolted out of the small classroom and rushed into my classroom next door. There was no need for his excited words – *"I did it – YES,"* his grin alone told me. Watching another student on the video monitor, I observed Bill putting his head down at the computer, with his arms raised high in victory. What these two high school students had just completed were industry certification exams that award the designation of certified computer specialists in computer networking.

These two young men have just accomplished a step toward becoming a computer technician. Although most people in a school or business work on computer networks, the average computer user (end-user) does not understand the complexity and knowledge base the computer technician must have to support his or her systems. Imagine this scenario: It is another busy day at work; a teacher's report is due to the principal by 3:00 p.m. The teacher turns on the computer and attempts to access a Microsoft Word® document from the network to finalize last minute changes. However, instead of the report, the computer beeps and the monitor screen turns blue, with the following message displayed:

An exception 0E has occurred at 0028:???????? in VxD VREDIR(01) + ????????. This was called from 0028:C0033AE8 in VxD IFSMGR(01) + 00001098. It may be possible to continue normally.

Who are you going to call? The technician or support person who responds may very well be a student or a recent high school graduate of one of the leading-edge Information Technology (IT) programs in place in the Virginia Beach City Public Schools.

Creating Life-long Learning The mission of the Technical and Career Education Center is to promote life-long learning. This statement rings true for students studying Information Technology skills in the Computer

Network Administrator (CNA) program. Computer technology changes daily, and in ten years the students will probably not be working on the networks and the computers on which they trained today. The CNA program provides the solid foundations needed to encourage continued education and knowledge of computer networks. By focusing the program on the industry as a whole and the software as the means to manage the computer systems, CNA students have the groundwork needed to expand their current training and become successful in their future careers.

Computers have revolutionized our entire lives; as a society we have become dependant on their daily use. It is only in the last decade that personal computers started appearing in our homes and their use turned from strictly business to a machine for personal finance, homework, and, of course, computer games. As computer costs decreased, the numbers found in businesses increased; as a result, the need to share computer peripherals such as printers and to share data was mandatory. As companies implemented this technology, they realized the need to have trained personnel on site to manage these increasingly complex networks.

As computer costs decreased, the numbers found in businesses increased; as a result, the need to share computer peripherals such as printers and to share data was mandatory.

Managing and maintaining personal computers and the related field of computer networking are growing technological fields, and according to the Information Technology Association of America (ITAA), Information Technology (IT) is one of America's fastest growing industries. IT encompasses computers, software, telecommunications products and services, Internet and online services, systems integration, and professional service companies.

The challenge of meeting the growing need of skilled computer technicians in the IT field, with the academic challenges of high school students, was met in 1994 when a convergence of three separate entities joined forces to bridge the gap. Virginia Beach City Public Schools; leading national IT solution providers, Novell, Inc. and Compaq, Inc.; and a local Value Added Reseller (VAR) Electronic Systems developed the first of its kind program world-wide by creating a new model of a Technical Education course: Computer Network Administrator. At the time, I was a certified instructor for Novell's networking products (CNI) and had been delivering authorized curriculum to corporate customers of Novell's products. During this initial year, we created a program that not only taught, but also challenged computer-oriented high school seniors in new facets of computers and their related technologies. This program also raised awareness in our community about the capabilities of high school students to maintain and manage complex computer systems. CNA students volunteered in the schools; they helped with installing software, running maintenance programs, answering questions, troubleshooting errors, and teaching an after school computer club for two years at an elementary school. Students also participated in internships in a diverse cross section of businesses and with the United States Navy.

The Early Years Throughout the early years of the program, I worked with the project and the students. Initially I was part of the program as a contract instructor. As a contract instructor, I was employed by a local computer integration company and remained employed by them while I taught at the Virginia Beach Technology Center. Being a contract instructor allowed me to continue my work in corporate and other businesses and bring to the classroom the educational competencies and relevant real-world problems and solutions. During the three initial years of the program, the computer industry was experiencing unprecedented growth. One of the driving factors was the evolution of today's Internet. The Internet evolved from a government "top secret" computer network to inclusion in most businesses and schools world-wide. As more people became "connected," the need to support the Internet with a company's computer network became a must.

On a given day, the students may be installing computer operating systems or servers; another day will find them on the Internet downloading software patches or searching for solutions for problems.

To be successful, the Computer Network Administrator (CNA) requirements had to change to meet the demands of current technology and the increasing need for training that goes beyond the basics for a new generation of technically savvy students. It was at this point that I became a full time staff member at the Technical and Career Education Center. As I migrated from teaching an adult audience already working in the computer field to teaching eager students who grew up with computers in their households, I faced many challenges. The students were savvy about computers but lacked the business acumen needed to work with businesses. Incorporating business practices into the curriculum has been exciting, but the biggest challenge is keeping an entire class focused on the same task. There is no typical day in the CNA classroom. On a given day, the students may be installing computer operating systems or servers; another day will find them on the Internet downloading software patches or searching for solutions for problems. For instance, they may be adding user accounts and setting up login restrictions, or they might take the computers apart, only to put them back together again. Although the primary focus of the CNA program is computer networks and their function, a successful CNA student must have a broad background on computer technologies as a whole.

A National Model Through continuous change and basic principles, we have developed this program into a national model. It was recognized by the National Center for Dissemination for Career and Technical Education as an exemplary program in the nation in December 2001. Our program is only one of four high schools to receive this designation, sponsored by the United States Department of Education.

Qualified Students This does not mean the student must be an advanced computer "guru." The ideal student is one who is eager to learn about computer technology and understands the basic responsibilities of a network administrator. While interviewing potential students for the 2002 academic school year, I met Adam. When I asked Adam what he liked about computers, his face lit up and he replied, "Servers, I love servers." Another student, Theresa, wanted to know "What goes on when I send that email to my friend?" and yet another student, Joe, eagerly brought a portfolio of sample work he had created in various applications and a summary of the classes he had taken. When asked if he had any other computer background, he became concerned and asked, "What else could I have done to get ready for this program?" All these students had one common theme; they wanted, almost needed, to know what else there is to learn about computers, for they already knew the basics. Eagerness to learn is the most important consideration for a prospective CNA student.

Industry Standards As with Virginia's Standards of Learning, computer areas of specialty have their own methods to verify the learning of students. In the IT world, computer certifications are the norm. Novell pioneered IT certification in 1986 with the Certified Novell Instructor (CNI) program. It has since expanded its own certification offerings, and most industry leaders have developed their own certification programs. The current focus of the CNA program is to offer instruction to prepare the students for Certified Novell Administrator and Microsoft Certified Professional certifications. Our CNA program not only meets the industry standards but exceeds them. Our standards are developed and reshaped yearly, through the implementation of an advisory board, which consists of industry professionals in the local Hampton Roads community. Our advisory board provides many additional aspects to the program. In addition to providing guest speakers, field trips, and computer donations, they become program mentors, serve as career advisors, and offer additional subject matter. We have incorporated such basic skills as maintaining daily logs and working with business forms, such as purchase orders and company memos. They also advise me on current industry trends and needs they are facing, which allows me to modify the program to meet the needs of local business and industry.

Industry partners also provide an important element of the CNA program — internships.

Industry partners also provide an important element of the CNA program – internships. The last nine weeks of the students' senior year, eligible students are placed in local businesses in an internship capacity. This work experience provides relevance to students and offers experiences in real-world settings. Many students have continued their internships after high school graduation, some resulting in full time employment.

Effective Use of Technology

Teaching technology-based solutions requires innovation and a "beyond the basics" approach to daily lesson plans. It is important to encourage "beyond the lesson" thinking, meaning that a student who does not have one foot grounded in the current technology and the other reaching for additional learning will soon find himself or herself less qualified and perhaps even left behind in the rapidly changing world of technology. Students are expected to use technology as they learn it. One method to promote that thinking is a week I call "Office Boot Camp." Although most students have had a keyboarding class or a basic Computer Information Systems class, they still only use about twenty to thirty percent of the capabilities of Microsoft Office®. Each day of Boot Camp is devoted to a program within the suite: Monday, Microsoft Word®; Tuesday, Excel®;

Wednesday through Friday, Access®, PowerPoint® and Publisher®. Real life projects are subsequently assigned through the program using each application. Students learn to write technical documents, such as FAQ (Frequently Asked Questions) for various computer questions, using business correspondence and more. Students develop an extensive vocabulary database using Access®, which they will put on CD-ROM and take with them upon graduation, and a series of four internal company newsletters related to computer usage and the company network using Microsoft Publisher®. In addition to developing Microsoft Office® proficiency, these assignments directly promote their language arts skills, which in turn support the Virginia English SOL. The students are encouraged to develop their skills and take the Microsoft Office® User Specialist exam(s) for the different products. This not only helps build proficiency in the applications but shows a prospective employer that the students are skilled in the application and will be able to work with a firm's end-users as well.

Internet-based lessons welcome each student daily; they include a summary of the lesson of the day, upcoming assignment(s) and announcements, a vocabulary word of the day, a Web site of the week (related to computers/networking/Internet), and Tip(s) of the week. Students also use email to deliver assignments to me or to collaborate with other students or business and industry members. They also research and develop an internal Acceptable Use Policy (AUP) for classroom email and proper Internet usage.

Students also use email to deliver assignments to me or to collaborate with other students or business and industry members.

Due to the tremendous amount of material presented, constant reviews are a must! To make this more enjoyable and challenging, I purchased a program that allows us to run such computerized games as *Jeopardy* and *Is That Your Final Answer*. Winners get prizes that are donated from industry partners or sample items I pick up at trade shows. Finally, it is important that the students know that their teacher is not just "talking the talk." I maintain certifications in every product I teach, as well as certifications in other areas of technology. This provides credibility for instruction.

Learning Relevant learning is paramount. If a student cannot relate to the subject matter being taught, he or she will not learn. Because these students only have real experience with the computer networks in their school, we often tie the subject matter to the VBCPS Local Area Network (LAN). Students can relate to printing problems, teacher complaints, and the use of the Internet and other applications. Equally important to their learning is the constant inclusion of "soft skills." These skills are more commonly referred to as speaking, writing and other customer service skills. No matter how technically skilled an individual can become, if he or she does not demonstrate customer service skills, he or she will not become or remain employed. I have added a unit on customer service into the overall curriculum, and students must practice skills during their two-year tenure in CNA.

Program Results The CNA program has been highly successful. Since the first graduating class in 1995, over 70 percent of all students have continued their education in either a two or four year school. Others have gone on to excel in other areas. Take Mike for example. He graduated from the CNA program in 2001 and entered the United States Navy. Due to his CNA training, he entered at the Cryptology rate. In his first technical school after basic training, Mike went on to have the highest score in training, due in no small part to the fact that the majority of training was replication from our program. He was subsequently offered a place in Naval Security Vulnerability Training in Washington, D.C. Brandon is another success story. He did not care whether he graduated from high school and during his junior year put in minimal effort in both the CNA courses and at his home high school. However, in June of his junior year, he successfully passed his Novell CNA certification. When he returned his senior year, he was more confident and out-going. He still did not care for regular school work, but through my encouragement and his mother's, he put in the extra effort he needed to pass his English course. When internship opportunities came around, employers all wanted Brandon on their payroll. He is still working at his internship site, has kept in constant touch with me, and has been offered full-time

In his first technical school after basic training, Mike went on to have the highest score in training, due in no small part to the fact that the majority of training was replication from our program.

employment. Another student, Matthew did such a great job during his internship that his company kept him as an employee and let his college courses dictate his hours for their firm; they adapted to his needs. Finally, there is Beth. Quiet during the two years in CNA, she studied hard but did not have confidence in her abilities. When she entered a specialized trade school for IT, not only did she realize how much she knew, but also the teachers and other students respected her and counted on her involvement in class. She returned to the Tech Center as my intern for a six-week period and returned threefold what she had learned through her interactions with the current students and me.

Conclusion

Computer networking is perhaps the most exciting technical field a student can enter in today's market. There are many different degrees of specializations students can achieve, both in the high school portion of their program and in the workplace as they hone their skills and work with additional technologies. The potential for learning is limitless. As technology changes, the need to maintain their current skill set and develop new skills will remain. To meet the changes, the CNA program has moved to a new facility, the Advanced Technology Center, which provides partnerships with Tidewater Community College and the City of Virginia Beach's Economic Development department. This enables the CNA program to remain closely aligned with higher learning and current workplace skill sets. The benefits to CNA students are enormous – this program builds the IT skills that are needed for a lifetime.

About Linda Lavender

Linda Lavender is the Computer Network Administration (CNA) instructor for the CNA program at the Technical and Career Education Center. She began teaching there eight years ago, on the pilot phase of the program, and continued in that capacity for an additional two years. Five years ago she became a full time teacher for the Virginia Beach City Public Schools. Prior to that, she was a systems administrator, computer technician, and a fully certified instructor for commercial networking and other technical products. She maintains certifications in Novell (Instructor, Administrator, Engineer), and Microsoft (Instructor, Professional) as well as vendor neutral certifications in Comptia's A+ and Certified Technical Trainer + programs.

This Is NOT Your Daddy's Oldsmobile!

by Patrick Konopnicki

Competition and Technology Create New Challenges

A recent national report indicated that global competition, the Internet, and the widespread use of technology will create new challenges for employers and workers in the twenty-first century. Meeting these challenges was the rationale behind the creation of the Advanced Technology Center (ATC). The ATC promises to change the face of technical and career education in Virginia Beach and may well serve as a national model. The evolution of this vast project is notable not only for its vision, but its strategic planning, partnerships, and marketing. What follows is a record of the journey from idea to reality.

Background

In 1989, the Tidewater Community College (TCC) Virginia Beach Campus, based on projected overflow enrollment figures for the 1990s, began planning to fund construction of a new academic facility to meet the requirement of providing functional and safe facilities for students, faculty, and staff. The proposed facility (as described in the 1998-2000 Biennium Capital Budget Request) would consolidate most of the Health Science activities and provide expansion for the rapidly growing enrollment in that division. The plan placed the building southeast of the proposed building site between the lake and existing parking areas.

Beginning in the late 1980s, the Virginia Beach School Board began discussing the need for an additional technical and career facility to meet the increasing demand by students for technical and career course offerings. A feasibility study was conducted and presented to the superintendent but was set aside due to budget constraints. With the election of a new School Board, the idea of a new center resurfaced and on November 29, 1996, the School Board approved the study of a new Technical and Career Education Center. In January 1997, a new feasibility study was completed and the architectural firm of Ballou, Justice, Upton, and Associates submitted plans which included the initial schematic design.

A feasibility study was conducted and presented to the superintendent but set aside due to budget constraints.

During the spring of 1997, staff from TCC and the Virginia Beach City Public Schools (VBCPS) met and began preliminary discussions of the possibility of TCC and the VBCPS pursuing a collaborative venture to construct an occupational/technical facility that would benefit the city schools, local businesses, the community college system, and the community itself. The facility could be used during the day by the school division and at night by TCC; weekend sessions could meet flexible needs. In May 1997, a planning group met and began formal discussions of the collaboration project to be constructed on the TCC/VB Campus. Preliminary research suggested that full funding should be requested from the state, given the project's overwhelming potential for education, community, and economic development. Initial discussions and a legal opinion resulted in several scenarios for ownership to include, but not be limited to, a lease buy back arrangement and bonded indebtedness. The cost of the building was estimated at $23,000,000.00 for approximately 137,000 square feet of space. Overlapping usage would be encouraged based on day and evening schedules.

Preliminary research suggested that full funding should be requested from the state, given the project's overwhelming potential for education, community, and economic development

In November 1997, the City Council passed a resolution supporting a partnership for the construction of a joint Tidewater Community College/Virginia Beach City Public Schools Technical and Career Education Center and committed local funding up to thirteen million dollars, at the same time urging maximum state funding. Grant and private funds would be solicited to reduce the local share of the cost. A month later, Governor George Allen announced his plan to allocate ten million dollars in his 1998-2000 state budget for a high-technology center jointly operated by the Virginia Beach City Public Schools and TCC.

Following that decision, planning discussions began to focus on the school division's delivery of three School Board advanced technology program areas: Telecommunications, Information Technology, and High Performance Manufacturing/Engineering. (Specific courses are listed in the Appendix.)

The name ATC came about as part of many discussions among the project team including the superintendent, school board members, city council members, the community college provost, Economic Development director, and the Technical and Career Education director. It was decided that it made sense to designate the facility as an ATC since VBCPS had been approved to join the National Coalition of Advanced Technology Centers Network, which includes about 200 community colleges around the country and one public school system, VBCPS.

In addition, the center was to include unique features such as Economic Development Department shell space, a local cable station, Virginia Beach TV, a technology theatre with a 250 seating capacity, and a Distance Learning/Teleconferencing Lab. Typically, such facilities as members of the National Coalition of Advanced Technology Centers are post secondary in nature and do not have the benefits of these extraordinary features. The ATC is unlike any other in the country.

Uniqueness As indicated earlier in this article, in the planning discussion, it was decided that the ATC should focus secondary training around three strands: Information Technology, Telecommunications, and High Performance Manufacturing. This train of thought parallels a Virginia Beach economic development study that outlines the strategic directions for the city's economic development. It is fortuitous that both directions of secondary training and economic development form a seamless transition. This enables the facility to fully maximize its potential for the educational skill development of the emerging workforce, the training and retraining of the existing workforce, and for pursuing new business recruitment.

> *This stipulation, that all Technical and Career programs at the secondary level subscribe to a higher level by organizing curriculum around nationally recognized skill standards, speaks volumes about the commitment of the state of Virginia to academic rigor in all disciplines.*

Certifications are another unique feature of the ATC and have become the standards of learning of technical and career education and the common denominator that workplace employers easily understand. In 1999, the Virginia General Assembly voted to change the Virginia Standards of Quality (SOQ) legislation to require all schools to align the occupational vocational programs with industry standards and professional standard certifications. This stipulation, that all Technical and Career programs at the secondary level subscribe to a higher level by organizing curriculum around nationally recognized skill standards, speaks volumes about the commitment of the state of Virginia to academic rigor in all disciplines. Technical and career programs at the secondary level have embraced this initiative as a way of improving programs. These new credentialing procedures offer a means of enhancing a graduate's employment opportunities and increasing educational options.

The Virginia Board of Education has approved certifications for eligible students to receive the Virginia Board of Education's Seal of Advanced Mathematics and Technology. This seal will be awarded to students who earn either a Standard or Advanced Studies Diploma, satisfy all of the mathematics requirements for the Advanced Studies diploma with a "B" average or better, and either pass an examination in a career and technical field that confers certification from a recognized industry or trade or professional association, acquire a professional license in a career and technical education field from the Commonwealth of Virginia, or pass an examination approved by the Board that confers college-level credit in a technology or computer science area. All Telecommunications and Information Technology programs at the ATC will carry industry certifications that have national recognition. Additionally, the ATC is unique because it not only offers industry certification programs but also training and professional development, customized contract programs, self-enrichment, and conference services with large technology theatre capabilities.

Partnerships

It is widely understood in the Virginia Beach Schools that it is in the best interest of the business community to help improve education. Business visions of strategic education alliances reflect their unique business values and the priorities of their organizations. Business-education partnerships can take on many different forms around a variety of issues. However, by carefully examining the goals of both the business and the education partners, and focusing on the critical areas in need, partnerships can have lasting effects on program enhancement and ultimately on business success.

The ATC was built upon the partnership concept that draws its strength from among its partners. The city (Economic Development Department and cable television station), TCC, and the VBCPS all have attributes that they bring to the table. In addition, each partner has symbiotic relationships with other partners that will eventually contribute to the overall good of the ATC.

One example of a lasting partnership is the Computer Network Administrator (CNA) program and Compaq computers. The Virginia Beach City Public Schools CNA course was the first program in the world to be offered to secondary students for certification by Novell. Compaq donated the original computer lab at the program's inception in 1994 and used their marketing connections to help the VBCPS tell the positive CNA story that appeared in the nationally syndicated *Business Week* magazine. In December 2001, the CNA program won the nation's highest award as an exemplary program for career and technical programs through the National Center for Career and Technical Education (NCCTE), sponsored by the United States Department of Education. This CNA program has helped VBCPS become designated as a Prometric testing site for national IT examinations, which for secondary schools is an extraordinary accomplishment. Recently, their marketing office in Atlanta contacted our office to help develop the continuing partnership between Compaq and the CNA program at the new ATC. Discussions are underway to repeat the computer donations to the CNA lab at the ATC.

Many partnerships involve student internships that give students real world insights into the needs of the business community. This can lead to direct employment, as in the case of a young CNA student named Daniel, who works for a local military firm. Being the youngest member of a 300-member team can have its challenges. For instance, when Daniel went to San Diego on a computer installation project, he was too young to rent a car, and taxis became quite expensive. His original interview three years ago occurred on the same day that he passed his CNA exam while still in high school. He has been with the firm ever since.

For instance, when Daniel went to San Diego on a computer installation project, he was too young to rent a car, and taxis became quite expensive.

Another successful internship example is John who started his internship with a national communications firm. After two years of full time service after high school, he was declared "head and shoulders" above his peers and is now responsible for a multi-million dollar computer contract that includes installation, contract negotiations, inventory control, and project management. Not bad for a twenty-year-old!

Other partnership examples abound. Cisco Corporation works with the Cisco Academy, which provides state of the art certification and free training to secondary students. In addition, Oracle Corporation is training prospective ATC instructors at their California headquarters, as well as providing curriculum valued at over $150,000. Locally, Cox Communications has worked with the new Telecommunications program to develop curriculum and provide instructor training. These efforts underscore the fact that the ATC curriculum is part of a real world effort which will teach students real world applications while mastering high standards content.

A virtual tour and site dedication to highlight the partnership that was being formed were held in December 2000. Members of the state department of education, city council, school board, and members of the business community attended a tent-covered ceremony on that cold December day. ATC momentum and anticipation had begun to spread. Since that time numerous presentations have been given to national businesses, localities around the state, local business and civic groups, and countless student audiences.

Conclusion

In February 2002, over 16,000 letters were mailed to rising tenth-, eleventh-, and twelfth-graders. Parents and students were informed of the dynamic opportunity that was available to them. The letters invited the students to attend a meeting at Landstown High School, located across the street from the ATC, to ask questions, and to receive greater program insights. On March 14, 2002, over 300 people attended the event, indicating significant public interest.

As the opening of the facility drew near and the paint began to dry, furniture and equipment were installed; 2,300 ports were activated and connected to over 1,000 computers! The latest piece of the academic village is now in place. Figure 1 shows a recent picture of the ATC. The pride of Virginia Beach and the excitement of 450,00 citizens can almost be heard. To have a mayor, city manager, school board, city council, Economic Development Department, businesses, parents and students all moving in an aligned strategic direction is a major feat. By now, we can really start to believe that this truly is "not your daddy's Oldsmobile."

Figure 1

SPECIFIC COURSE OFFERINGS AT THE ADVANCED TECHNOLOGY CENTER

- Microsoft Windows and Visual Basic
- Electronic Commerce
- Computer Network Administrator
- Digital Design
- Cisco Networking Academy
- CADD
- A+ Computer Repair
- Telecommunications
- Oracle Internet Academy
- i-NET+
- Modeling and Simulation

HIGH PERFORMANCE MANUFACTURING AND ENGINEERING PROGRAM

- Engineering Principles I
- Engineering Principles II
- Computer Interpreted Manufacturing (CIM)
- Programmable Logic Control (PLC)
- Engineering Materials
- Total Quality Management (TQM)
- Statistical Process Control
- Case Study
- Engineering Research
- Modeling and Simulation
- Engineering Materials

About Patrick M. Konopnicki Patrick M. Konopnicki, Ed.D., Director of Technical and Career Education, Virginia Beach City Public Schools, has been in education for thirty-one years. He is a former classroom teacher and is currently an adjunct professor with The George Washington University. He has been a member of the National Alliance of Business Advisory Board for Advanced Technological Education, vice-president of the Virginia Vocational Association, and a member of the Hampton Roads Quality Management Council, as well as a member of the Virginia Beach Quality Alliance. He has also served on the Governor's Advisory Council for School/Business Partnerships and is a past vice-president of the Virginia State Partnership Association. In spring of this year, he received the outstanding service award from the National State Association of Technical and Career Education Directors.

Currently, Dr. Konopnicki helped to lead the Virginia Beach City Public Schools' creation of an Advanced Technology Center in partnership with Tidewater Community College, which opened in the fall of 2002.